THE BEATLES
WHO'S WHO

THE BEATLES
WHO'S WHO

BILL HARRY

Delilah
BOOKS

DISTRIBUTED BY
THE PUTNAM PUBLISHING GROUP
NEW YORK

Copyright © 1982 Bill Harry

A Delilah Book
Delilah Communications Ltd.
118 East 25 Street
New York, New York 10010

ISBN: 0-933328-51-6
Library of Congress Catalog
Card Number: 82-71918
First printing 1982

All rights reserved. No part of this book may be reproduced or transmitted in any form or by any means, electronic or mechanical, including photocopying, recording or by any information storage and retrieval systems, without permission in writing from the Publisher.

Designed by Neil H. Clitheroe and Giulia Landor

Typeset in the UK by Bookworm Typesetting, Manchester, England
Printed in the USA

The author would like to thank the following for providing photographs for this book: The *Mersey Beat* Archives; the Clive Epstein Collection; the press officers at EMI records, Charly Records, WEA Records, RCA Records; Tony Adler at Polydor; Hal Carter; Joe Flannery; Liz and Jim Hughes of Cavern Mecca; Dick James; Mike McCartney.
Photographs supplied by Bill Harry on pages 4-5, 6, 8-9, 10-11, 12-13, 18, 20, 24, 27, 28, 31, 38, 39, 42, 44, 45, 53, 60, 61, 62-3, 65, 66-7, 69, 70, 74-5, 76, 78, 81, 82, 88, 93, 94, 110, 112-13, 115, 129, 134, 142-3, 148-9, 153, 159, 160, 166, 179, 189; Tom Hanley: 16, 29, 32, 56-7, 80; Freda Kelly: 50-1; Keystone: 14, 122-3; Pictorial Press: 102, 108-9, 128, 130-1, 156-7; Popperfoto: 42-3, 78-9, 96-7, 100, 105, 118-19, 136, 138, 140-1, 155, 164, 165, 182; Rex Features: 48-9, 86-7, 98, 99, 106, 107, 114-15, 120-1, 126, 145, 150-1, 169, 174, 175, 177, 180-1; Graham Spencer: 37, 40; Syndication International: 17, 35, 36, 90, 92-3, 97, 102-3, 124, 133, 140, 146-7, 185; John Topham Picture Library: 27, 172, 187.

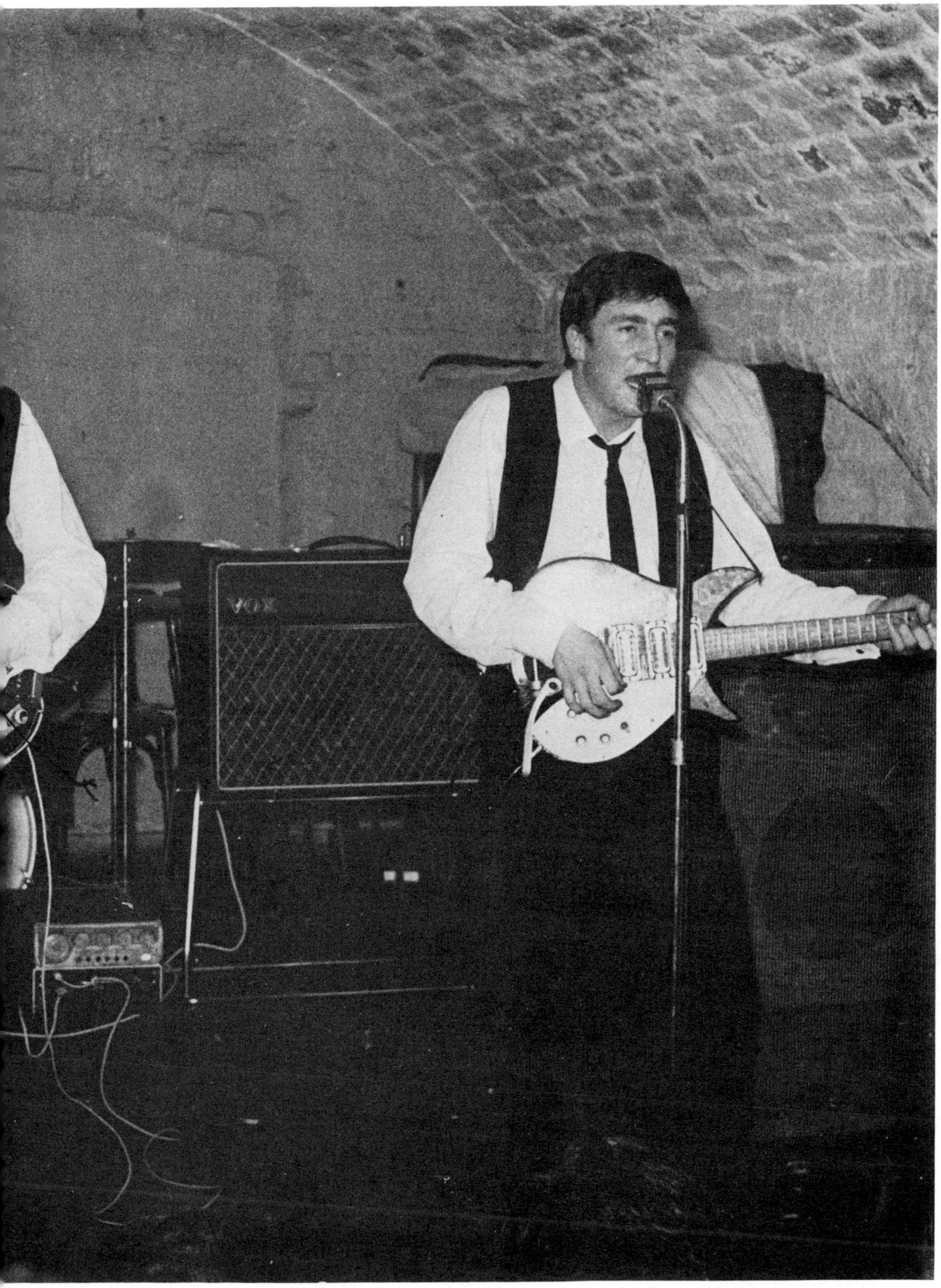
VOX

INTRODUCTION

Following a tiff with his girlfriend, an art student wandered around a red light district, was attracted to some music — and his life was never to be the same again; a trainee accountant decided to drive a van for his former schoolmates and ended up running a multi-million pound business; an accountant bought himself a small cellar-club, booked some leather-clad rockers and found himself owning the most famous venue in the world; a struggling music publisher was introduced to a dapper young man from the provinces and ended up as the head of one of the world's major music publishing companies.

The personal stories of Klaus Voorman, Neil Aspinall, Ray McFall and Dick James are typical of the many people whose lives were not merely touched but totally transformed by The Beatles. The group affected millions throughout the world with their music: inspiring, entertaining, exciting. But to a few hundred other folk who were directly involved, they brought something more personal. These were the wives, lovers, relatives, business associates, childhood friends and others who, through luck or circumstance, found themselves part of The Beatles Story.

Over the years, in offices, at clubs and receptions, I have bumped into many of them and we have always had a mutual topic of conversation. I've witnessed at first hand their lives transformed, remembering some of them when they 'didn't have two halfpennies to rub together' and now seeing them glide by in their executive cars. There were also those, of course, who were left behind and never shared the fame or the wealth. These people had their part to play in the early Liverpool days and remained in that dark city on the Mersey to struggle with life as best they could: Bob Wooler, Pete Best, the many friends and sweethearts who weren't among the chosen few. There were those too who were overtaken by tragedy: Brian Epstein, Stu Sutcliffe, Mal Evans, Rory Storm and several more.

The story of those four young men whose talent changed the face of popular music has been written into history by many different people. I was lucky enough to have known them from the start of their career, and perhaps through my eyes and the experiences of the hundreds of characters in this book, you may taste some of the flavour of those exciting days when The Beatles ruled the world!

The Toxteth area of Liverpool achieved notoriety in 1981 because of the riots. I was brought up there and we just called it Liverpool 8 in those days. It was a grim area of broken buildings and bombed sites, tenements and warehouses, little terraced streets and old decaying houses. Many people still had gaslight, most had outside toilets and a bathroom was almost unknown. The jobless used to hang out on street corners, forming gangs such as The

Bill Harry in 1963. Apart from a beard and a twinkle in his eye, he looks much the same today!

Chain Gang and The Peanut Gang. No one had a television, crackling radios were tuned into *Family Favourites* or *Worker's Playtime*, and the only entertainment was in the local flea pits (cinemas) where ancient films flashed across grey screens. I attended a dockside school, St Vincent's, but was taken away and placed in a private school after a gang had kicked in my appendix. Every night I'd sit at a battered typewriter and write letters to pen pals from San Francisco to Sweden, compose short stories and while away the evening hours with creatures of my own imagination. A cousin introduced me to science-fiction fandom and I was soon art-editing over two dozen fanzines. Then I got a place at the Junior Art School, where I began their first magazine, which I called *Premier*. It was then that I formed the first threads of Beatle association: also at the school was Cynthia Powell, later to marry John Lennon, and Les Chadwick, who was to take many of the early Beatle photographs. The school was situated in a Georgian terrace called Gambier Terrace where John Lennon was later to rent a flat. When I entered the Liverpool College of Art in Hope Street I continued to produce magazines, this time specialising in jazz. I was asked to write, draw and design for a magazine financed by Frank Hessy's, the local music store, and thus began to frequent the clubs and halls of Liverpool reporting on the music scene. There was a lot of jazz, a lot of skiffle. Chris Barber and other popular traditionalists would appear on venues promoted by the late Albert Kinder, such as The Pavilion in Lodge Lane, and jazz clubs catered for either trad or modern jazz, whilst The Temple in Dale Street presented both. When the Cavern opened in 1957 it was strictly a jazz venue, with skiffle groups supporting the bands.

Skiffle was the biggest musical mania Britain had ever experienced and kids throughout the country had taken to making music on a scale previously unheard of. The instrumentation was simple: guitars, plus home-made bass (take a tea-chest, attach a rod and some bass strings) and kazoos (if you couldn't afford a few pence for a kazoo, use comb and paper). Numerous British skiffle bands entered the charts and a singer from Chris Barber's band, Lonnie Donegan, hit the No. 1 spot in the States with 'Rock Island Line', the first British artist to crack that elusive market. It was his gig at the Pavilion that inspired a lot of Liverpool kids to become involved in skiffle – including Paul McCartney, who was in the audience.

Skiffle was much in evidence at the art college. I remember going into the Life Rooms during lunchtime to practise in a skiffle group with Rod Murray. As I hummed away on a kazoo I noticed John Lennon and some of his friends rehearsing in the other corner of the room. John was now a student at the college and invited his friends Paul McCartney and George Harrison from the Liverpool Institute next door to join him at rehearsals.

John and Stuart Sutcliffe were two of the few friends I made at the art college. I'd first noticed John in the canteen, an imposing figure with a Teddy-boy hairstyle and clobber (clothes), out of place yet strangely at ease, stalking around with his friend Jeff Mohammed looking as if trouble was his middle name. As I was to discover, he had a tough exterior which harboured the soul of a poet. Girls were drawn to him and he didn't take his studies too seriously.

Coming from my type of background I found it difficult to mix with the middle-class dilettantes who formed the main bulk of the student body. I was never happy with dabblers but I was completely fascinated by anyone who had a spark of creative ability, and I warmed to Stuart and John. We used to get together in a pub called Ye Cracke or in student flats in the area, to talk about the things that moved us. At one time we decided to call ourselves The Dissenters and articulate the problems that existed in our own environment. The big 'in' thing with students was America's Beat Generation and the San Francisco poets, but John, Stuart and I weren't interested in parroting their work, we wanted to create something based on our own experiences in the area in which we lived.

At the art college I became a member of the Student's Union Committee, and also on the Committee with me were Stuart and Alan Swerdlow, a neatly dressed, bespectacled youth with a very precise manner who later photographed The Beatles and designed handbills for Brian Epstein promotions. Stuart told me that John's group were experiencing difficulties because they had no money and couldn't buy a PA system, so we put it to the Committee that we should lend them the money to buy some amps and the group could, in exchange, play at our local college dances.

The dances were held on Saturday evenings, a couple each term, and usually comprised a bill with a trad jazz band and a skiffle group. John's band (they weren't called The Beatles then) performed a different kind of music, and although I'd been a jazz freak their type of material appealed to me. I got to

THE NORTH'S ONLY ENTERTAINMENT PAPER
THIS IS IT!
MERSEY
MERSEY
MERSEY
MERSEY
MERSEY
MERSEY
MERSEY
MERSEY BEAT
'MERSEY BEAT'
A BOON TO ADVERTISERS

know John's two friends from Liverpool Institute, Paul and George, and started going to some of their gigs.

Then, in 1960, I decided to start a newspaper and began to gather material and information about the local music scene. The name I'd come up with was 'Mersey Beat': I'd visualised an area I wanted to cover, in the manner of a policeman's 'beat'. Little did I realise that the name would appear in the *Encyclopaedia Britannica* and inspire an entire musical movement.

Naturally enough, I began to plug the group nearest to my heart, who had now decided to call themselves The Beatles — and John wrote a piece for me called 'On the Dubious Origins of Beatles', which I ran in the first issue. By the second issue they were spread across the front cover — and I continued writing about them and plugging them in virtually every issue until a year later they became the best known group in Liverpool. Bob Wooler told me that the other bands resented my plugging The Beatles so much that they had begun to call the paper the Mersey Beatle — a name that I was later to use for a special supplement each issue.

I was writing the entire copy, designing the layouts, delivering copies to distributors, shops, clubs, venues, music stores and record shops. The manager of NEMS in Whitechapel was impressed with how quickly *Mersey Beat* sold and by the second issue was taking 144 copies. His name was Brian Epstein. He became my record reviewer and would ask polite questions about the local groups and venues, and one day phoned me to ask if I could arrange for him to go to the Cavern. That was the first time he saw The Beatles.

Because *Mersey Beat* was expanding so fast I had to have working capital. It had been a success from the first issue and was solvent on paper, but the immediate bills had to be paid. Ray McFall, owner of the Cavern, offered to come in as a silent partner, providing financial backing — and the services of Paddy Delaney as bouncer. The paper grew until it was a full-colour weekly with a circulation of 75,000 per issue, and it was the first British music paper to be distributed in America. Its success inspired so many other publications that it became the most imitated newspaper in Britain (probably the world), with at least eighteen papers throughout the country which were based on it.

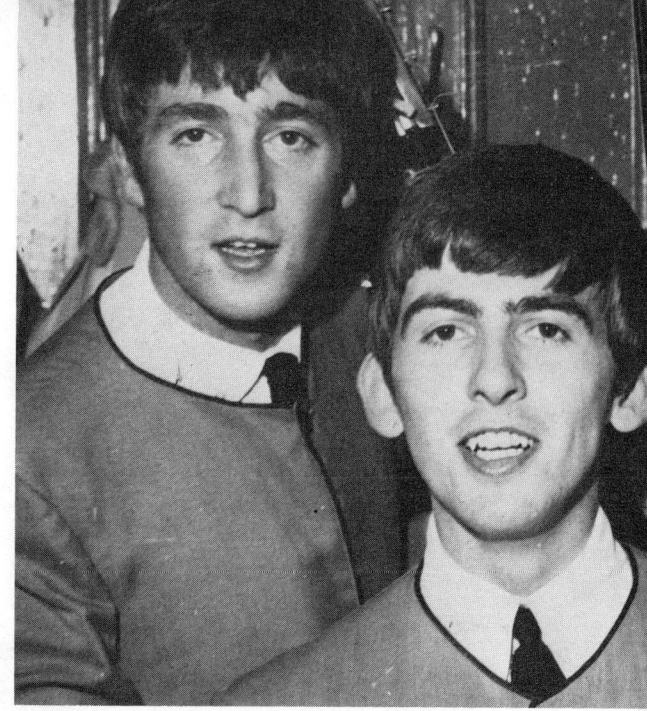

In Liverpool The Beatles were treated like gods. The entire city was obsessed with Beat music: it engulfed the city like a tidal wave and exploded into a gathering of almost 200,000 people who took to the streets to line the pavements from Speke Airport to the Town Hall when The Beatles were fêted at a civic reception.

The fan fever spread to all parts of Britain and eventually received acknowledgement following the Beatles' London Palladium appearance, when the phrase 'Beatlemania' was coined, and they hit the front pages of every national newspaper — where they were to remain for almost a decade.

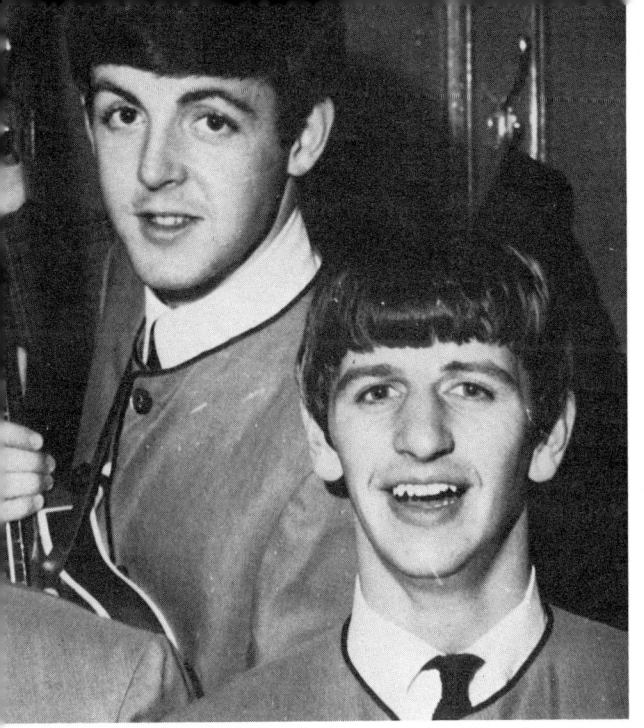

Like young Alexanders they conquered Europe and then hit the United States for six, becoming the most famous quartet in modern history. Their music, their clothes, their accents, their hair, their private lives, were put under the microscope and emerged in large type across the covers of papers and magazines in almost every language. They influenced fashions and trends, helped to launch the Swinging Sixties in London and created an image of that decade which people will refer to with nostalgia until the century comes to a close.

I have selected some 300 people to feature in this book. There could have been many more. Some of them only dwelt on the periphery of the Beatles world, others never even met them, while some were instrumental in their rise to fame.

I have included a number of the Liverpool bands in order to portray something of the flavour of a time when 350 groups were competing for attention in a small area of the north-west of England and The Beatles were just one of them.

Numerous wives and girlfriends are featured. In the early days there were shop assistants and hairdressers, later models and film stars, indicating that the rich and famous eventually marry the rich and famous — and in between became fodder for the gossip columnists.

There is a new generation of Beatle fans, Mark Lapidos and Liz and Jim Hughes, for example, who were only babies at the height of Beatlemania but who have been sufficiently gripped by the legend of the Fab Four to continue to keep their name alive today.

Brian Esptein's circle of friends — Peter Brown, Geoffrey Ellis, Terry Doran — suddenly found themselves in another world, and after Brian's death they remained in show business. They are an example of the people who were 'brought in', so to speak; they weren't prime movers.

Although my own life was not transformed by The Beatles, I was the first person ever to write about them and have continued to do so for the past 20 years, amassing an unparalleled amount of information on them and their circle.

Within these pages is a wide variety of Beatles people: recording producers and engineers, musicians, singers, parents, publishers, writers, disc jockeys and personal friends. Welcome to their world!

BILL HARRY
London, April 1982

James McCartney Father of Paul and Mike. Jim McCartney was born on July 7th, 1902. At the age of 17 he formed a band called The Masked Melody Makers and he was to continue his interest in music during the years he worked as a cotton salesman. In the thirties he had his own semi-pro outfit called Jim Mac's Band and he composed a song called 'Walking In The Park With Eloise'. Paul recorded the number in Nashville in 1972, accompanied by Linda, Denny Laine and country musicians Chet Atkins, Floyd Cramer, Vasser Clements and Bobby Thompson. The instrumental was issued as a single with the musicians using the name The Country Hams.

Jim's wife Mary died on October 31st, 1956 and he did not remarry until November 24th, 1964, when he wed 35-year-old Angela Williams. Jim died on March 18th, 1976 and his life is lovingly retold in Mike McCartney's book *Thank U Very Much*.

Mary McCartney First daughter of Linda and Paul, born on August 28th, 1969. Named after Paul's mother.

Julia Lennon John's mother and from all accounts a lively, somewhat eccentric lady who, for a giggle, once walked the streets with a pair of knickers on her head and sometimes wore spectacles with no glass in the frames — a sense of humour which John seemed to inherit. Her family name was Stanley and her sisters were Mimi, Anne, Elizabeth and Harriet. She married Freddie Lennon at Mount Pleasant Register Office on December 3rd, 1938 and was left literally holding the baby when John was born because he went to sea and by the time the boy was six had more or less

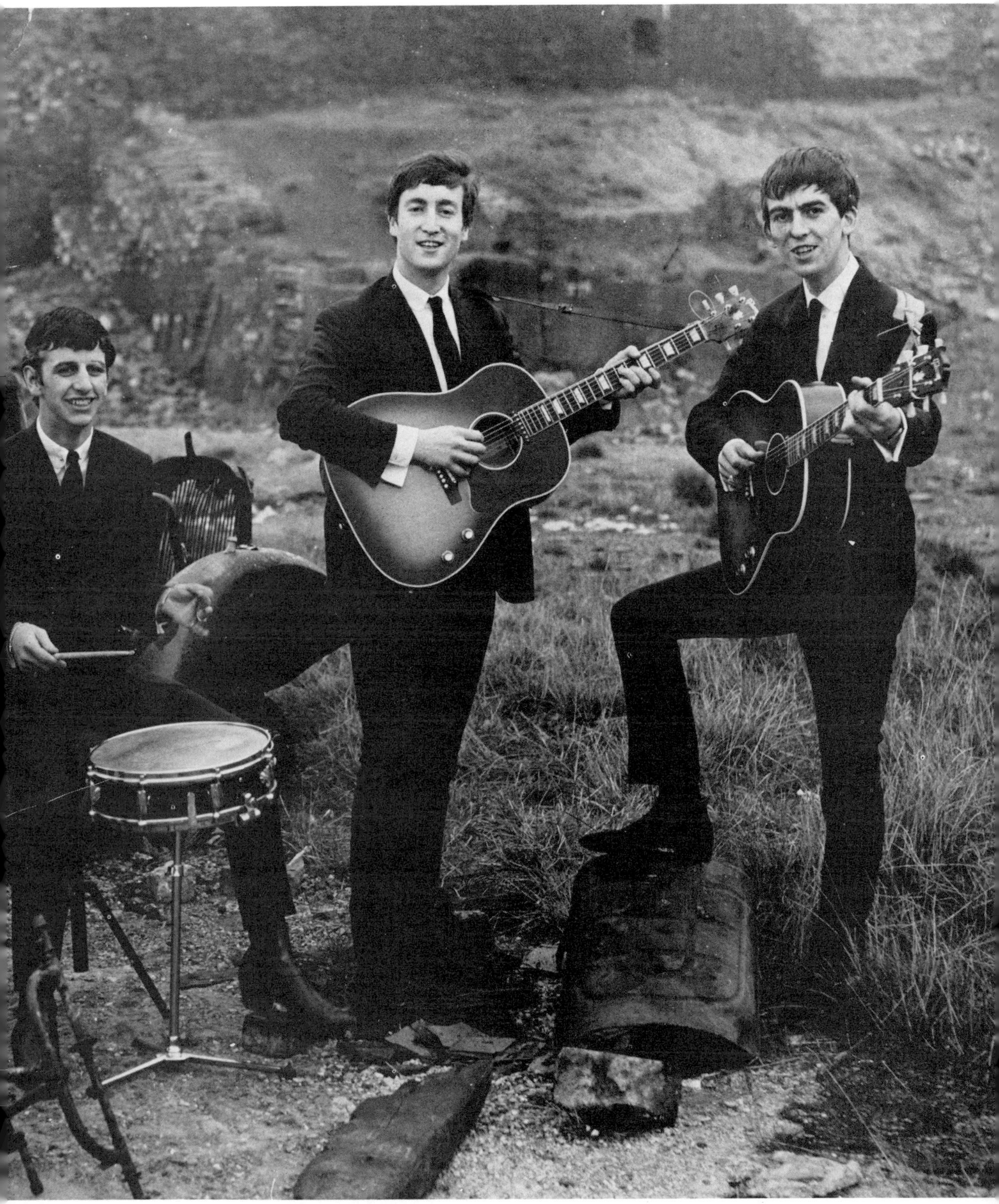

deserted her and his son. Julia fell in love with a waiter and went to live with him. He had children of his own and was not too happy with the idea of Julia bringing her own offspring into the household, so she gave John to Mimi to bring up. They lived quite close together in Woolton and Julia began to visit John regularly. John used to call the man she lived with 'Twitchy' and Julia had two daughters by him — Julia and Jacqueline. One day, following a visit to Mimi's house, on July 15th, 1958, she was run down by an off-duty policeman and died on the way to hospital. John did not show his emotions openly, but it was apparent that her death had a profound effect on him and he wrote a number of songs dedicated to her, including 'Julia' and also named his son Julian in memory of her.

Alfred 'Freddie' Lennon John Lennon's father who left home when John was 6 and didn't see his son again until 17 years later. Freddie came from such a large family that he was placed in an orphanage and lived there until he was 15. After a short time working in an office he went to sea at the age of 16 as a bell boy and spent a total of 25 years as a mariner. He married Julia when he was 25 and John was born three years later. When he eventually abandoned his life at sea he worked as a waiter, then took a job at various holiday camps. When The Beatles became famous, the British press began to seek John's long-lost father and the *Sunday Express* discovered him working as a kitchen porter in a hotel in Esher. John didn't want to meet him initially, but later on a relationship developed between them and they were in contact with each other until Freddie's death in 1970.

When Freddie was discovered and hurled into the limelight he suggested that John's musical talent was part of the family heritage as his own father was a member of the original Kentucky Minstrels. Fred found himself a manager in Tony Cartwright, who co-wrote an autobiographical song with him, 'That's My Life (My Love And My Home)'. It was issued on Pye's Piccadilly label in December 1965 with 'The Next Time You Feel Important' as the flip side and released in the States in February 1966 on Jerden 792.

Freddie married a 19-year-old university student, Pauline Jones, and they both became visitors to John's house prior to Freddie's death.

Harold Harrison George's father. A sea-faring man who was in the Merchant Marine. He married Louise on May 20th, 1930 at Brownlow Hill Register Office and settled down to a land-based job, first as a bus conductor, then as a driver. Their first child, Louise, was followed by Harold, Peter and George. His wife died in 1970 and Harold himself passed away in May 1978.

Louise Harrison George's mum. She first met his father, Harry, in 1929 and they were married at Brownlow Hill Register Office on May 20th, 1930. They then moved to 12 Arnold Grove in Wavertree where they lived for 18 years before moving to Speke. Louise worked in a greengrocer's shop until Louise, her first child, was born in 1931, to be followed by Harold in 1934, Peter in 1940 and George in 1944. Louise took an interest in George's music and visited the Cavern to see The Beatles and offer her encouragement. She died of cancer in 1970.

George and Patti with George's parents and Patti's mum at their wedding reception

Elsie Starkey Mother of Richard Starkey (Ringo Starr). Her maiden name was Gleave and she married Richard Starkey in 1936. Both of them worked in a bakery at the time and after they were married they moved to No. 9 Madryn Street, Dingle, where their son Richard was born on July 7th, 1940. By the time Ringo was 3 his father had deserted the family home, although he continued to send a sum of money each week. But it wasn't enough, and Mrs Starkey had to move to a smaller house in Admiral Grove. When Ringo was 11, a Romford-born painter and decorator, Harry Graves, entered their lives. Ringo took to him straight away and was quite pleased when, on April 17th, 1953, Harry married his mother. The relationship between the boy and his stepfather was very strong and it was Harry who bought Ringo his first drum kit. When Ringo used to go out with petite, blond Pat Davis, Pat would visit Elsie along with her friend Cilla White (later Black). Mrs Starkey now lives in a very

John's beloved Aunt Mimi

pleasant area of Liverpool — and her close neighbour is Cilla's mum.

Mimi Smith Née Stanley. John Lennon's aunt, one of Julia Lennon's four sisters. Married to George Smith and nicely settled in Mendips, a semi-detached house in Menlove Avenue, Liverpool, she agreed to take John into her home when he was five years old as Julia was estranged from her husband and wished to live with a man who had children of his own. Mimi took her responsibilities seriously and brought up John with care, at times upset by the knowledge that he was something of a rebel. George died when John was 12 and Mimi had to care for the boy single-handedly: and he was certainly something of a handful! She did not entirely approve of his interest in rock music and attempted to dissuade him, but on realizing that he was so determined, she bought him a guitar. She was particularly upset when he left the art college and was disappointed in his determination to go to Germany. He returned broke, despite his assurances to her that he would make a lot of money. She even went to the Cavern to see if there was anything behind John's passion but decided that she didn't like the sound of The Beatles very much.

Despite this, an affection between the two of them was very strong and she was thrilled when he achieved success. In October 1965 John bought her a bungalow for £25,000 in Poole, near Bournemouth, overlooking the harbour. She was initially reluctant to leave her home and friends in Liverpool, but he was anxious to repay her for so many years of care and she eventually moved into the house in the south. She was proud to hear the news of the MBE award and John presented her with the actual medal, which she displayed in her living room. She was to be disappointed again when John sent a chauffeur to pick it up from her as he'd decided to return it to the Queen.

Over the years, 'Aunt Mimi' rarely discussed John with the press but following his death she agreed to speak in a series of articles in the *Daily Star* newspaper in 1981 because she was so upset at the false and inaccurate stories of his life which were appearing in the media.

George Smith Husband of John Lennon's Aunt Mimi whom John called Uncle George. In June 1953 when John was almost 12 and had just begun attending Quarry Bank Grammar School, George had a haemorrhage one Sunday and died suddenly. George had been a dairy farmer and his brother Alfred was a teacher at Liverpool Institute, the school which George Harrison and Paul McCartney attended. George remembers Alfred who was nicknamed 'Cissy' Smith because he was such a smart dresser.

Mrs Millie Sutcliffe Mother of Stuart, born in Scotland and now a widow residing in Sevenoaks, Kent. Millie Sutcliffe did much to perpetuate her son's reputation as an artist by organizing exhibitions of his work. She also attempted to put the record straight about the numerous erroneous stories and pieces of gossip that appeared in the press about Stuart — for instance, the oft-repeated story that he slept in a coffin at Gambier Terrace. In fact, Stuart slept in a camp bed which Mrs Sutcliffe bought after his death. Millie has passed on all Stuart's artwork that she possessed to one of her two daughters, Pauline, who has allowed them to be displayed at several Beatles conventions in England.

Mike McCartney I first remember Paul's brother, Mike, as a snappily dressed young hairdresser who used to provide some fine photographs for *Mersey Beat*.

He had a ready wit which came in handy when he joined The Scaffold, a highly creative trio who combined satire, comedy, poetry and music in a unique way which proved very successful for a number of years on stage, TV and

Jane Asher, Paul and Jim McCartney at Mike McCartney's wedding

record. He used to work in André Bernard's, a ladies hairdressing salon in the centre of Liverpool and changed his name to McGear so as not to trade-in on his brother's reputation (although the national press continued to overplay the fact, much to his frustration). Born in Walton Hospital on January 7th, 1944, he enjoyed a close relationship with his family, although he and Paul suffered from the premature death of their mother.

When Mike decided to team up with poet Roger McGough and humourist John Gorman in The Scaffold, they were to enjoy almost immediate success with a regular spot on the television show *Gazette* in 1964. George Martin produced their first single '2 Day's Monday' c/w '3 Black Jellyfish' and numerous other singles, with different producers and various record companies, followed over the years. They included 'Goodbat Nightman' c/w 'Long Strong Black Pudding'; 'Thank U Very Much' c/w 'Ide B The First'; 'Do You Remember' c/w 'Carry On Krow'; 'Lily The Pink' c/w 'Buttons Of Your Mind'; 'Charity Bubbles' c/w 'Goose'; 'Gin Gan Goolie' c/w 'Liverbirds'; 'All The Way Up' c/w 'Please Sorry'; 'Busdreams' c/w 'If I Could Star All Over Again'; 'Do The Albert' c/w 'Commercial Break'; 'Woman' c/w 'Kill'; 'Liverpool Lou' c/w 'Ten Years After On Strawberry Jam' and 'Leave It' c/w 'Street Baby'. Mike then made a number of solo singles for various independent companies.

The group had a number of strong hits, the biggest being their chart-topper 'Lily The Pink' and others included 'Thank U Very Much' and 'Liverpool Lou'. In 1974 Paul and Linda, together with Jimmy McCulloch, Denny Laine and Jerry Conway performed on Mike's solo album *McGear* for which Paul wrote a few songs. Paul also produced an earlier album, *McGough and McGear*, as well as their 'Liverpool Lou' single, and co-wrote some other songs with Mike. For a short time, Mike joined Grimms and toured and recorded with them. Apart from himself, the group comprised John Gorman, Andy Roberts, Neil Innes, Roger McGough, Viv Stanshall, Zoot Money and Gregory Conway. They cut two albums for Island Records in 1973: *Grimms* and *Rockin' Duck*. The Scaffold continued to make occasional appearances and cut records but made their final appearance together on an *All Fool's Show* on April 1st, 1977. Mike concentrated on writing children's books for a time, in addition to bringing out independent single releases.

Paul was best man at Mike's wedding to Angela Fishwick in north Wales on June 8th, 1968. Mike reciprocated by being best man at the wedding of Paul and Linda. Although estranged from his wife, he is the proud father of three lovely daughters.

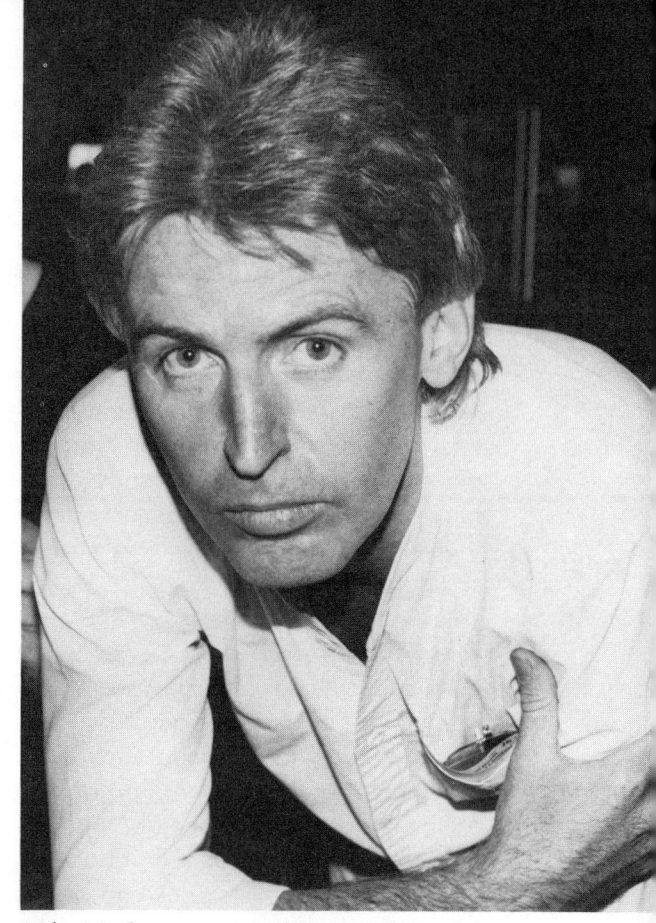

Mike McCartney, using his own name after eighteen years as Mike McGear

His 1981 book, *Thank U Very Much: Mike McCartney's Family Album*, is a lavish production and the best so far published on the early life of the McCartneys. In it Mike announced that he had now reverted to his real name after being known as Mike McGear for almost 18 years.

We should be grateful that Mike is an inveterate collector of even the slightest memento, whether it be a concert ticket stub or a visiting card, providing a wealth of memorabilia for posterity. A number are reproduced in his book: family photographs tracing the McCartney and Mohin clans; sketches; holiday snaps; the pics of all the McCartney Liverpool homes; the set of photographs of the two brothers growing up, unfolding in almost documentary fashion; the schools; the school reports; the little firsts – bike rides, girlfriends, school uniforms; the forms; letters; adverts; portraits of girlfriends; postcards; early Beatles pics; letters; newspaper cuttings; doodles; contracts; handbills; programmes – all produce a tour-de-force of memorabilia of the McCartneys' life.

Mike continues to live in Hoylake, regularly travelling across the Mersey to produce records by new Liverpool bands, in addition to his writing activities. Roger McGough lives in London and continues to publish and perform his popular poetry. John Gorman remains a television humorist, regularly appearing in long-running TV series such as *Tis Was* and *Over The Top*.

The Nurk Twins Name used by Paul and Mike McCartney when the two of them entertained the family circle as children. John Lennon and Paul McCartney were to use the name on an occasion when they accepted a gig as a duo.

Pete Shotton Arguably, John Lennon's closest friend. Blond-haired Pete lived close to John in Vale Street, Liverpool and they went to primary school together, formed their own gang and were reputed to have got into a lot of mischief, a habit which seems to have persisted when they both went to Quarry Bank Grammar School. When The Quarrymen were formed, Pete played washboard, even though he was not particularly interested in music. It came as something of a relief one evening when, at a party, John got drunk and smashed the washboard over Peter's head – all in good fun of course! Sans washboard Pete left the Quarrymen, but the mutual affection they shared continued. When John achieved financial success he bought Pete a supermarket in Hayling Island which he managed for a number of years. When Apple was launched, John asked him to leave the supermarket and run the Apple Boutique. This was in 1968. Unfortunately, the shop didn't do too well and John Lydon replaced Pete who became John's personal assistant for a short span of time.

Nigel Whalley School chum of John Lennon and Pete Shotton since early childhood. Nigel, who lived in Vale Street, close to Menlove Avenue, was a member of John's gang and affectionately nicknamed 'Whalloggs'. When the Quarrymen formed he originally played tea-chest bass, but then decided that he would become their manager. As an apprentice golf pro he figured he had important contacts. It was while he was calling on John one day that he witnessed the accident in which Julia Lennon was run down and killed by an off-duty policeman.

John 'Duff' Lowe A former pianist with The Quarrymen, John had vanished from Beatles history almost before it had begun and then reappeared in 1981 when he attempted to sell at auction a record he claimed was the first disc ever made by John, Paul and George. It was an amateur disc they made in the Quarrymen days with 'That'll Be The Day' sung by John and 'In Spite Of All The Danger' by Paul and George. Paul McCartney made him an offer for the disc, which he wanted to include in the Beatles museum he is starting. Lowe refused as he preferred to offer it in a sale to the highest bidder.

McCartney then instructed his solicitors to take action and a court ruled that the disc had to be placed in the hands of McCartney's solicitors until the niceties of the law had been sorted out. Lowe, now a stockbroker in the Midlands, then claimed that he had lost the record.

Rod Davis A schoolboy friend of John Lennon's who was in the Fourth Form with him at Quarry Bank Grammar School. When John formed The Quarrymen, Rod joined the group as banjoist. On occasions his father drove The Quarrymen to their bookings.

Len Garry One of the Liverpool Institute boys who was introduced to John Lennon by his friend Ivan Vaughan. When Nigel Whalley decided to become the skiffle group's 'manager', his place as tea-chest bass player was taken by Len.

Colin Hanton Drummer with John Lennon's first group, The Quarrymen, a skiffle band in which he qualified as a member purely because he possessed a drum kit. He was the youngest boy in the group and looked it. Colin always took his birth certificate around with him to prove his age in pubs where he used to down his favourite drink: Black Velvet. One of the many drummers associated with Lennon in the early days, prior to the permanent engagement of Ringo Starr in August 1962.

Ivan Vaughan In his pre-teen years, Ivan, who lived in the Dovedale area of Liverpool, joined a gang comprising John Lennon, Pete Shotton, and Nigel Whalley. Later, when a skiffle group called The Quarrymen was formed, Ivan played occasional tea-chest bass, sitting in when Nigel Whalley didn't feel like playing, and vice versa. When Ivan attended Liverpool Institute he discovered that one of his classmates, Paul McCartney, was interested in the guitar and invited him to meet John and his skiffle group. He'd already previously introduced another Institute schoolmate to John: Len Gary, who'd also become a member of The Quarrymen. Paul eventually agreed to go along with Ivan and the pair went to a church fête at St Peter's Parish Church in Woolton where Ivan was to arrange for Paul and John to meet for the first time. The actual date of this affair has been the cause of some confusion. The second issue of *The Beatles Monthly* magazine stated that the date was June 15th, 1955, which is the date mentioned by George Tremlett in both *The John Lennon Story* and *The Paul McCartney Story*. It is also the date quoted by Philip Cowan in his Book *Behind The Beatles Songs*. John Swenson in *The Beatles — Yesterday And Today* claims it was June 15th, 1957 and Hunter Davies in *The Beatles — The Authorised Biography* claims it was June 15th, 1956. Philip Norman in *Shout: The True Story of The Beatles* and Ray Connelly in *John Lennon 1940–1980* say it was July 6th, 1957. Ivan joined Paul McCartney and Tony Bramwell on a trip to America in 1968.

The Quarrymen Group formed by John Lennon when he was in the Fifth Form at Quarry Bank School. The name came from a line in the school song: 'Quarrymen strong before our birth'.

Pete Shotton (left) and John Lennon (third left) were founder members of The Quarrymen, who eventually became The Beatles

Initially John just got together with his friend Pete Shotton to learn the skiffle songs that were popular at the time. John played guitar, Pete, washboard. Another Quarry Bank pupil called Rod Davis joined them on banjo and their drummer was called Colin Hanton. Their old friend Nigel Whalley, who now attended the Bluecoat Grammar School, occasionally played tea-chest bass — and Ivan Vaughan played the instrument when Nigel didn't feel like it. Nigel eventually decided to become the group's manager and got them bookings at various local venues. Eric Griffith played lead guitar and when Pete left the group after John had broken his washboard, the group had found a new member, Len Gary, to play tea-chest bass. They performed skiffle numbers such as 'Cumberland Gap' and 'Railroad Bill' and pop tunes such as 'Twenty Flight Rock' and 'Let's Have A Party' and appeared at the Sixth Form school dances, at the youth club belonging to St Peter's Parish Church and at various socials and church fêtes. Ivan, who'd brought Len Gary into the group also introduced Paul McCartney to John and a week later Paul was asked if he'd join the band. When they appeared at Wilson Hall in Garston they were watched by George Harrison, a young guitarist friend of Paul's who was asked to join the skiffle group a year after Paul had become a member. They entered a 'Discoveries' competition at the Empire Theatre, hosted by Carroll Lewis, won the Liverpool heat and travelled to Manchester under the name Johnny and The Moondogs. The Quarrymen fluctuated from time to time, once becoming The Rainbows and often folding for short periods. By the end of 1958 Colin had ceased to be their drummer and Rod Davis had drifted away. Then Nigel Whalley contracted tuberculosis and Len Gary had meningitis and they never returned to the band. George joined The Les Stewart Quartet who were to begin a residency at a new club, the Casbah and when Stewart decided not to do the gig, George and the Quartet's guitarist, Ken Brown, were joined by John and Paul and the Quarrymen began their stint at the Casbah. A dispute led to the loss of Brown and they used temporary drummers such as Tommy Moore, changing their name to The Silver Beatles.

William Edward Popjoy Headmaster who took over the running of Quarry Bank Grammar School in 1956. At the time both John Lennon and Pete Shotton had a bad reputation in the school for their unruly behaviour. Rather than treat them in a strict disciplinarian fashion, Mr Popjoy took a sympathetic approach and began to help John and encourage his talent for drawing. It has been reported that he helped John in securing a place at Liverpool College of Art.

The Rebels A five-piece group, originally formed by George Harrison in 1957 for an appearance at the British Legion Club in Liverpool. The fee was £2 10s for the entire group in which George, his brother Peter and Arthur Kelly were the guitarists, supported by a boy on tea chest and someone else playing mouth organ.

The Rainbows Short-lived group name used by John, Paul and George in 1958 when they appeared with guest drummers. They selected the name because each member wore a different coloured shirt on stage.

Johnny and The Moondogs The name which John, Paul and George thought up when they entered the Carroll Levis show *Discoveries* as a trio. Although they beat competitors such as Billy Fury, they were pipped at the post in the finals by a band called The Gladiators. At the time the trio were very much under the influence of Buddy Holly and performed numbers such as 'Think It Over' and 'It's So Easy'.

Tommy Moore Liverpool drummer who played with The Silver Beatles for a short time in 1959. At 25 years of age he was several years older than them and worked at Garston Bottle Works. Casey Jones (Valence), leader of Cass and The Cassanovas, put The Silver Beatles in touch with him and he travelled up to Scotland for their two-week tour with Johnny Gentle. The group's van crashed at a crossroads near Banff and Tommy was hit in the face by a guitar case. He was taken to hospital where his face required stitches but although he was in pain, having had his front teeth knocked out, he played with the group that night. He left them on their return to Liverpool, settling for the security of his job at the bottle factory. Tommy died from a stroke in 1981, soon after joining a local jazz band.

Ken Brown For a brief spell in his life, a potential member of The Beatles. Ken was a rhythm guitarist who lived in the West Derby area of Liverpool and was a member of The Les Stewart Quartet, along with George Harrison. Hearing from George's girlfriend, Ruth Morrison, that one of his neighbours, Mrs Mona Best, was going to open a club in Heyman's Green, he approached her and began to help in preparing the club for opening night. As a result, Mrs Best offered to book his group as resident band. The Les Stewart Quartet had, until that time, appeared mainly at working men's clubs and Ken was pleased that he had obtained the residency. However, when he went to discuss it with Les Stewart, Stewart was so piqued that he had spent time fixing up the Casbah and had thus missed out on rehearsals at the Lowlands Club that he refused to do the gig. George was present at the flare up and left with Ken. He told him he'd find two mates and turned up with John Lennon and Paul McCartney. The four of them, together with various drummers, appeared at the Casbah for the next nine months as The Quarrymen, performing numbers such as 'Long Tall Sally' and 'Three Cool Cats'. The group received £3 which meant a payment of 15s for each of them. One night Ken was feeling ill and Mrs Best suggested that he could collect the money at the door rather than play on stage. At the end of the night she paid him 15s from the money due to the band. John and Paul strongly disagreed with this and an argument ensued during which Ken found himself without a group to play in. He was later able to continue playing at the Casbah as a member of The Blackjacks, Pete Best's group.

Ruth Morrison According to Ken Brown, ex-member of The Quarrymen, Ruth was George's first girlfriend. In interviews he recalled that one of her suggestions indirectly led to The Beatles teaming up. In the company of George and Ken, she told them of the plans Mrs Mona Best had of turning her basement into a club called the Casbah. George and Ken were members of The Les Stewart Quartet and after Ken had

Pete Best with his own group shortly before recording 'I'm Gonna Knock On Your Door'

made arrangements for them to begin a residency at the club, Les Stewart refused to play and George asked John and Paul to join Ken and himself. It was during the Casbah residency that George, aged 16, refused to take Ruth to the cinema, an incident that led to their breaking up. Ruth moved to Birmingham to become a nurse.

The Eddie Clayton Skiffle Group
Eddie Clayton did not exist. This was a name picked by Ringo Starr's neighbour Eddie Miles when the two of them, joined by another friend, formed a skiffle band during the fifties craze. Initially it comprised Eddie on guitar, Roy Trafford on tea-chest bass and Ringo on drums. They made their début at the Labour Club in Peel Street, Liverpool and soon enlarged the band with the addition of three more members. Ringo also sat in with other bands during the Ed Clayton period, including The Darktown Skiffle Group and The Raving Texans. When Eddie Miles left the group to get married, Ringo began to play mainly with Rory Storm's group, The Raving Texans, who eventually became Rory Storm and The Hurricanes.

Eddie Clayton was also the name used by Eric Clapton on the *Ringo* album.

Mona Best Dark-haired, handsome woman, born in New Delhi, India, who settled in Liverpool after marrying Johnny Best, a former boxing promoter. In

August 1959 she transformed the basement of her large house in Heyman's Green, West Derby, into a club which she called the Casbah (inspired by the Paul Henreid film *Algiers*). Among those involved in last-minute preparations, helping to paint the cellar area, were John Lennon, Cynthia Powell and friends. The original band, The Les Stewart Quartet, didn't take up their residency because of some obstinacy on Stewart's part and two members of his group, George Harrison and Ken Browne teamed up with John Lennon and Paul McCartney in another variation of the Quarrymen line-up and made their début there. One night, noticing that Ken Browne had a cold/was ill/absent (there are different versions of the actual reason) she paid him the 15s which was a quarter of the £3 nightly fee for the Quarrymen. There was a disagreement about this among the group and Ken was out. For a time they replaced him with Mona's younger son, the dark, brooding Pete Best. He formed his own band The Blackjacks for a while but when The Silver Beatles (as they now were) decided to go to Hamburg, he joined them. Two years later he was sacked and Mona, who had championed the group all along, was furious. She reckoned that as Pete was the most popular member of the band locally, there was some jealousy involved. She also wanted to clear the slur from her son's name when the excuse was given that George Martin had suggested he wasn't a good enough drummer (which Martin later denied).

Pete Best Pete was the youngest son of Mona Best and first began his association with The Beatles when they started their residency at his mother's club in Heyman's Green, West Derby. They were then known as The Quarrymen. Having performed there for some months they had a dispute with their drummer and Pete sat in with them. They were suitably impressed. Pete formed his own band — The Blackjacks — and The Beatles, who had been using various drummers such as Tommy Moore, felt they had to have a permanent member, particularly as they had a Hamburg gig coming up, so in August 1960 Pete became a Beatle. The effect was amazing. Girls went berserk over him, the fan following grew.

Apart from his good looks — and everyone regarded him as the most handsome Beatle — he was reticent and his reluctance or shyness in speaking to people gave him an aura of mystery. They would hang around the town centre during the day, visiting coffee bars, trying to kill time until the gigs in the evening. In the Jacaranda Pete would sit alone by the corner window, dressed in black leathers, silent, uncommunicative. His popularity began to increase and at one time there was an attempt to put him in the forefront of the band, but when his drum kit was moved to the front of the stage the girls kept trying to grab hold of him and the idea had to be abandoned. At one stage girl fans slept in his front garden just to be near him.

The cruel blow was struck when The Beatles were on the verge of success. Following their first EMI recording session, Pete was told that he was to be replaced by Ringo Starr. The announcement had come out of the blue. He was stunned. Everyone in Liverpool was stunned. Hundreds of letters began to pour into the *Mersey Beat* office. The outcry was more than Brian or The Beatles had expected and they began to get worried, particularly as the fans were turning hostile. Some limp suggestion that George Martin had thought he wasn't good enough as a drummer was trotted out — but this didn't stand up. In the first major analysis of The Beatles' local success in *Mersey Beat* in August 1961, Bob Wooler had written: 'Musically authoritative and physically magnetic, example the mean, moody magnificence of drummer Pete Best — a sort of teenage Jeff Chandler.' In fact, Pete was the only Beatle mentioned by name in the article.

Lots of local people began to discuss the controversy. Pat Delaney, the Cavern doorman, told me: 'Before The Beatles recorded, Pete was inclined to be more popular with the girls than any other member of the group. There were several reasons why I believe he was so popular. Girls were attracted by the fact that he wouldn't smile, even though they tried to make him. They also tried to attract his attention on stage but he wouldn't look at them.'

I'd witnessed Pete's hypnotic power over girls on numerous occasions. When I accompanied The Beatles and their fans on a coach trip to Manchester for their first radio broadcast, Pete was the only member of the group to be mobbed by the Manchester girls and he was trapped outside the theatre. On the evening the group were to make their first appearance at the Cavern with Ringo Starr, Matthew Street was crowded with Pete Best fans and the group had to run the gauntlet. Brian Epstein was terrified and George Harrison received a black eye.

Pete next joined The All Stars but success eluded him. He formed his own band, The Pete Best Four, whose first record 'I'm Gonna Knock On Your Door' c/w 'Why Did I Fall In Love With You' was issued by Decca on Decca F11929 on July 3rd, 1964. It was unsuccessful. In mid-1966 an album was issued on Savage BM 71 called *Best Of The Beatles*. He appeared on some American TV shows such as *I've Got A Secret*, but it all seemed in vain. He gave up the business, hung up his drumsticks and went to work in a local bakery. He married and bought a house with the proceeds he'd received after taking legal action regarding a *Playboy* interview in which a member of The Beatles suggested that he'd taken drugs.

The circumstances of his dismissal have remained a puzzle over the years, but Pete has put the record straight, having finally written his autobiography, which he completed in 1982. With the rise in nostalgia for The Beatles era, Pete has become of interest to researchers and TV and radio producers, as well as to the fans themselves, and acted as consultant for the made-for-TV movie *The Birth Of The Beatles*.

Larry Parnes Major London rock-and-roll impresario of the late fifties. He managed a string of British rockers, giving each member of his stable a prefabricated surname: Tommy Steele, Georgie Fame, Marty Wilde, Billy Fury, Dickie Pride, Johnny Gentle, Nelson Keene, Vince Eager, Johnny Goode and Duffy Power. On a trip to Liverpool to find a backing group for Billy Fury he auditioned several Mersey bands at the Wyvern Club, Seel Street, including The Beatles. He offered them the job on condition that they drop Stuart Sutcliffe, but they turned him down. He booked them on their first-ever tour, a two-week ballroom stint in Scotland as backing band to Johnny Gentle.

Billy Fury Born Ronald Wycherley on April 17th, 1941, Billy Fury became Liverpool's first-ever rock star. Fury, who had shared the same class as Ringo Starr in Dingle Vale Secondary School, had a string of hits, including 'Maybe Tomorrow', 'A Thousand Stars', 'Wondrous Place', 'Halfway To Paradise' and 'Letter Full Of Tears'. At one time his manager, Larry Parnes, considered The Beatles as a possible backing band for him. Together with Ringo Starr he appeared in the film *That'll Be The Day* in a holiday camp scene which was reminiscent of Ringo's stints at Butlin's with Rory Storm and The Hurricanes.

Duncan McKinnon Scottish promoter of the two-week ballroom tour in October 1962 in which The Silver Beatles, on their first major stint outside Merseyside, backed the Larry Parnes singer, Johnny Gentle. McKinnon was so unimpressed by the Liverpool quartet that he intended to sack them during their first week but was dissuaded from doing so by Gentle.

Johnny Gentle Moderately successful British singer of the late fifties who was one of the Larry Parnes stable of artists. The five-piece Silver Beatles provided backing for him on a two-week tour of Scotland in October 1960. Gentle wasn't too pleased with the group, who were appearing on their first major gig outside Liverpool. Gentle commented: 'When I first saw them I wondered what on earth Parnes had sent me.' Despite the initial impression, he decided to help them out, provided them with some stage clothes and talked the promoter out of firing them. Johnny later changed his name to Darren Young.

Johnny Hutchinson One of the most popular Liverpool drummers in the Mersey Beat days. He occasionally played with The Silver Beatles in the

Johnny Gentle, who fronted The Silver Beatles on a two-week tour of Scotland

period during which they had no regular drummer and sat in with the group when they auditioned for Larry Parnes in the Wyvern Club when Tommy Moore was late. Johnny made his début on drums at the age of 18 at the Corinthian Club, Slater Street with Cass and The Cassanovas and he also did the occasional gig with a modern jazz band. When Cass left the group it became The Big Three and Johnny turned down a two-year contract with Johnny Kydd and The Pirates to remain with them. Their line-up was Adrian Barber (lead), Johnny 'Gus' Gustafson (bass) and Johnny 'Hutch' Hutchinson (drums). Brian Epstein took over their management and as Adrian didn't want to become part of NEMS Enterprises he left the group to become stage manager at the Star Club in Hamburg and was replaced by Brian 'Griff' Griffiths, reputed to be the best guitarist on Merseyside — and an amazing drinker. He is said to have drunk the group's entire month's allocation of free drinks at the Star Club in a single night! Brian changed their aggressive image to a smooth, mohair-suited style and they didn't appreciate the grooming. As one of the most dynamic bands on Merseyside they also objected to the type of material Brian was making them record, such as Mitch Murray's pop tune 'By The Way' and they split from him. There were various changes in personnel with Hutch as the only consistent member. Among the interesting records they produced before their eventual split was an EP: *The Big Three At The Cavern*, recorded live at the best of cellars and containing an introduction by Bob Wooler.

Tony Bramwell teamed Johnny Gustafson and Brian Griffiths with Elton

Hutch, Gus and Griff — a red-hot Mersey trio. Johnny sat in with The Beatles on several occasions before Pete Best joined the group

John's drummer, Nigel Olssen, some years later to produce an album for Polydor, but it was unsuccessful.

Neil Aspinall The man whom The Beatles affectionately call 'Nell' was with the group longer than any other person and is one of that élite set of people who, from time to time, have been dubbed 'the fifth Beatle'. Originally born in Prestatyn, north Wales on October 13th, 1942, Neil then moved to Liverpool where he attended West Derby School before enrolling at the Liverpool Institute where he shared the same class as Paul McCartney for Art and English Lessons. George Harrison also attended the school but was in the class one year behind Paul and Neil. Neil became close friends with the two of them and kept in touch when he left in July 1959 with eight 'O' levels to study accountancy as a trainee earning £2 10s per week. When the group began to appear on regular gigs locally, Neil spent £80 on a second-hand van to drive them to the bookings, charging then 5s per man, per gig. At the time he was living at 8 Heyman's Green, the home of Mrs Best and her two sons. He remained behind when the Fab Four left for their first trip to Hamburg but decided that he was earning more money driving them around than he was as an accountant and packed in his job, helping Mrs Best to run the Casbah while they were in Germany. On their return to Liverpool, Neil had prepared posters for their appearances at Brian Kelly's gigs at Litherland Town Hall and began to work with determination as their road manager and general factotum. However, it must have been a particular strain on him when Pete Best, one of his closest friends, was sacked.

He was now their official road manager and continued in this post for a number of years, although Mal Evans was hired to take charge of the physical labour of handling equipment and Neil became something of a personal assistant to the boys. When Apple was launched, Neil was appointed managing director in January 1968, involving himself in all aspects of the company — even setting himself the task of producing their film *Let It Be*. When Neil was married to Susan Ornstein at Chelsea Register Office on August 30th, 1968, Paul McCartney attended the ceremony. Neil continues to run the Apple office in London on behalf of the individual members.

Jim Gretty Friendly, rotund chief salesman at Frank Hessy's music store and the person who sold guitars to most of the Mersey Beatsters in the late fifties and early sixties. It was Jim who sold a guitar to Mimi Stanley when she dropped in one day with her nephew, John Lennon, and Jim was later to book The Beatles on a number of dates in local social clubs — on whose circuit Jim himself was quite well known as a country music singer/guitarist. Jim offered lots of advice to all the groups and he once built a 'wall of fame' — a panorama of photographs of all the local bands stretching along the showroom wall.

Iris Caldwell Blond sister of the late Rory Storm. Her first boyfriend was George Harrison, in the days before he was interested in music. Iris was only 12 at the time. When she was 17 her boyfriend was Paul McCartney and she claims that Paul wrote 'Love Me Do' specially for her. Rory was one of the most popular group leaders in Liverpool and his association with drummer Ringo Starr was a close one. Iris recalls: 'Brian Epstein phoned my Mum and said he wanted to contact Ringo. He told her that Pete Best was leaving the group and The Beatles wanted a new drummer — Ringo. By then Rory was halfway through his summer show and when my Mum explained it to Brian he said, "We can wait, so long as we know he is going to join."

'It came at a funny time for Ringo because his parents hadn't wanted him to go down to Skegness for the summer and Ringo had agreed to give it all up so that he could become an apprentice joiner. At the beginning of the season Rory had gone round to his parents and persuaded them to let Ringo go to Skegness — and now here they were a few weeks later and Ringo was being asked to leave. Rory was a bit upset about it but you couldn't blame Ringo because everyone could see that The Beatles were going to go a bit further, though no-one had any idea of what was about to happen. What caused some bitterness was that Ringo wouldn't wait until the season at Skegness had finished and insisted on joining The Beatles at once — which left Rory without a drummer . . . and the group got the sack at Skegness.'

Iris married Shane Fenton who later changed his name to Alvin Stardust. They had a son, Sean, but Alvin divorced her to marry television celebrity Lisa Goddard.

Allan Williams Eccentric and funny — definitely one of Liverpool's famous characters who has successfully exploited his early associations with The Beatles by travelling around the world on lecture tours and appearing as guest-of-honour at Beatles conventions. His entrepreneurial skills were evident at one convention, where he sold mugs with the slogan 'The mug who lost The Beatles'. His personal card reads: 'The world's only talking head on the formation years of the cult of The Beatles. Available world wide. Beatles convention lectures with rare Beatles films. After-dinner speaker.'

Allan ran a club called the Jacaranda in Liverpool. He had a steel band playing for him and occasionally, because they were so cheap, he had a few bands play for him. He launched an Arts Ball at the George's Hall and booked Gene Vincent at Liverpool Stadium. Then his promotional activities seemed to wane as he concentrated on running his new club, the Blue Angel, situated on the premises formely occupied by a social club called the Wyvern. By booking a few gigs for some of the bands he was not acting as a manager in the true sense — if that were the case, there are numerous people who could claim to have managed The Beatles in the early days, ranging from Bob Wooler to Brian Kelly. When he booked Derry and The Seniors into the Kaiserkeller in Hamburg, The Beatles weren't even his second choice, but he nevertheless booked them and drove them over in a minibus. Since they arranged their own gig at the Top Ten Club, they wrote to him saying that they didn't think he was entitled to any commission. He threatened to make sure that they would never work again and apart from the fact that they used to come down to the Blue Angel to socialize, he had no real connection with them again. He had a local writer Bob Azurdia ghost a book about him in the sixties. I read the original manuscript and The Beatles are hardly mentioned. I wrote a feature on him for the *Mersey Mirror* which I called 'The Man Who Missed The Beatles' and soon after, Bill Marshall got together with Allan and they came out with a book called *The Man Who Gave The Beatles Away.*

His big love in the sixties was the Blue Angel Club which, in my opinion, was the best club that Liverpool ever had. Initially it was to be an up-market place with an exclusive membership and featured cabaret-type acts such as a scantily clad snake-charmer. Gradually, the groups began to come down there and we had lots of fun. When the Mersey sound became famous, the 'Blue' was the 'in' place, frequented by celebrities ranging from Judy Garland to George Melly. Allan was a great club host and it's a pity that the Blue Angel had to close.

Sam Leach Sam was one of that small but important group of Liverpool promoters who were part of the birth of the Mersey sound, booking the local groups rather than engaging chart names. Sam differed from the others in his efforts to present bigger and better bills, grandiose concerts with hosts of local bands,

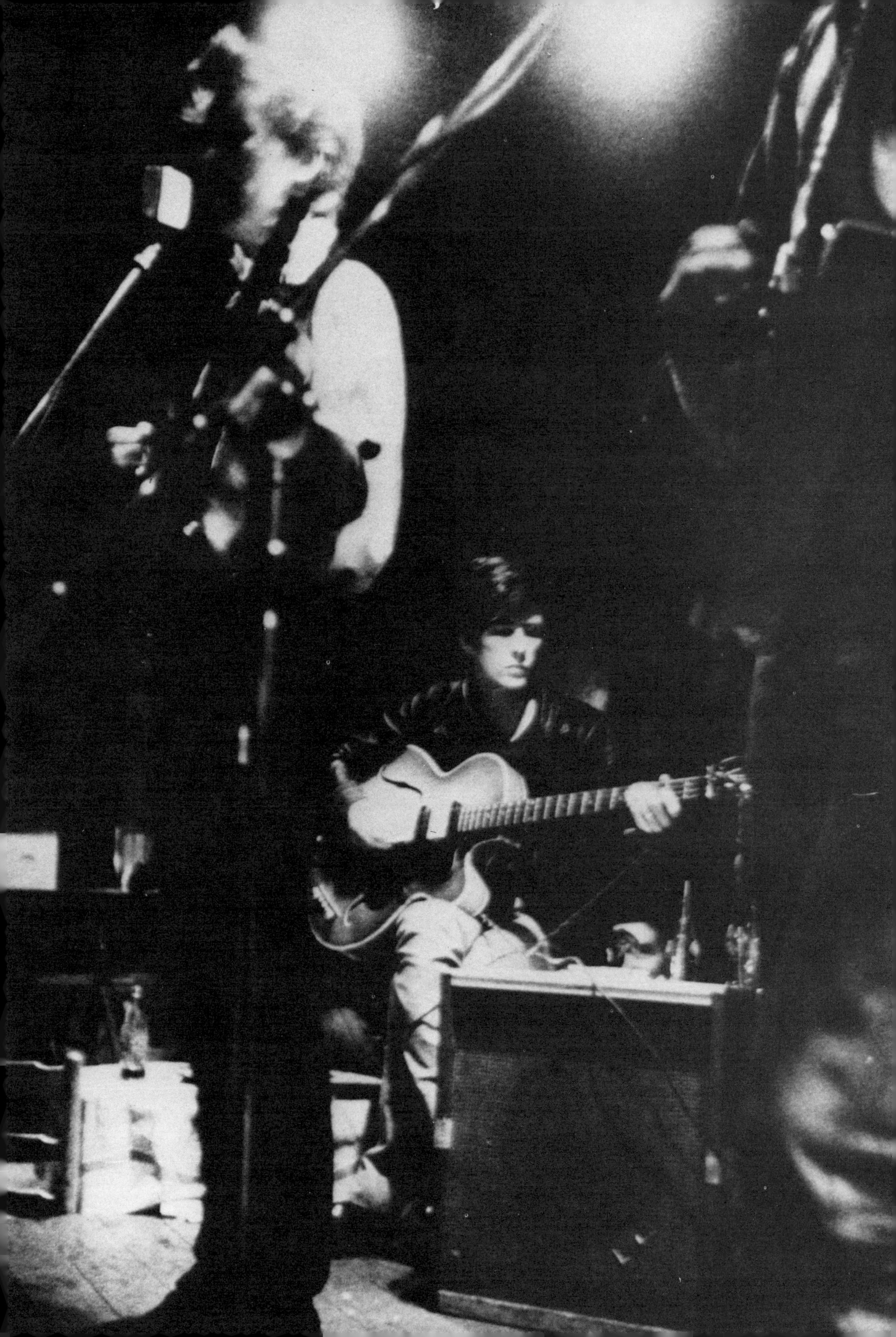

despite the financial constraints. On some of his larger concerts, at venues such as the Tower Ballroom, his initial payments would go towards the hire of the hall and then to the bouncers. Anything left over would be split between the groups with a larger fee promised for their next appearance. His creditors would often gather at the Jacaranda Club on a Saturday afternoon and Sam would invariably turn up with a scheme in which he promised to recoup their money on yet another big concert. His promotions at St George's Hall were sabotaged. Rival promoters hired some girls to jump on the stage and perform a striptease while a group was playing and he was barred from booking the hall again. Following the death of John Lennon he organized the large gathering in Liverpool's Lime Street to pay tribute to the city's famous son and he also organized a further event on the first anniversary of John's death.

Lord Woodbine Nickname of Liverpool-based West Indian, one of Merseyside's genuine 'characters' who was given the name because of his habit of chain-smoking a famous brand of cigarettes. He ran several 'shebeens' and managed the strip club at which The Beatles appeared, backing Janice. Such clubs were illegal in those days as striptease was forbidden by the local Watch Committee. He also accompanied The Beatles on their first trip to Hamburg.

Stuart Sutcliffe Many people throughout the years have been called

Stu Sutcliffe in Hamburg, shortly before leaving The Beatles to return to his art studies

'the fifth Beatle', but Stuart Sutcliffe was genuinely the fifth member of the band. He was born in Edinburgh on June 23rd, 1940. His parents moved to Liverpool and I first met him at Liverpool Art College in 1959.

Students began talking about a brilliant new artist in their midst and I was intrigued. He was in a different class to me but I was eager to see what his paintings were like. The first one I saw was a painting of a church, displayed in the entrance hall. I couldn't believe it: was this the product of the brilliant new student everyone was talking about? It was done in the style of Vincent Van Gogh. Stuart and I met and became friends and together with John Lennon and Rod Murray we'd get together for drinks in Ye Cracke or at various flats in the area and spend hours together in conversation, at one time calling ourselves 'The Dissenters'. Stu got a ground floor flat in Percy Street and I used to visit him there. We were all short of money in those days as the grants were small and if your parents weren't rich enough to support you, you had to work in the holidays to earn a crust, or live a very frugal existence indeed. Stu opted for painting during his vacations while I worked at a variety of jobs. He liked a jacket I'd bought with my wages, so I exchanged it with him for an oil portrait he did of me — in his Van Gogh style, once again.

We were both voted onto the Students' Union Committee and together with Alan Swerdlow, proposed to buy a PA system for John's band to use at the art college dances. Stuart was small, pale-faced and appeared fragile. He had striking features and his dedication to his art seemed to be burned into his eyes. He grew very close to John and was invited to join the group. Having no money he was unable to do so until he entered some paintings in the annual John Moore's Exhibition at the Walker Art Gallery. John Moore himself paid about £65 for one of the paintings and Stu was able to buy a bass guitar and join the band. It has been suggested that Stu was the one who came up with the name The Beetles, the 'a' being introduced by John later. He started making appearances with them locally at clubs such as the Jacaranda, even though he was not particularly expert at his instrument. But he looked good — and there was an intensity about him. The group auditioned for impresario Larry Parnes who was looking for a backing group for Billy Fury. He didn't hire them, but he booked them on a short tour of Scotland to back Johnny Gentle. Parnes, by the way, has denied that he ever said that he turned the Beatles down because Stuart couldn't play bass.

During the Scottish tour Stuart called himself Stu de Stijl, George became Carl Harrison and Paul called himself Paul Ramon.

When the opportunity came to visit Hamburg they were all ecstatic, having never been abroad before. When they appeared at the Kaiserkeller, Klaus Voorman, Astrid Kirchnerr and Jurgen Vollmer entered their lives. Astrid has said that she fell in love with Stu as soon as she set eyes on him and in November 1960, within two months of their first meeting, they became engaged.

On his return to Liverpool, Stuart was depressed because he was not allowed to return to the art college. His passions were art and beat music, but if he had to choose between them, art was the winner. On his next trip to Hamburg he continued to play with The Beatles but his heart was no longer in it and there were flare-ups with Paul McCartney who wanted to take over on bass guitar. When they returned to Liverpool, Stuart was no longer with them. Eduardo Paolozzi had arranged for him to study at the Hamburg State Art College and had also managed to secure him a grant. He lived with Astrid and her parents in the suburb of Altona and had his own attic studio. The only problem in this idyllic existence was the constant pain he had from headaches. Soon, he began collapsing in agony. At Christmas 1961 he took Astrid to visit his mum in Liverpool and introduced her to his friends. I saw them sitting together in the Jacaranda, both dressed in black, both as pale as ghosts. That was the last occasion I ever saw Stu. He returned to Hamburg and the pain continued. Doctors examined him, X-rays were taken. On April 10th, 1962 Astrid called for an ambulance and Stu died on the way to hospital of a cerebral haemorrhage. The Beatles arrived in Hamburg to open at the Star Club that same week to be met at the airport by Astrid who told them what had happened.

There have been several posthumous exhibitions of his work, the first major one taking place at the Walker Art Gallery. Surprisingly, Mrs Sutcliffe was unable to get a single member of the group to attend any of them — although they actively supported exhibitions by other artists, such as Jonathan Hague.

Although he was only 21 when he died, Stuart left behind a large volume of work, most of it created in those pain-stricken days in Hamburg.

John with former art college mate Jonathan Hague

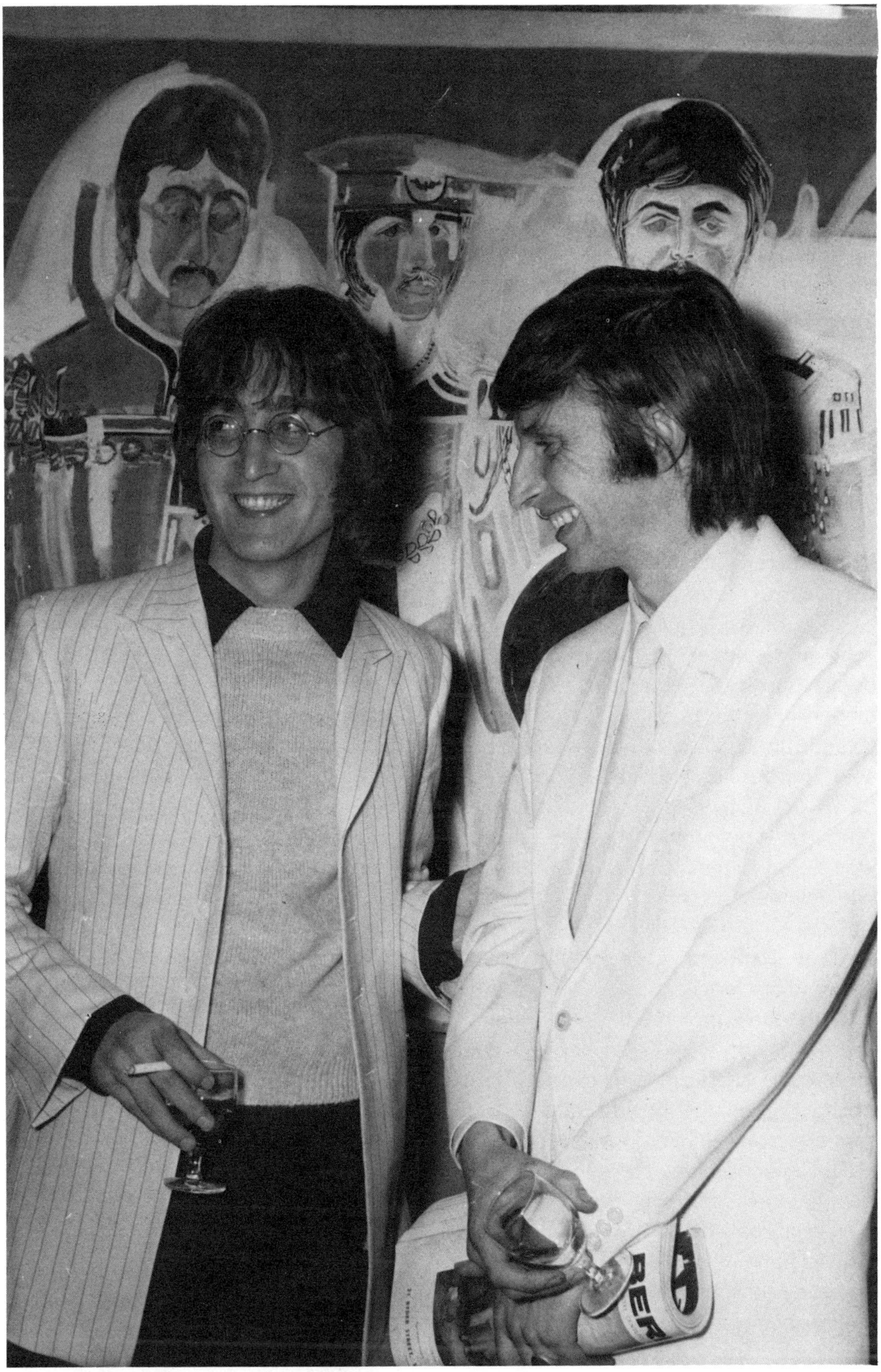

Jeff Mohamed One of John Lennon's closest friends at Liverpool College of Art.

Sam Walsh Liverpool painter who was a friend of John Lennon in his art school days. During the mid-sixties he received encouraging reviews for his large-scale oil portraits of Paul McCartney.

Jonathan Hague Friend of John Lennon from Liverpool College of Art. John and Paul sponsored an exhibition of his paintings in 1968 at the Royal Institute Gallery. His pictures included portraits of The Beatles, Mick Jagger and Vincent Van Gogh.

Rod Murray Student friend of John Lennon and Stuart Sutcliffe at Liverpool College of Art. He shared a flat with John in Gambier Terrace where The Beatles used to rehearse. When he moved from the premises he was presented with a bill for damages which he said The Beatles had helped to incur. Stuart paid off 50 per cent of the bill. Among the belongings they left behind was a copy of the *Daily Howl* which was later returned to John.

Arthur Ballard One of the most outstanding teachers at Liverpool Art College and a painter in his own right. There was something of a furore when the Walker Art Gallery hung one of his abstract paintings upside down. For some reason, Arthur always reminded me of Jean Gabin. He joined in the activities of his students, from boxing to having a drink at Ye Cracke, and was able to communicate with them because he genuinely looked upon them as human beings. Due to some personal problems there was a period in which I hardly attended the college and it was decided that I should be expelled. Arthur found out the reasons why I'd been absent for so long, talked the teachers round and made my life at college a lot easier. He also prevented John being expelled. Whereas Arthur managed to get me placed as the first student in the new Commercial Art Department at the college, the same department refused to take John. Arthur aided John in much the way Mr Popjoy did at Quarry Bank — finding out the reasons why he was regarded as the tearaway and then communicating.

In 1981, a few months after John had been killed, Arthur confessed to me that one of the reasons why he took so much interest in John was because of Stuart Sutcliffe, whom Arthur regarded as the most talented student he'd ever come across.

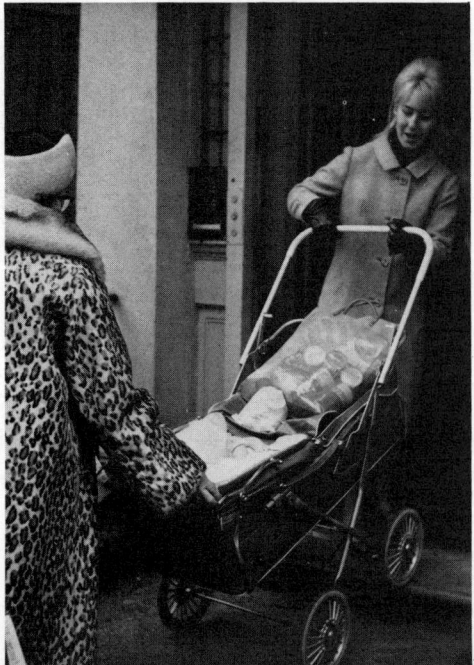

Cynthia Lennon Born Cynthia Powell in Blackpool on September 10th, 1939 where her mother and two brothers had been evacuated during the war. The family returned to their home in Hoylake where Cynthia spent her childhood. At the age of 18 she enrolled at Liverpool College of Art where she met John Lennon. Cynthia stayed very much in the background during The Beatles' rise to fame in Liverpool and on August 23rd, 1962 the couple were married in an unpublicized ceremony at Mount Pleasant Register Office in Liverpool. In attendance were Cynthia's brother Tony and his wife, Brian Epstein, Paul McCartney and George Harrison. Cynthia was pregnant at the time and her son John Charles Julian Lennon was born at Sefton General Hospital on April 8th, 1963. In the meantime, the couple had been living in a flat loaned to them by Brian Epstein, but as The Beatles were on the road and Cynthia was alone, she moved in with Mimi Smith, John's aunt. When Julian was six months old, Cynthia returned to Hoylake to stay with her mother. Later, news of Julian was revealed in the press and Cynthia and her son then moved in with John in a flat in Knightsbridge, London. Following The Beatles' American tour, John bought a house in Weybridge, Surrey.

During the height of Beatlemania, Cynthia travelled with John to various places, including America and India and, at one time, a Cynthia Lennon Fan Club was launched by Beatles fans. On returning from a holiday in Greece in 1968, Cynthia found John and Yoko together in her home and she left to stay with friends for a few days. She returned and there was a temporary reconciliation. John left on a business trip to America whilst Cynthia went on holiday to Italy with her mother and Julian. Whilst there, Alexis Mardas, a friend of John's, arrived with a message that John was divorcing her. Cynthia's attempts at a further reconciliation failed and on October 28th, 1968 she petitioned for divorce and this was granted on November 8th. On August 1st, 1970 she married Italian restaurateur, Roberto Bassanini, but this marriage also ended in divorce. In 1976 she married businessman John Twist and the couple moved to Ireland for a short time with Julian. The marriage didn't last and Cynthia settled in Ruthin, north Wales. Her biography *A Twist of Lennon*, under the name Cynthia Lennon Twist, was published in paperback in April, 1978 and featured a number of drawings illustrating her life with john. The book was republished following John's death and became quite a big seller. Cynthia then began touring America with her paintings, reverting to the name Cynthia Lennon and making personal appearances at special exhibitions in major cities.

Peter Mackey Peter was bass guitarist with Liverpool's premier R&B band, The Roadrunners. When George Harrison talked to Dick Rowe at the Philharmonic Hall beat contest he said: 'We've seen a great band down in London called The Rolling Stones who are almost as good as our own Roadrunners.' Pete became President of the Students' Union at the Liverpool College of Art and was commissioned to recoup the art college PA equipment lent to The Beatles which was needed for the art college dances. He travelled to Manchester on the fan club coach and approached John Lennon, who said: 'We've hocked it in Hamburg. If you need to know anything about it, just contact our manager.' Peter is now a freelance illustrator in London.

Lu Walters Bespectacled bass guitarist/vocalist with Rory Storm and The Hurricanes, Lu had been a member of the group since their formation at the end of the fifties as The Raving Texans. Their drummer was Ringo Starr. In 1960 The Hurricanes were appearing at the Kaiserkeller in Hamburg at the same time as The Beatles were at the Indra Club. Lu visited the Indra to watch the Beatles and took the stage to sing several numbers with them. Allan Williams was watching the show and was so impressed with Lu's singing voice that he arranged for him to make a record in a local studio with The Beatles backing him. Pete Best was feeling ill at the time so The Hurricanes' drummer, Ringo, replaced him for the session. Lu, together with John, George, Paul and Ringo recorded 'Fever', 'Summertime' and 'September Song'. When they finished the session The Beatles asked Allan if they could record a few numbers themselves, but he turned them down as the extra time in the studio would have cost him more money.

When I interviewed Lu for *Mersey Beat* in 1963 he had a fund of anecdotes and stories about Ringo and how their ebullient drummer began to sing in the act during their seasons at Butlin's, a British holiday camp. Ringo first started singing numbers such as 'Alley Oop' and later had his own spot in their show called *Ringo Starrtime*. Other incidents Lu recalled included the time they saved Ringo from drowning in the 12-foot end of the swimming-pool and how Ringo left The Hurricanes during a Hamburg trip to join Tony Sheridan's band, only to return to Liverpool a few months later and rejoin them.

The Beatmakers The Beatles and Gerry and The Pacemakers combined to form The Beatmakers who made a single appearance as a group at Litherland Town Hall, Liverpool on October 19th, 1961. Gerry Marsden wore George Harrison's leather outfit and George, who played lead, wore a hood. Paul played bass and wore a nightie and Freddie Marsden and Pete Best played one drum each. The numbers they performed that evening were: 'Whole Lotta Shakin';' 'What'd I Say?', 'Red Sails' and 'Hit The Road, Jack'.

Brian Kelly Liverpool promoter who was very active on the Mersey scene in the late fifties and early sixties promoting various local bands at venues such as Litherland Town Hall and Aintree Institute. He first booked The Silver Beatles at Litherland Town Hall on Boxing Day

1960 and was so impressed that he used them continually on all of his venues. He also ran an amplification business called Alpha Sound and provided the group with amplification equipment.

Bob Wooler Merseyside disc jockey who was particularly active in promoting The Beatles' career in their pre-recording days. At the beginning of the sixties Bob was compering numerous shows at the main Mersey jive hives such as Aintree Institute, Litherland Town Hall and Hambleton Hall and was instrumental in gaining bookings for the band from such promoters as Brian Kelly. His enthusiasm for The Beatles was spotlighted when he devoted his column 'Well Now — Dig This!' in *Mersey Beat* dated August 31st, 1961 to the first-ever published review and analysis of the group. Bob had a good turn of phrase and his 'Woolerisms' were well known locally. He was responsible for thinking up catch phrases for many Mersey Beat personalities including 'The Nemperor' (Brian Epstein), 'The Panda Footed Prince Of Prance' (Faron of Faron's Flamingoes), 'Mr Showmanship' (Rory Storm) and 'The Boswell of Beat' (Bill Harry). His original column was enlivened by phrases such as '. . . in the Beatles was the stuff that screams are made of', 'the mean, moody magnificence of Pete Best — a sort of teenage Jeff Chandler' and '[The Beatles are] rhythmic revolutionaries'.

Allan Williams, when involved with the opening of two of his clubs, the Blue Angel and the Top Ten, suggested that Bob become The Beatles' manager. When Brian Epstein signed up the group, he relied initially on Bob's advice concerning many aspects of their career locally. Bob also produced a number of NEMS Enterprises promotions for Brian. Despite being such a Beatles champion, Bob was badly hurt when physically attacked by John Lennon at Paul McCartney's 21st birthday party over an alleged remark and had to spend a few weeks in hospital. He took up Ray McFall's offer to work full time at the Cavern and introduced The Beatles on stage more times than any other person. During his Cavern days he also compered a weekly radio show for Radio Luxembourg and involved himself in managing a few local acts.

Currently he writes for a Liverpool newspaper and involves himself in local Beatles conventions.

Bernard Boyle Liverpool fan who formed a Beatles Fan Club in September 1961 prior to Brian Epstein managing the group and a few months before an official fan club was sanctioned. Bernard was president, Jennifer Dawes, treasurer and Maureen O'Shea, secretary.

Beryl Marsden Real name Beryl Hogg. Liverpool singer who first began performing with local groups at the age

A picture from the Mersey Beat *files: Gerry and The Pacemakers, having tidied up their image after signing with Brian Epstein*

of 14. Generally regarded as the best female vocalist of the Mersey Beat period, she was originally promised the opportunity of recording 'Love Of The Loved', but the song went to Cilla Black when she signed with Brian Epstein. Beryl recorded several numbers, a few of which entered the lower region of the charts and she appeared with The Beatles on their last British concert tour in December 1965. She moved to London and became a member of Shotgun Express with Rod Stewart and Peter Bardens and later returned to Liverpool, married and became a housewife. She returned to her career as a vocalist with several Mersey bands in the seventies and is still appearing as a singer in London and Liverpool.

Adrian Barber Yorkshire musician, based in Liverpool in the late fifties and early sixties. A member of Cass and The Cassanovas and The Big Three, he was an electronics wizard who designed huge amplifiers, nicknamed 'coffins', for several Mersey bands, including The Beatles. He based himself in Hamburg and was stage manager of the Star Club, single-handedly building a complete sound system for the club. Adrian used to record the various bands, among them The Beatles. The tapes he recorded and gave to Kingsize Taylor were released in 1977 as the album *The Beatles Live! At The Star Club In Hamburg, Germany, 1962*. Joey Dee was so impressed with Adrian's sound system in Hamburg that he invited him to America to build a similar system for The Starliter Club. Adrian later became successful as a recording manager and now lives in Brighton, Massachusetts.

Arthur Dooley Ebullient Liverpool sculptor. Alan Owen once used him as the inspiration for the leading character in a TV play and he was the subject of a *This Is Your Life* programme. A friend of The Beatles during their early career, he was one of the many local artists to use the group as a theme for his work. Arthur created the statue dedicated to The Beatles which was erected in Matthew Street in April 1974. Disc jockey Peter Prince launched an appeal to raise £500 to enable Arthur to work on his tribute. £1,300 was raised, the balance being donated to a Liverpool boys' club. The work is fixed to the wall above a club in Matthew Street. When the Cavern was knocked down to make way for an underground shaft, a new Cavern opened on the opposite side of the street, although it has since undergone several changes of name. The sculpture depicts a Madonna holding three babies, a fourth is separated from the group and is flying away. The three represent John, George and Ringo and the solo babe is Paul. Five initials surround the piece: M.J.P.G.R. (the M standing for Madonna). Directly above the piece is a reproduction of a Liverpool street sign: 'Beatle Street. Liverpool 2'.

Gerry and The Pacemakers Friendly rivals of The Beatles in the popularity stakes during the Mersey Beat days. Leader Gerry Marsden had been a musician since the age of 14 when he formed Gerry and The Mars Bars. As a rock-and-roll band they were highly popular in both Liverpool and Hamburg. They became the second band to be signed by Brian Epstein but, unlike The Beatles who were left to develop in their own way, Gerry and The Pacemakers were transformed from a rock band to a pure pop group but nevertheless had tremendous success and a hat trick of No. 1 hits with their first three releases: 'How Do You Do It?', 'I Like It' and 'You'll Never Walk Alone', an achievement which remains unsurpassed in Britain. For a short period of time they trod a similar path to The Beatles with their own Christmas show, a film: *Ferry 'cross The Mersey* and international tours. The other members of the band were Les Maguire (piano), Les Chadwick (bass) and Freddie Marsden (drums).

Royston Ellis British author/poet of the early sixties who earned short-lived fame as an English exponent of the American 'Beat Generation' poetry. Whilst on a trip to Liverpool to appear at Liverpool University for poetry readings he met and became a friend of The Beatles, who played host to him at the Gambier Terrace flat. They also made an appearance with him, backing him on a 'Poetry-to-Beat' session at the Jacaranda Club, Slater Street. As a writer, his books included *Jiving To Gyp,*

Brian with Gerry and The Pacemakers and Billy J. Kramer and The Dakotas

Driftin' With Cliff Richard (co-authored with Jet Harris) and *The Big Beat Scene*. Although he wrote a paperback biography of The Shadows, he never attempted a book about The Beatles.

Davy Jones American singer based in Europe during the early sixties. The Beatles provided the backing for his Cavern appearances in 1961.

Billy J. Kramer Kramer, whose real name was William Ashton, was active on the Mersey scene at the beginning of the sixties as lead singer with Billy Forde and The Phantoms. He changed his name to Billy Kramer and fronted The Coasters. The group became very popular in Liverpool under the wing of pensioner Ted Knibbs who transferred the management to Brian Epstein after Billy was voted third most popular act on Merseyside in the *Mersey Beat* poll. As The Coasters would not turn professional, Epstein secured a top Manchester band, The Dakotas, who had been backing Pete MacLaine, as Billy's regular band. Epstein added the J. to his name and arranged for him to record a number of Lennon/McCartney numbers with George Martin as his recording manager. Billy J. then had immediate success with the Lennon/McCartney material which included 'Do You Want To Know A Secret?', 'I'll Be On My Way', 'Bad To Me', 'I Call Your Name',

'I'll Keep You Satisfied', and 'From A Window'. The Dakotas comprised Mike Maxfield, lead; Robin McDonald, rhythm; Ray Jones, bass; and Tony Mansfield, drums.

Dick Matthews Dick was one of the people who helped launch *Mersey Beat*. When he heard that I was looking for finance to start a paper he introduced me to his friend Jim Anderson, who lent me £50. Aware that we were running the newspaper with virtually no working capital Dick decided to help by taking photographs for us — and thus he takes his place in history. He was the person who took all the early shots of The Beatles performing on stage at the Cavern. They were published in *Mersey Beat* and they have since appeared throughout the world as a record of how the Fab Four looked in those early days. Without Dick, a part of rock history would be sadly missing.

At one time he took a small room on the same floor as the *Mersey Beat* office which he converted into a darkroom. Despite his seeming disorganization, he always provided us with great Beatles shots. Sometimes he'd come to the office and begin to root about in his top pocket for negatives. Once, he even discovered one of his negatives attached to the sole of his shoe!

Peter Kaye Business name for a compact, dedicated photographic studio run by Bill Connell, who provided *Mersey Beat* with much of its early photographic material. Bill's assistant at the time was Les Chadwick, a former school chum of mine from the Junior Art School. Les took most of the early Beatles sessions for Brian Epstein, which have since been reproduced throughout the world. Bill still runs his Peter Kaye business from a prestigious shop in Liverpool's Bold Street and Les is manager of Kodak factories in the north-west of England.

LIVERPOOL'S GREATEST DISCOVERY SINCE YOU KNOW WHO

the ESCORTS

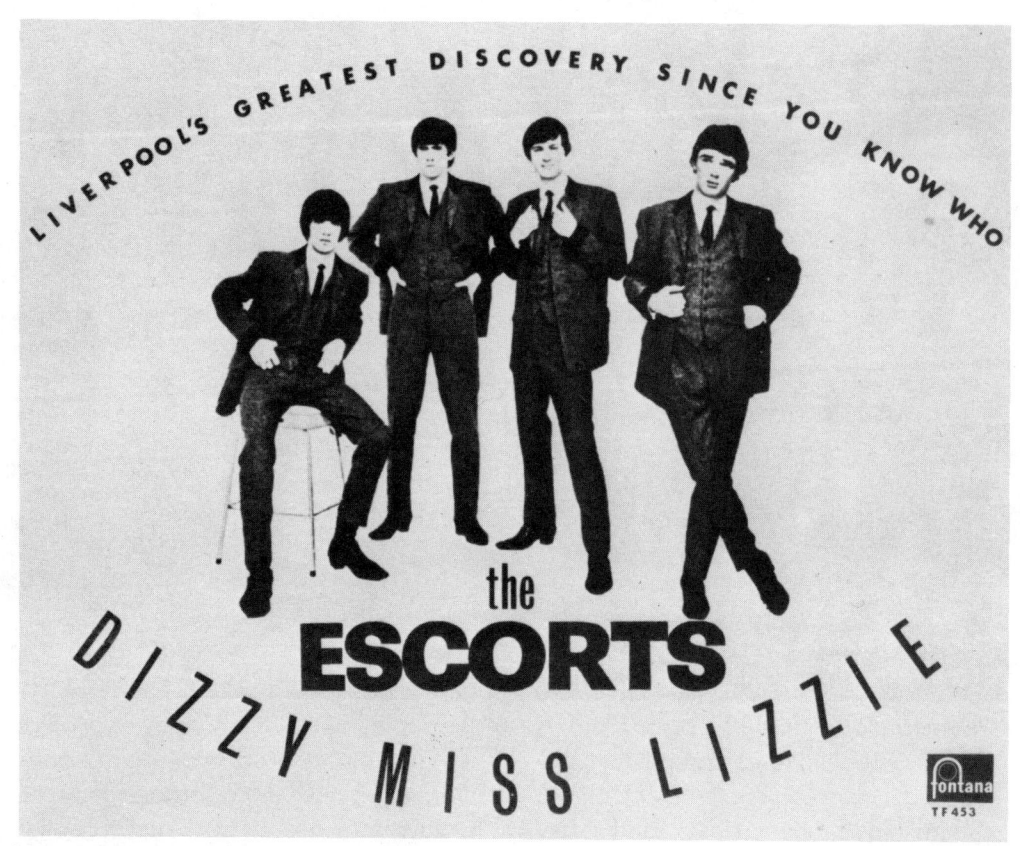

DIZZY MISS LIZZIE

fontana
TF 453

Graham Spencer Liverpudlian who was one of the main *Mersey Beat* photographers in the early sixties. When I approached him about the book he began to search for some photographs and discovered four boxes of material which he hadn't looked at for nearly 20 years. Together with his wife Irene he unearthed about 70 previously unpublished pics of The Beatles, together with a number of Beatles colour transparencies and numerous pics from the Mersey Beat days, including some of John Lennon and myself, Freda Kelly with Paul McCartney, and Lennon and McCartney with TV producer Johnny Hamp. Graham's son Paul was named after his favourite Beatle. From his shop in Childwall Fiveways, Liverpool, he has built up a successful photography business based on the early recognition he received for his work in the *Mersey Beat* newspaper.

Steve Aldo Liverpool vocalist who first started singing at the age of 13 in *The Backyard Kids* at the Pavilion, Lodge Lane. When 14 he sang at the Holyoake Hall and, when on holiday in the Isle of Man, sang with the Ivy Benson Band. Later he sang occasionally with Howie Casey and The Seniors before moving to Cardiff to become a ladies' hairdresser. He worked at Raymonde's (Mr Teasy Weasy) in London before going away to sea for a year. He returned to Liverpool and joined The Challengers, then moved to Germany and sang occasionally with The Dominoes. On returning to Liverpool he joined The Nocturnes for a short time before becoming a member of The Griff-Parry

Five. He was booked to appear on The Beatles December tour of Britain in 1965 and currently manages a public house in Liverpool.

The Escorts Popular Mersey band who never quite made it into the top league. They comprised Terry Sylvester (guitar), John Kinrade (guitar), Mike Gregory (bass) and Pete Clarke (drums). Paul McCartney produced their single 'From Head To Toe' c/w 'Night Time', issued on November 18th, 1966 on Columbia D.B. 8061, but it fared no better than their previous releases. The group appeared on the bill with The Beatles at several Cavern appearances, including The Beatles' very last gig there on August 3rd, 1963. Terry Sylvester later joined The Hollies.

Lee Curtis Stage name of Peter Flannery. Lee originally appeared on the Liverpool scene in 1961 in a group called Lee Curtis and The Detours, managed by his brother Joe, who was a friend of Brian Epstein. When Pete Best was fired from The Beatles he joined Lee in a new band called Lee Curtis and The All Stars. Lee was the first member of the Mersey Beat scene to record a solo single and moved to Hamburg where he appeared for several years and recorded a number of albums and singles. Later he moved to Manchester as manager of a club.

The Fourmost The group started life in 1959 as The Four Jays and comprised Brian Redman (drums), Joey Bowers (vocals/rhythm guitar), Billy Hatton (vocals/bass guitar) and Brian O'Hara (vocals/lead guitar). They played rock, jazz and included comedy in their act and by 1962 they had called themselves The Four Mosts and their line-up was Brian O'Hara and Billy Hatton with Mike Millward (rhythm guitar) and Dave Lovelady (drums). They played R&B, C&W, jazz and standards and were interested in the cabaret circuit. Brian Epstein signed them up and shortened their name to The Fourmost. They made their recording début with the Lennon/McCartney number 'Hello Little Girl' c/w 'Just In Case' which was issued in Britain on August 23rd, 1963 on Parlophone R5055 where it reached No. 9 in the charts with a 17-week chart life. It was released in the US on Swan 4152 on September 16th.

The group, whose records were produced by George Martin, recorded another Lennon/McCartney song: 'I'm In Love' c/w 'Respectable' on Parlophone R5078 on November 15th, 1963. It was issued in the States on ATCO 6285 on February 10th, 1964. This reached No. 17 in Britain with a chart life of 12 weeks. Their EP *'The Fourmost Sound'* containing the four tracks was issued on Parlophone GEP 8892 on February 14th, 1964. Their biggest hit was not a Lennon/McCartney number but a song called 'A Little Loving' which reached No. 6 in the

British charts. They had several minor chart entries with 'How Can I Tell Her', 'Baby, I Need Your Loving' and 'Girls, Girls, Girls'.

The Fourmost appeared on *The Beatles Christmas Show* at the Finsbury Park Astoria in December 1962. They performed 'Hello Little Girl', then Brian O'Hara sang 'White Christmas' during which he did impressions of Gracie Fields, Elvis, Dean Martin, Adam Faith and The Beatles.

In 1969 Paul McCartney produced their British single 'Rosetta' c/w 'Just Like Before', a number he had suggested they record. It was issued on February 21st on CBS 4041.

The group still perform on the cabaret circuits of the north of England.

Casey Jones Although he wasn't a Liverpudlian, Casey (real name, Casey Valence) was the leader of one of the most popular, although relatively short-lived Liverpool bands, Cass and The Cassanovas, who made their début at the Corinthian Club, Slater Street in 1959. Casey played lead guitar/vocals, Adrian Barber, guitar, and Johnny Hutchinson, drums. Soon after their formation they decided they needed a bass guitarist and Hutch brought Johnny Gustafson to see the group and suggested he join. Johnny didn't have a guitar but Adrian converted a Hoyer acoustic for him and put bass guitar strings on it. They appeared at the Liverpool Stadium with Gene Vincent and also ran their own venue, the Cassanova Club.

Before launching *Mersey Beat* in June 1961 I'd spent the previous year building notebooks of information about the Liverpool scene. Casey gave me his version of how Mersey bands came to go to Hamburg. At one time, Casey Jones used to sleep overnight in Allan Williams' Jacaranda Club in Slater Street. Cass, who was a hustler and had his contacts in London, heard about a German promoter who was looking for British groups to appear in Hamburg. Without Allan knowing, Cass had been making long-distance calls to a promoter in Hamburg, trying to fix up a gig for The Cassanovas. One afternoon, when he wasn't there, the promoter phoned the 'Jac'. Allan talked to him, found what had been going on and told him that he could supply all the groups that were needed.

Cass left The Cassanovas and moved to London, the band became The Big Three and Casey formed a new outfit. He later moved to Germany and had a number of hits with Casey Jones and The Engineers. It's interesting to note the line-up of the band between August and October 1963: Casey Jones (vocals), Eric Clapton (guitar), Tom McGuiness (guitar), Dave McCumisky (bass) and Ray Smith (drums).

Incidentally, Cass once suggested to John Lennon that the group should call themselves Long John and The Silver Men because he didn't like the name The Beatles.

Janice The Stripper (Full name unknown.) One wonders how successful she would have become exploiting her 'art' on the circuits if she had advertised the fact that The Beatles provided backing music for her. Lord Woodbine ran a private strip club in the Upper Parliament Street area of Liverpool in 1960 at a time when strip clubs were banned by the local Watch Committee. One of the early Beatles stints was at the club backing Janice. Paul wrote me a letter about the experience which I subsequently printed in *Mersey Beat*. Paul wrote: 'At the end of the act she would turn around and . . . well, we were all young lads, we'd never seen anything like it before, and all blushed . . . four blushing red-faced lads.' But the fact was that John Lennon and Stuart Sutcliffe, as students at the art college, had to spend several hours every week sketching nude females in the college life rooms: 'To tell you the truth, it was a bore for most of the time and we tried to get out of the chore by sagging from the life lessons.'

It was shortly before the experience of The Beatles' first trip to Hamburg in which, ensconced in the St Pauli district, they were probably surrounded by more strippers per goose pimple than anywhere in the world. Stu Sutcliffe was a member of the group at the time and Paul commented further: 'Janice brought sheets of music for us to play all her arrangements. She gave us a bit of Beethoven and the 'Spanish Fire Dance'. So in the end we said: "We can't read music, sorry, but instead of the 'Spanish Fire Dance' we can play the 'Harry Lime Cha-Cha' which we've arranged ourselves, and instead of Beethoven you can have 'Moonglow' or 'September Song' — take your pick . . . and instead of 'The Sabre Dance' we'll give you 'Ramrod'." So that's what she got. She seemed quite satisfied anyway.'

Janice is not to be confused with Jan Carson, the stripper from Raymond's Revue Bar who performed a striptease dance in *Magical Mystery Tour*.

Rory Storm and The Hurricanes
Rory Storm was one of the most memorable characters of the Mersey Beat scene. Dubbed 'Mr Showmanship' by Bob Wooler, he was a sheer professional dedicated to achieving the success which eluded him and 100 per cent committed to providing entertainment.

His real name was Alan Caldwell, but he so identified himself with his stage persona that he changed his name officially to Rory Storm and dubbed his house in Childwall 'Stormsville'. He held open-house at Stormsville and would regularly bring friends home in the early hours of the morning, waking up his mum, who'd make chip butties for the guests. Regulars at the early morning chat sessions included Paul McCartney, Jimmy Tarbuck, Johnny Guitar and myself.

An all-round sportman, he was captain of the Mersey Beat XI football team. Rory had courage and it was amazing how he became one of the most popular vocalists on Merseyside despite the impediment of a severe stutter, though he never stuttered on stage. Telephone conversations, in particular, were hard to conduct with Rory.

He was a night bird — and he was also publicity conscious. On one occasion I was woken up in my flat at four o'clock in the morning by a tremendous hammering on the front door. The pounding was so intense that people on every floor poked their heads out of the windows to discover what the emergency was. When I opened the door, a police car had pulled up and was shining its light on the steps to see what all the fuss was about. Rory took his time explaining that he'd just come across a photograph of himself and had brought it around because he wanted me to use it in *Mersey Beat*.

He originally formed his band during the skiffle craze in 1957. Called The

One of Liverpool's finest groups, Rory Storm and The Hurricanes: Ty Brian, Johnny Guitar, Rory Storm, Lu Walters and a tiny Ringo Starr

Raving Texans, they comprised Rory, Ringo Starr, Johnny Guitar, Ty Brian and Bobby Thomson. They were very popular at Butlin's, Skegness, where they appeared for three summer seasons. They received many offers to appear in Italy and France and became very popular in Hamburg where they featured on many occasions.

When the Beatles asked Ringo to join them, Rory was intensely upset. They'd had a very close rapport and the group never really recovered from Ringo's departure. Rory commented: 'During the four or five years Ringo was with us he really played drums — he drove them. He sweated and swung and sung. Ringo sang about five numbers a night, he even had his own spot — it was called "Ringo Starrtime". Now he's only a backing drummer. The Beatles' front line is so good he doesn't have to do much. This is not the Ringo Starr who played with us.

'When Ringo first joined The Hurricanes (we were called The Raving Texans then), he didn't have any rings and we just called him Ritchie. During our first year at Butlins we all chose fancy stage names and that's when he became Ringo Starr.'

Despite their popularity on the Continent, they never achieved any degree of success on the recording scene. Hurricanes tracks were included on the *This Is Mersey Beat* albums. On Volume One they perform 'Dr Feelgood' and 'Beautiful Dreamer' and on Volume Two 'I Can Tell'. The group were also filmed during a Cavern session by the late Charlie Squires for his TV documentary *Beat City*, but they were generally ignored by the A&R men who made the trek to Livepool.

Late in 1964 it seemed that luck had touched Rory and his group at last. They were signed to an agency and management contract with the powerful Arthur Howes organization in London and Brian Epstein personally recorded them. It was the only time Brian produced a record and also the last record The Hurricanes ever made. On November 13th, Parlophone released their version of 'America' from the musical *West Side Story*.

When The Hurricanes broke up, Rory began to carve a career for himself as a disc jockey (yes, he still had his stutter) and was popular in both Spain and Holland. His sister Iris, a former girlfriend of Paul McCartney was married to Shane Fenton. When Rory's father died, his mother never recovered from the shock. In 1972 Rory took time off from his job in Amsterdam to visit his mother and they were both found dead. At the scene of the suicide it was found that they'd consumed alcohol and pills. One

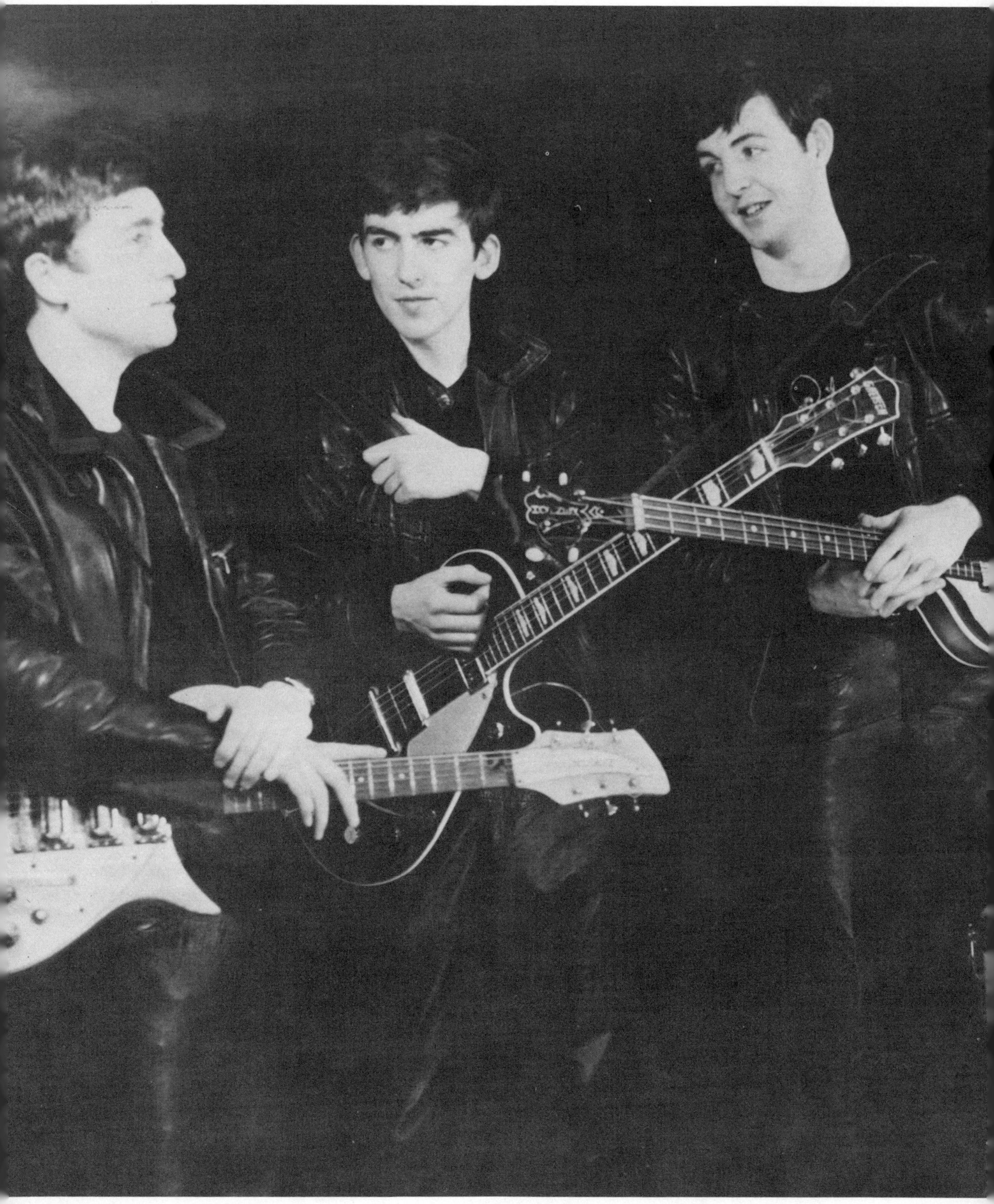

can only speculate on what happened but my own theory is that Rory was trying to console his mother who was still in a deep depression over the loss of her husband. I'd recently talked to Rory and he was enthusiastic about his DJ job, and I don't think he would consciously have attempted suicide.

Kingsize Taylor Liverpool singer/guitarist, real name Edward Taylor, who first began to appear on the Mersey scene following the skiffle boom in the fifties with groups such as The James Boys. His most noted band was Kingsize Taylor and The Dominoes. He spent several years in Hamburg during which time he asked for and was given the tapes of The Beatles at the Star Club, recorded by Adrian Barber. Fourteen years late, having settled down as manager of a butcher's shop in Southport, he was asked to appear on a show in Liverpool. He mentioned the tapes to Allan Williams and together they began hawking them around. They were eventually accepted by Paul Murphy, a Liverpudlian then running Buk Records in London and the resulting album *The Beatles Live! At The Star Club In Hamburg, Germany: 1962* was released on May 1st, 1977.

Ron Appleby Merseyside compere at the beginning of the sixties who claimed he was the first person to announce the Fab Four on stage as The Beatles when they shortened their name from The Silver Beatles. This caused much amusement in Liverpool at the time as Bob

One of the early photo sessions commissioned by Brian Epstein. The photographer was Albert Marrion, who retired in 1979

Wooler also claimed that honour and the two of them were always arguing about it.

The Swinging Bluejeans The Swinging Bluejeans, still alive and kicking and very popular on the Continent of Europe, have proved to be Liverpool's longest surviving group, having originally formed in 1957. They were then known as The Swinging Bluegenes and were a skiffle band. They had their own guest night at the Cavern, didn't play rock and roll and liked trad jazz and swing numbers of the twenties. In June 1961, John Carter left the band and the line-up then was Ray Ennis (lead), Ralph Ellis (solo), Les Braid (bass) and Paul Moss (banjo). The group began to do a three-quarters-of-an-hour spot every Friday, Saturday and Sunday and opened their Tuesday evening guest nights in 1961. On March 21st they welcomed The Beatles to their first-ever Cavern gig. The Bluegenes were held in high regard in Liverpool and when Bob Woolver compiled a Top Ten list in the October 5th, 1961 issue of *Mersey Beat*, with The Beatles placed at No. 1, he qualified this by writing: 'My list of what I rate to be the ten most popular rock groups on Merseyside — excluding the Bluegenes, of course. They are beyond comparison. They are in a class of their own.'

With the growing popularity of the groups and the death of the trad jazz boom, they altered their name to The Swinging Bluejeans and began to play rock and roll. Their line-up was Ray Ennis (guitar), Ralph Ellis (guitar), Les Braid (bass guitar) and Norman Kuhlke (drums).

After the success of The Beatles, Mersey groups were hot and The Bluejeans made their recording début with 'It's Too Late Now' c/w 'Think Of Me', released in June 1963. At the time I was suggesting various rock numbers for local groups to record in my *Mersey Beat* editorials and one which I plugged was called 'The Hippy Hippy Shake', which The Bluejeans recorded. When it was released it was reviewed on the all-Beatles edition of *Juke Box Jury*, held at the Empire Theatre, Liverpool on December 7th, 1963. Remembering that I championed the number, John Lennon commented, 'I prefer Bill Harry's version' and that weekend thousands of youngsters throughout Britain were plaguing record shops with requests for Bill Harry's version of 'The Hippy Hippy Shake'.

The Bluejeans' success continued for some years: they appeared in a special film for Pathé Pictorial, had their own weekly Radio Luxembourg show *Swingtime*, appeared on the Christmas 1963 edition of *Z Cars* performing 'Hippy Hippy Shake', 'Angie' and 'Money' and also appeared in the film *Circularama Cavalcade* which had its London premier on March 11th, 1964.

Their current line-up is Ray Ennis (guitar), Les Braid (bass guitar), Colin Manley, ex-member of The Remo Four (guitar) and Ian McGee (drums).

Harry Bostock Enterprising manager of the Plaza, St Helens, a ballroom in a small town close to Liverpool which opened in 1956. Harry began featuring groups in 1958 and in 1959 began to use groups exclusively and was open four nights a week: Friday, Saturday, Sunday and Monday. There were usually three groups per night and admission charges varied from 2s 6d to 3s 6d. Most of the top Mersey groups appeared there, including The Beatles,

Gerry and The Pacemakers, The Merseybeats and The Searchers.

Jackie Lomax One of Liverpool's early rock bands was Bob Evans And The Five Shillings. They changed their name to Bob's Vegas Five but when they turned up at Litherland Town Hall one night to find that an unknown group called the Undertakers was billed — the promoter, Brian Kelly, told them that they were it. They adopted the name, dressed in sombre undertaker's garb, complete with top hats and began their set with a rendition of 'The Death March'. All the members had nicknames at the time: Shine was lead guitarist Chris Huston; Big Bow was drummer Bob Evans; Boots was saxophonist Brian Jones; Mush was bass guitarist Davy Cooper; Trad was solo guitarist Geoff Nugent; Spam was vocalist Jimmy McManus. Bugs Pemberton took over the drum seat in September, 1960 when Bob was in hospital for an operation and Jackie Lomax also joined as vocalist, using the nickname Max. They became one of the leading Liverpool bands and a major rival to The Beatles, developing their sinister image by having photographs for *Mersey Beat* taken in a hearse. They began to gather a large following in Hamburg.

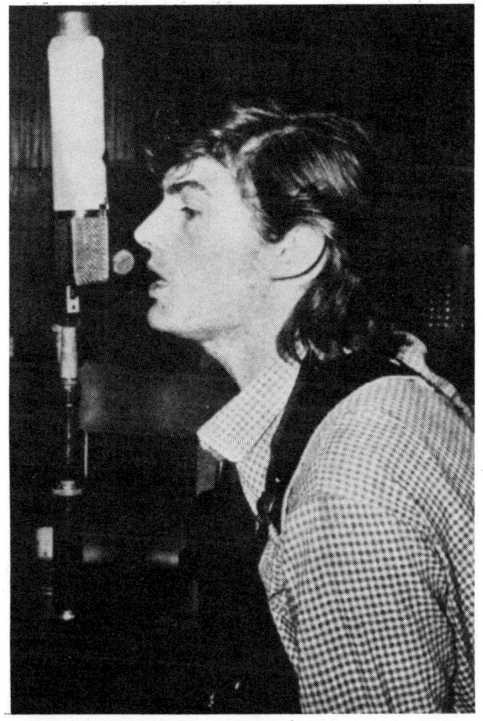

When the Mersey Beat scene became a national craze, Pye Records signed the group up. They recorded 'Mashed Potatoes' and 'Money' but despite *Mersey Beat's* recommendation that 'Money' become the 'A' side, Pye put the track on the 'B' side, thus giving Bern Elliott and The Fenmen an opportunity to record 'Money' and have a massive hit with it. Other records followed but they were not successful and although they changed their name to The 'Takers in September 1964, the group never made it and eventually disbanded.

Jackie made a solo single, 'Genuine Imitation Life' and then teamed up with two Americans in 1967 to form the Lomax Alliance who issued 'Try As You May' c/w 'See The People' on the CBS label. The trio were signed up by Brian Epstein but when he died they didn't wish to remain with Robert Stigwood and disbanded. Jackie signed with Apple in 1968 and George Harrison took an interest in his career. George wrote 'Sour Milk Sea' for him and also produced it at Trident Studios on June 24th and 26th with Paul McCartney on bass guitar, Ringo Starr on drums, Eric Clapton on lead guitar, Nicky Hopkins on piano and George Harrison and Jackie on rhythm guitars. Jackie's number 'The Eagle Laughs At You' was the flip and the single was issued in the US on Apple 1802 on August 26th and in the UK on Apple 3 on September 6th. Jackie then went on a promotional tour of the States in October, accompanied by Mal Evans.

His first album was called *Is This What You Want?*, also produced by George, and was issued in Britain on Apple Sapcor 6 on March 21st, 1969 and on May 19th on Apple ST 3354 in the States. His other Apple singles included 'New Day' c/w 'I Fall Inside Your Eyes' — both Jackie's compositions — and he co-produced the tracks with Mal Evans. It was issued in Britain on May 9th, 1969 on Apple 11 and in America on June 2nd on Apple 1809. His next single, 'How The Web Was Woven', was produced by George, although Paul produced the 'B' side, 'Thumbin' A Ride', completing the record on the eve of his wedding to Linda. Another of the singles Jackie made at Apple, 'Going Back To Liverpool' was never released. With the coming of Allen Klein, Apple seemed confused; the artists didn't know where they stood and drifted away. Jackie moved to the States and recorded two albums for Warners, then returned to Britain in 1974 to become a member of Badger, a band which included Tony Kaye, Paul Pilnick, Roy Dyke and Kim Gardner. When Badger folded he returned to America where he has remained. He signed himself to Capitol and his début album for them was called *Livin' for Lovin'*.

Harry Watmough Liverpool photographer, specializing in show-biz acts, who was commissioned to conduct a special photo session with The Beatles soon after Brian Epstein had signed them up. John, Paul, George and Pete appeared very sartorial in their mohair suits in complete contrast to their previous rough-and-ready image. The photos have been rarely seen outside the pages of *Mersey Beat*.

The Remo Four They first formed as a vocal group, The Remo Quartet, in 1958, playing at social clubs and weddings, then became known as Liverpool's Fendermen because they were the first group on Merseyside to have a complete line-up of Fender guitars. They comprised Keith Stokes (vocals/rhythm), Colin Manley (guitar), Don Andrew (bass) and Harry Prytherch (drums). They had their own residency at the Cavern and became backing band for Johnny Sandon, former lead singer with The Searchers. They made a few singles for Pye and there were various personnel changes with Phil Rogers (bass), Roy Dyke (drums) and Tony Ashton (keyboards) joining Colin. Brian Epstein hired the group to provide backing for Tommy Quickly who made various tour appearances with The Beatles in 1963. The Remo also appeared on The Beatles' tour of Britain in the autumn of 1964. George Harrison used the group as session musicians on his *Wonderwall* album and later reciprocated by producing an album for them. When the group had undergone another change and slimming operation to emerge as Ashton, Gardner and Dyke, with Kim Gardner on bass, George Harrison played guitar on the 'I'm Your Spiritual Breadman' track on their *The Worst Of Ashton, Gardner and Dyke* album.

Joe Flannery Childhood friend of Brian Epstein who was active on the Mersey Beat scene in the early sixties, primarily to manage his brother Lee Curtis (real name Peter Flannery). Joe had become so enamoured of the scene that he sold his lucrative grocery business to concentrate on artist management and agency with his Carlton-Brooke Agency and at one time managed the Mersey scene's most promising girl singer, Beryl Marsden. He masterminded the move to have Pete Best join Lee in Lee Curtis and The All Stars and when Lee became a popular artist at the Star Club, moved to Germany for several years to book groups into Hamburg. He returned to Liverpool in the late sixties and once again started a successful business. In the eighties he teamed-up with Clive Epstein to launch a Liverpool-based management agency with acts such as Motion Pictures and Phil Boardman.

A few weeks before John Lennon's murder, Joe talked to him on the phone and John expressed his enthusiasm for a forthcoming British tour in which he would return to Liverpool. Joe was so depressed by news of the killing that he wrote a poem 'Much Missed Man' in tribute to John. This was put to music, recorded by Phil Boardman and issued on Joe's own independent Mayfield label in February 1982.

Pat Davis Petite, blond Liverpudlian with a devastating sense of humour. A girlfriend of Ringo Starr when he was a member of The Hurricanes. Pat was also Cilla Black's close friend and moved to London in the mid-sixties to work at Polydor, leaving the company in the late seventies. Polydor was the company which first recorded The Beatles and had Tony Bramwell working in an executive position.

Howie Casey Derry and The Seniors were the first Liverpool band to play in Hamburg and their leader was saxophonist Howie Casey. The band soon became known as Howie Casey and The Seniors. Howie told me that he remembered The Silver Beatles performing at the Wyvern Club during the Larry Parnes auditions. 'Quite frankly, I wasn't too impressed and can't remember the group singing. I believe they played a lot of instrumentals and Shadows numbers.' When the group went over to Hamburg, Howie was furious to learn that Allan Williams intended to send the Beatles across after them and wrote him a stiff letter indicating that the scene would be ruined for the rest of them if such a bad group as The Beatles came over. When they did arrive, Howie commented: 'They had very, very pointed shoes in grey crocodile. They had mauve jackets with half-belting at the back. The length of their hair caused a great stir around the area — it was thick at the back, almost coming over their collars.'

Howie's two lead singers were Derry Wilkie and Freddie Starr and the group became the first Mersey band to be recognized in Britain when they signed with the Fontana label and set off on tour. They were also the first Merseyside band to release a single and album and appeared at the prestigious Inn At The Top Club in Ilford where they recorded an album *Twist At The Top*. Despite the initial success, the group disbanded and they all went their own ways: Freddie Starr forming various groups such as Freddie and The Delmonts and Freddie Starr and The Midnighters and Derry leading bands such as The Pressmen. Howie joined Kingsize Taylor and The Dominoes and spent many years in Germany before returning to England and becoming a successful session man in London. Paul McCartney asked him to join Wings on their 1975 world tour and

1979 tour of Britain. He also played on a number of Wings recordings, including the albums *Band On The Run* and *Back To The Egg*.

Tony Sheridan A musician who had such a profound effect on Merseyside groups such as The Beatles and Gerry and The Pacemakers that Liverpool bands dubbed him 'The Teacher'. Born in Cheltenham in 1940, Tony joined a skiffle group called The Saints whilst he was at art school and during 1958 began to appear with them at various London coffee bars, including the famous 2 I's. Later the same year he became a member of The Playboys, backing group for British rock 'n' roller, Vince Taylor. Tony was part of the 1960 tour featuring Gene Vincent and Eddie Cochran, on which Eddie Cochran was tragically killed in a road accident.

The bill headed by Gene at the Liverpool Stadium featured several Liverpool groups including Rory Storm and The Hurricanes (with Ringo Starr). In the audience were John Lennon and Stuart Sutcliffe. Stuart bemoaned the fact that The Beatles weren't on the bill to local promoter Allan Williams. In May 1960, Sheridan made his Hamburg début at Bruno Koschmeider's Club, the Kaiserkeller, the only beat club in Hamburg at the time. He was supported by his group, The Jets, and when the other members of the band returned to Britain he remained to perform as a solo artist. He began to appear at a new club in the Reeperbahn, the Top Ten, as resident singer and backing was provided by various Mersey bands who were then beginning to dominate the Hamburg scene.

Many say that the style in which he played and held his guitar on stage was

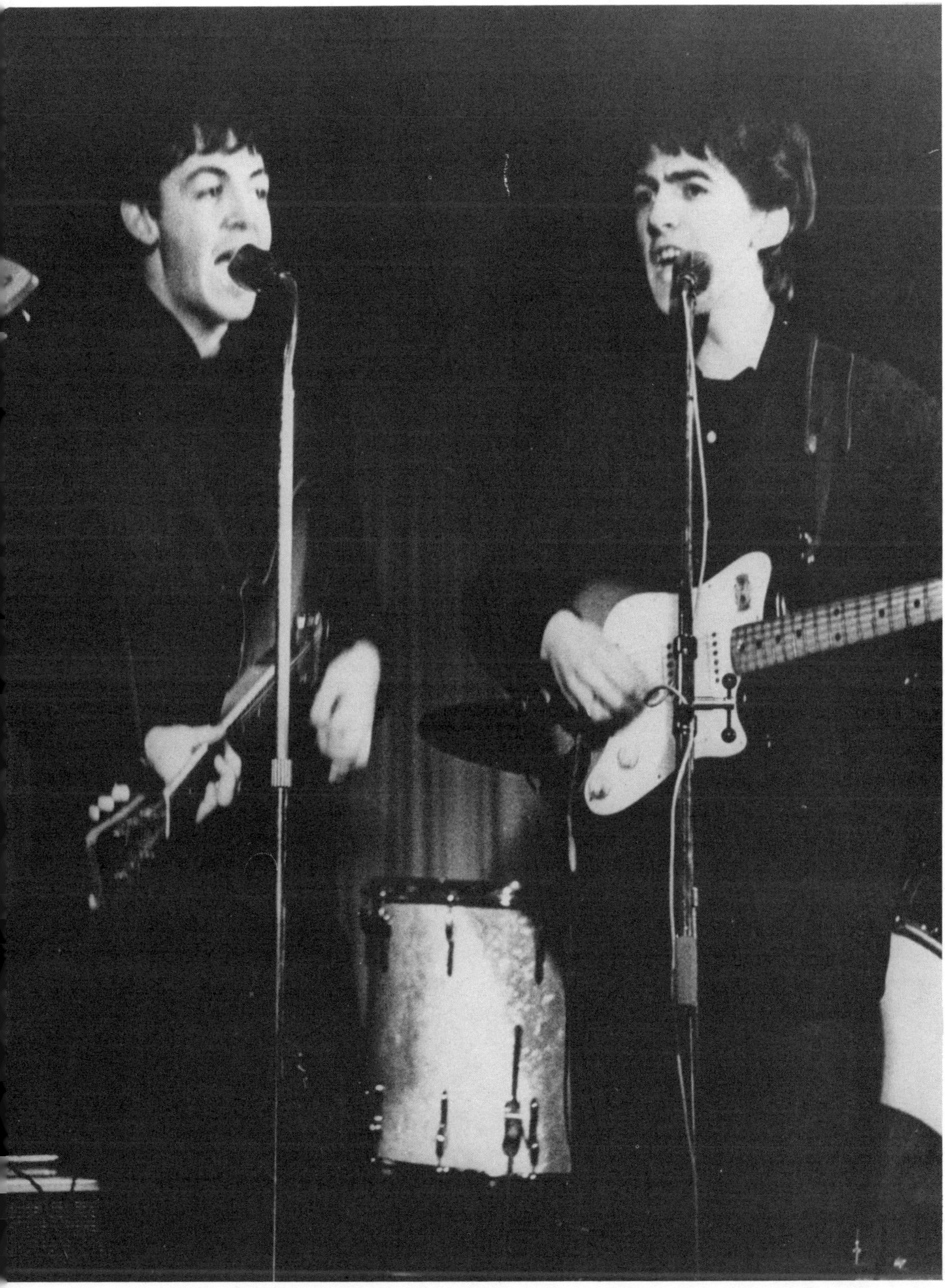

copied by John Lennon and Gerry Marsden and there is no doubt that he was a great influence on both bands. On their second trip to Hamburg from April to July 1961, The Beatles became backing group to Tony at two Polydor recording sessions produced by Bert Kaempfert. The group backed Tony on the numbers 'My Bonnie', 'The Saints', 'Why', 'Nobody's Child', 'Take Out Some Insurance On Me Baby' and 'Sweet Georgia Brown'. The Beatles also recorded the George Harrison instrumental 'Cry For A Shadow' and 'Ain't She Sweet', on which John was lead vocalist. News of the session was reported on the cover of Mersey Beat in July 1961 and the coupling of 'My Bonnie' and 'The Saints' was released in Germany in September 1961 with The Beatles' name replaced by that of The Beat Brothers.

Jurgen Vollmer When The Beatles began their appearances at the Kaiserkeller in 1961 they attracted three particularly enthusiastic students who became dedicated followers. The first was Klaus Voorman and on his third visit to the club he brought along Astrid Kirchnerr and Jurgen Vollmer. Fortunately, both Astrid and Jurgen were excellent photographers and have provided posterity with some brilliant photographs of The Beatles in their early years. A number of the photographs were first printed in Mersey Beat and pics were later to grace the pages of prestigious American magazines at the height of Beatlemania. One of them was used as the sleeve of John Lennon's Rock 'n' Roll album. A collection of his early photographs was published in a slim 80-page book by Editions de Nesle, Paris, in 1980. Entitled Rock 'n' Roll Times it included ten pages devoted to The Beatles, taken during their early Hamburg appearances. There is also a foreword by John Lennon who describes Vollmer as 'the first photographer to capture the beauty and spirit of The Beatles'.

Iain Hines Keyboards player who appeared with The Jets, the first British band to appear in Hamburg. Other members of his group included Tony Sheridan (guitar/vocals), Del Ward (vocals), Ricky Richards (rhythm), Colin Milander (bass) and Pete Wharton (rhythm). Iain met Bruno Koschmeider in the 2 I's Club in Soho where the German promoter was seeking British rock-and-roll bands. Although he had no set group at the time, Iain convinced Koschmeider that he had and made a name up on the spot. Koschmeider booked the group to appear in Hamburg immediately and Iain gathered his musician friends who were present at the 2 I's to undertake the Jets booking.

His experiences in Hamburg were serialized in an interesting set of articles in the girlie magazine Fiesta under the title 'Hamburg Rock'. Although the sexual nature of the St Pauli area is dwelt upon at length due to the nature of the magazine, the articles are nevertheless an atmospheric and interesting insight of the Hamburg period from the point of view of a musician. Beatle reminiscences abound, including the times Iain and Paul regularly dated two German blondes. Paul's girlfriend was a barmaid called Liane who, Iain related, eventually ended up working in the Herbetstrasse, the famous street-of-windows. Paul was also bitten by Asso, a Boxer dog nicknamed 'the Hound of Hell', whose particular fancy was to stick his fangs into the legs of musicians.

Iain contributed articles of The Beatles' Hamburg period to *The Beatles Book* in the sixties and when the magazine was revived as *The Beatles Appreciation Society Magazine Book*, he wrote three articles under the title 'The Beatles Hamburg Days' in the April, May and June 1977 issues. He also contributed 'The Truth About Those Early Beatles Recordings' in the November 1976 issue of the same magazine.

Klaus Voorman Klaus was the son of a Berlin doctor and moved to Hamburg in 1956 to study art. His girlfriend was a pale, blond-haired girl called Astrid Kirchnerr and one day, after having a minor argument with her, he went walking along the Grosse Freiheit in the St Pauli district where he was attracted by the sound of rock-and-roll music, performed by Rory Storm and The Hurricanes at the Kaiserkeller. Klaus went inside to listen and was even more intrigued by the next group to appear: The Beatles. In his excitement he talked Astrid into joining him and, despite her reluctance, brought her down to the seedy district to listen to the group. They both became wrapped up in the band and struck up a conversation with them, in spite of their poor English. In an attempt to communicate, Klaus brought along some record sleeve covers he'd designed. Soon they encouraged other students to join them and youngsters began to pour into St Pauli to see 'der Peedles'. Astrid deserted Klaus for the frail-looking bass guitarist Stuart Sutcliffe, but this didn't alter Klaus's interest in the group. He kept in touch with them, even travelling to Liverpool to meet them on their home ground and when they were based in London he went to live in England taking up the same instrument as Stu Sutcliffe: bass guitar. Teaming up with two Liverpool musicians to form Paddy, Klaus and Gibson, he found himself sharing the same manager as The Beatles, Brian Epstein, but the group disbanded and he joined Manfred Mann. In the meantime he continued with his artwork and was to win a Grammy Award for his design of the *Revolver* album sleeve. He also designed a number of lithographs illustrating songs on the *Ringo* album and did the artwork for the cover of George's *Wonderwall* album.

Over the years Klaus performed on many records supporting The Beatles on their solo projects and has become a popular guest at Beatles conventions.

Astrid Kirchnerr I first met Astrid in the Jacaranda Club when Stuart Sutcliffe brought her over on a trip to Liverpool at Christmas 1961. With her ashen face and black clothes she reminded me of pictures I'd seen of French existentialists. Stu also sported the pale look and sombre mode of dress.

At the time I was very impressed with her talent. When I launched the first issue of *Mersey Beat*, which included John's famous 'On The Dubious Origins Of The Beatles', he also gave me lots of photographs. Among them were shots taken by Astrid which displayed a character and style. I used one on the front cover of the second issue — the first photograph of The Beatles ever published.

Astrid had seen the group on their first trip to Hamburg. Her boyfriend Klaus Voorman had drifted into the St Pauli district after they'd had an argument and had been attracted by the sounds he heard emanating from the Kaiserkeller. He was spellbound by The Beatles and brought Astrid to see them. Soon the couple were meeting The Beatles regularly and Astrid and Stuart fell in love. She began to take the group around the streets of Hamburg, taking photographs which are among the most atmospheric pictures of the group in existence. She also invited them to her home and the close relationship between her and Stuart grew so intensely that Stu left the group and remained in Hamburg to study at the art school and lived in the attic of Astrid's parents' house. She changed the way Stu's hair fell, adapting a French style which appealed to the other members of the group, who followed suit — and thus the famous 'moptops' were born.

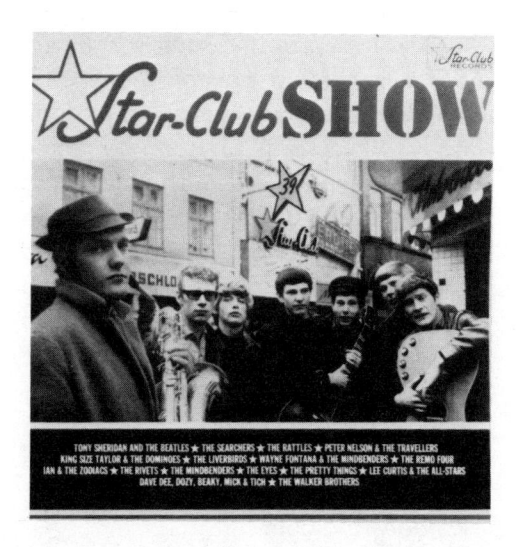

Fiction could hardly invent such a strange young couple, their deep love steeped in tragedy: he a brilliant painter, she a photographer of rare talent, both of them startlingly beautiful. At the age of 21 Stuart died tragically of cerebral bleeding and the haunting romance was brought to an end. The Beatles kept in touch with Astrid who married Liverpool drummer Gibson Kemp, and when the group visited Hamburg in 1966 she presented John with some of Stu's letters.

Bruno Koschmeider Small, burly club owner from Hamburg who began to hire bands for his venues the Indra and the Kaiserkeller and thus began the trek of Liverpool groups to Hamburg and into history. Koschmeider originally booked a London group called The Jets. Next to set off for Germany were the Liverpool band Derry and The Seniors, who were booked for the Kaiserkeller, followed by The Beatles, who appeared at the Indra Club. Koschmeider didn't pay much money to the bands and the accommodation he provided for the groups left much to be desired. The Beatles were given a squalid room at the rear of his cinema, the Bambi. Koschmeider had hired Horst Fascher, one of St Pauli's toughest characters, as his bouncer. When Fascher moved on to the Top Ten Club in the Reeperbahn, Koschmeider found that his former bouncer had inveigled the groups to go there with him. Furious that The Beatles were playing at the rival club, Koschmeider informed the police that they tried to burn down his cinema. This had been as a result of an insignificant fire that The Beatles had started — and it terminated their first Hamburg season. Once the Star Club opened, Koschmeider and other promoters didn't attempt to rival the bills presented by Manfred Weissleder.

Horst Fascher A fascinating man who was one of the principal characters in The Beatles' adventures in Hamburg. On my frequent trips there I came to like Horst and his brother Freddie very much. They were friendly, polite, courteous and Horst had a great sense of

Bill and Virginia Harry, Manfred Weissleder and Mr and Mrs Ray McFall outside the Star Club during a Cavern trip to Hamburg

humour, which belied their reputation as ogres. I knew for sure that when I wore a Star Club badge I was completely safe in that tough area. Yes, Horst and his brother had a fearsome reputation and Horst had been a boxer, imprisoned for manslaughter. When he went to live in the St Pauli district he was employed as a bouncer and no one interfered with anyone connected with him. Initially he worked for Bruno Koschmeider at the Kaiserkeller where he first fell in love with the Mersey sound, particularly that of The Beatles (known to German audiences as 'der Peedles'). He next went to work for Peter Eckhorn at the newly opened Top Ten Club and his very presence ensured that there were no reprisals against acts that may have reneged on their Kaiserkeller contracts. Later, he was to join Manfred Weissleder at the Star Club, the best and greatest of the Hamburg beat clubs, later to become a legend. The Beatles loved him and he was appointed manager of the club. In the late seventies he opened a new Star Club in the St Pauli area but it only had a short life span.

Peter Eckhorn The Reeperbahn is the main street running through the St Pauli red-light district of Hamburg and the Hippodrome was a strip club which also featured some circus acts. The club was owned by Peter Eckhorn's father who retired and passed the running of the venue over to Peter. He decided to transform it completely and turn it into a rock-and-roll club called the Top Ten. He poached Horst Fascher from the employ of rival club-owner Bruno Koschmeider and Horst helped him to prepare the club, painting it black and inveigling the groups to leave Koschmeider's establishments. The London band The Jets had completed their Hamburg contract and were ready to go home but some of them decided to stay and began playing at the Top Ten Club. They left two months later, apart from guitarist Tony Sheridan who decided to accept an offer to stay on as resident singer. Gerry and The Pacemakers were the next band to appear. Eckhorn had, in fact, employed The Beatles for a short time, enticing them with better sleeping accommodation and more Marks than they were earning at the Kaiserkeller. However, Bruno Koschmeider put a stop to that and they were sent back to England, Pete Best leaving behind his drum kit and some clothes in the Top Ten attic. They were therefore pleased when Eckhorn booked them again and they appeared there on their second trip to Hamburg in April 1961, playing from 7 in the evening until 2 in the morning, with an extra hour on Saturday evenings. They had a 15-minute break each hour. Liverpool groups had established themselves in Hamburg by that time and Peter Eckhorn travelled to Liverpool later that year to re-book some of the more popular bands. Brian Epstein had just signed The Beatles and asked for more money than Eckhorn was prepared to pay. He also had difficulty in convincing Gerry and The Pacemakers that the trip was worthwhile and ended up booking Ringo Starr as backing drummer for Tony Sheridan.

Manfred Weissleder Tall, blond-haired club-owner who launched Germany's legendary beat venue, the Star Club, in January 1962 with The Beatles topping the bill. Once Liverpool groups began to attract their own following in Hamburg from 1960 onwards, the way was open for an enterprising promoter not only to book the bands but to provide exciting bills and specifically to have a policy of encouraging the beat movement. Manfred, who also owned a

Bill Harry (left) with journalist Gordon Pitt conducting Bert Kaempfert's last series of interviews at the Churchill Hotel, London

string of strip clubs, secured a number of legendary American acts who were appearing at US bases in Germany; they included The Everly Brothers, Little Richard and Bo Diddley. He hired Adrian Barber as stage manager and Adrian built a complete sound system to enable all the bands to be recorded live on stage. Manfred had a Star Club record label, produced a magazine, *Star Club News*, and launched promotions in different parts of West Germany. Sadly, he died in 1980.

Eduardo Paolozzi Internationally renowned Scots-born sculptor, who took Stuart Sutcliffe under his wing when Stu wished to remain in Hamburg and continue with his art studies. Paolozzi saw Stu's potential, believed in his talent and not only arranged for him to become one of his students at Hamburg's State High School in June, 1961, but also approached the Hamburg authorities to arrange for Stuart to receive a grant.

Bert Kaempfert A quiet, gentle man, Bert Kaempfert died in Spain in June 1980. He suffered a heart attack a few days after appearing in concert in London at a time when I was just beginning to know him, having been hired as his press officer during his stay in England. Most of the interviews I arranged took place in the large, comfortable lounge of the Churchill Hotel and during the various chats with journalists (Philip Norman and Chris White among them) we were able to talk about his early experiences with The Beatles. I showed him the cover of issue No. 2 of *Mersey Beat*, dated July 20th, 1961, which read: 'Bert Kaempfert, who may be remembered for his golden record "Wonderland By Night" which reached the top of the American hit parade, contracted The Beatles for Polydor, Germany's top recording company. Under the contract they will make four records per year for the company.'

Bert told me that he'd first come into contact with the group when they were appearing at Peter Eckhorn's Top Ten Club. As A&R man for Polydor in Hamburg he was seeking a new sound. The actual recording sessions were conducted with Tony Sheridan as lead vocalist and the initial releases tagged The Beatles as The Beat Boys. He arranged for them to come to his home to discuss and sign their recording contract. They arrived before he got there and his housekeeper was so appalled by their appearance that she shunted them out to the patio with some cokes. They signed a three-year contract with him and when he went to pick them up at a pre-arranged spot for their recording session, there was no sign of them. He traced them to their attic room where they were still fast asleep. He told me that he was amazed at the spartan conditions in which they lived: a stark room with bunk beds and some chairs on which they piled their clothes.

Later, when Brian Epstein signed up the group and discovered that they had a legal recording contract, he wrote to Bert asking under what conditions he would release them. Bert discussed it with his bosses at Polydor who told him that they were only interested in Tony Sheridan and he was able to write to Brian releasing them from their contract with no strings attached and no payment required. Once The Beatles began to achieve their success, Polydor were anxious to track down any further material that Bert had and he found a number of tapes which he had stored away.

During our discussions in 1980 I suggested that as it was 20 years since he first recorded The Beatles, it might be a good idea for him to record an album of their numbers. The idea appealed to him as he had finally decided that we wished to become more active in his career.

Bert was born in Germany and his first

million-seller, 'Wonderland By Night', reached the No. 1 position in America. Over the years he wrote a number of major hits, such as 'Strangers In The Night', 'Bye Bye Blues', 'Swinging Safari', 'Spanish Eyes', and 'Danke Shoen' and when The Beatles were appearing at the Ernst Menck Halle in Hamburg on June 26th, 1966, he went backstage to see them and they all began whistling 'Strangers In The Night'.

Erika Hubers German girl who claims she had a love affair with Paul McCartney in Hamburg over a two-year period from 1960 and bore him a daughter, Bettina. She made the claim when Bettina reached the age of 18 and also stated that a financial settlement had been made at the time of Bettina's birth which obliged her not to reveal details of the affair.

Ray McFall Accountant, proprietor of the Cavern from 1959. I approached Ray McFall at the Cavern to try and raise some working capital for *Mersey Beat* and he agreed to become my silent partner. He also bought a van, to be shared between the Cavern and *Mersey Beat* and donated the services of Paddy Delaney to drive the van and deliver copies of the paper for us.

Ray's policy with the Cavern was an important factor in the development of the Liverpool sound. He took over the running of the enterprise on October 1st, 1959 and in the summer of 1960 made a radical departure: he introduced rock and roll. Ray also pioneered lunchtime sessions. By the end of February 1961 he'd stopped the modern jazz nights as the artists had failed to get the support they deserved. The club was now almost exclusively rock and roll, with The Bluejeans running their customary guest night. It was during a Bluejeans guest night that The Beatles made their début on March 21st, 1961. Thus began a stream of appearances which included their 'Welcome Home' session on Friday, July 14th, 1961 with Johnny Sandon and The Remo Four and the White Eagles Jazz Band. The Beatles began their own series of resident nights on Wednesday, August 2nd, 1961 and made a total of 292 appearances until their last one on August 3rd, 1963.

As success began to spread across the Mersey scene, Ray undertook a policy of expansion and the Cavern soon became the most famous club in Britain. There was even a group called The Caverners (Kenny Smith, lead; Steve Roberts, bass; Mark Farrell, rhythm and Colin Roberts, drums) and Beatles PR man Tony Barrow wrote a book *The Cavern*, which was published by Souvenir Press. Ray organized a Cavern trip to Hamburg in which 36 members of the club flew to the German city for two days to visit the Star Club and see The Kubas (later Koobas) and Ricky Gleason and The Top Spots from Liverpool and Tony Sheridan backed by The Bobby Patrick Big Six. Ray was to forge a friendship with his counterpart at the Star Club, Manfred Weissleder. He carried a letter from the Lord Mayor of

Liverpool to the Burgomeister of Hamburg which read: 'I have heard with interest that during the last few years groups of young Liverpool Rock and Roll musicians have visited Hamburg. I feel confident that these visits will result in the formation of friendships amongst members of the younger generation, a happy augury for the future.'

The Cavern now had a Junior Cavern

Brian Epstein with several of his acts, including Gerry and The Pacemakers, Sounds Ibc, The Dennisons, The Fourmost and Tommy Quickly

discs, was strictly for 13 to 16 year-olds and began on February 1st, 1964.

Ray continued his expansion plans and launched a management/agency called Cavern Artists Ltd, representing a number of acts, including The Michael Allen Group, The Clayton Squares, The Excelles, The Hideaways, The Kubas, The Notions, Earl Preston's Realms and The St Louis Checks.

On November 3rd, 1963 he bought the premises next door to the Cavern, extended the width of the club and began building a recording studio, Cavern Sound, which opened on October 15th, 1964 with £10,000 worth of equipment. The studio handled demonstration tapes, tape-to-disc transfers, master recordings, pressings, pressings for distribution to major labels, recordings for commercial radio. The first group to record there was The Clayton Squares and the studio was run by engineers Peter Hepworth and Nigel Greenburg. During alterations the old stage had to go and Ray had the idea of selling pieces of the original stage as 'Beatleboard' to Beatle fans who would like a souvenir of the stage on which the group had performed so many times. Beatleboard cost 5s a piece, the proceeds being donated to Oxfam. There were so many requests from all over the world that it took four months to fulfil the orders.

Club, membership of which cost 6d and admission cost members 2s and visitors 2s 6d. The sessions took place between 1 p.m. and 4 p.m. each Saturday and featured two groups and Top Twenty

On Saturday, 12th September, 1964 there was a 'Caverncade' — a parade through the streets of Liverpool by groups on decorated floats, the proceeds being donated to Oxfam.

There was even a regular half-hour weekly radio show which took place at the club. Called *Sunday Night At The Cavern*, it was broadcast on Radio Luxembourg each Sunday at 10.30 p.m. commencing March 15th, 1963. The show was hosted by Bob Wooler who played the latest chart records and introduced a group live from the Cavern stage each week.

Unfortunately, Ray had taken on too many enterprises and stretched his capital too far, with the result that he had to declare himself bankrupt, and the Cavern was sold. Part of the problem was that Ray had been conned by people he trusted. As the Cavern had become famous, Ray had become something of a celebrity and began to travel a lot. He joined The Beatles on their first trip to America, and whilst he was away some people he left in charge swindled him. It's sad that he had to give up his club because it was never the same after he left. He moved to London soon after and has remained there ever since. The Cavern itself was torn down in 1973 to make way for an air vent for the underground railway.

Paddy Delaney Paddy was one of the Liverpool legends, a giant of a man, always dressed in an evening suit, who was the main bouncer/doorman at the Cavern throughout the Mersey Beat years.

Initially, the Cavern took to rock and roll reluctantly, preferring the respectability of jazz which, unfortunately, didn't prove economical. There were certain rules and regulations at the various clubs in Liverpool. For example, no blokes were allowed into the dances at the Locarno without a tie. At the Cavern, jeans were out. Paddy once attempted to prevent George Harrison entering the Cavern because he wore jeans.

When Ray McFall became involved in *Mersey Beat* he offered us the services of Paddy as driver. Since he used to deliver copies for us we gave him the title of Circulation Manager, and since he liked the theatre we appointed him Theatre Critic. He was a warm friendly person with an engaging sense of humour.

The Beatles always treated him with affection and he is now Warden at Netherley Centre in Liverpool. He recently showed me the manuscript of a book he'd been writing about his experiences at the Cavern, which he'd called 'The Best Of Cellars'.

Brian Epstein Brian was The Beatles' only true manager. He was born in Rodney Street, Liverpool on September 19th, 1934 to Harry and Queenie Epstein. During the war he was evacuated to Southport and attended Southport College, returning to his home in the Childwall area in 1943 when he began to attend Liverpool College. He complained to his parents about anti-semitism in the school and they then sent him to a Jewish prep school, Beaconsfield, near Tunbridge Wells in Kent. At the age of 13 he failed the exams and was sent to a school in Dorset and in 1948 began attending Wrekin College in Shropshire. On September 10th, 1950, at the age of 16, he started work at his first job, a sales assistant in his parents' furniture store in Walton Lane, Liverpool at a wage of £5 per week. On December 9th, 1952 he was called up for National Service, received an A1 medical pass

The young Brian Epstein, whose early aspiration was to become an actor

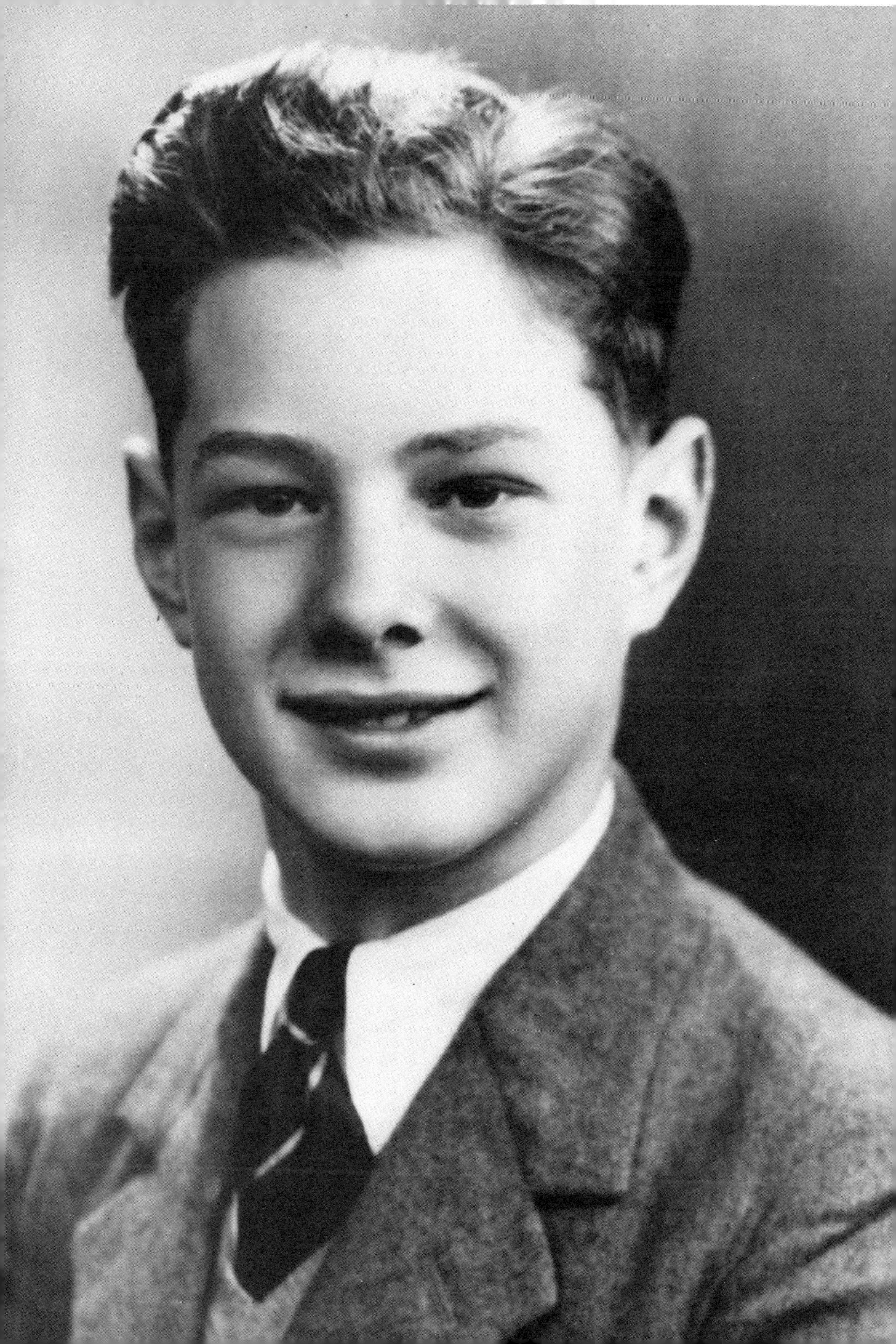

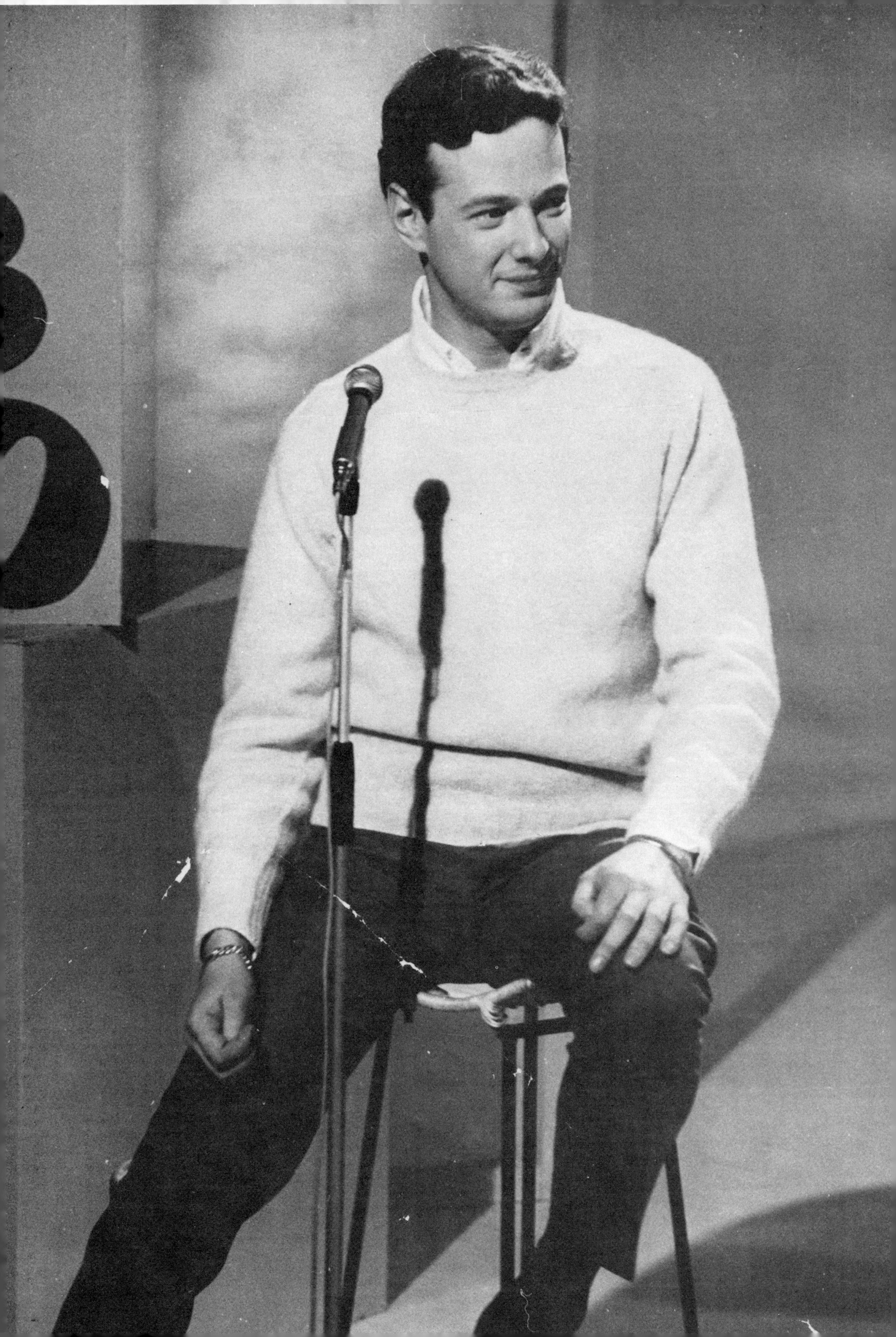

and was sent to the Royal Army Service Corps as a clerk. He couldn't take to service life and was examined by a psychiatrist and discharged after serving ten months.

He had visions of becoming an actor and at the age of 22 auditioned and was accepted as a student at the Royal Academy of Dramatic Arts. It didn't work out and he returned to Liverpool. In 1959 he took charge of the Whitechapel branch of NEMS.

In early June 1961 I went out into Liverpool city centre with a bundle of copies of the first issue of *Mersey Beat* under my arm. Arriving at NEMS Record Store in Whitechapel, I asked if I could see the manager. I was taken to some fairly plush upstairs offices and introduced to Brian Epstein. It was the first time he had met anyone connected with the local music scene and I showed him *Mersey Beat* and told him of the background behind the paper. he agreed to take a dozen copies. I then received a telephone call from him asking for more copies and when I delivered them we had another talk. He told me he was surprised at how quickly they'd sold, within an hour of his putting them on display: in contrast to some of the other publications which didn't attract nearly as much attention.

He was eager to know about the local music scene because he was ordering 144 copies of issue No. 2, published on July 20th. This was the issue with The Beatles on the cover and the story of them making a record in Germany. *Mersey Beat* fascinated him and he asked if he could contribute a record

Brian wished to become a celebrity in his own right and once hosted his own TV chat show

review column, which he did, starting in the third issue on August 3rd. It was headed: 'Stop The World — and listen to everything in it. Brian Epstein of NEMS.' He mentioned George Martin's *Beyond the Fringe* album, various LPs of stage musicals, a classical album and discs by Elvis Presley, Bobby Rydell and Chubby Checker. We used to discuss the activities on the local scene and one day he phoned me and said he'd like to go to the Cavern; could I arrange it? The Cavern was only about a hundred yards away from his shop but I called them and they said he'd be welcome. Brian, accompanied by his assistant Alistair Taylor, dropped in at a lunchtime session on November 9th, 1961 and saw The Beatles for the first time.

He then became fired with enthusiasm and was keen to sign the group up and become involved in the local music scene. He began sending me various notes about The Beatles' activities, in addition to phoning regularly. He contacted Bert Kaempfert and obtained a release from their German commitment to Polydor. The group seemed quite delighted that such an influential businessman was taking an interest in them and he made a promise that he would obtain the largest fee ever paid to a local Liverpool band: £15. And he succeeded! He also began making statements to the effect that The Beatles would become bigger than Elvis — and people scoffed at him.

On January 1st, 1962 he joined them in London where they had their first audition for a British record company at Decca's West Hampstead studio. The same month The Beatles topped the *Mersey Beat* poll and Brian was thrilled, sending out notices about their success on leaflets. Throughout the year he kept me informed of his dealings and on May 9th sent me a telegram: 'HAVE SECURED CONTRACT FOR BEATLES TO RECORD FOR EMI ON PARLOPHONE LABEL 1ST RECORDING DATE SET FOR JUNE 6TH BRIAN EPSTEIN.' Although he provided me with some excellent stories, he also kept mum about various things, such as the sacking of Pete Best. He also sent John Lennon to see me at the office to retrieve some photographs taken in Hamburg that John had given to me: pictures of him in the Reeperbahn in his underpants, on stage with a toilet seat around his neck and such like. I returned them to him. Brian had polished up their image, replacing the leather suits with mohair ones, sending them to his hairdresser at Horne Brothers and advising them to stop smoking on stage and to cut out their swearing. He also supplied me with special reports of their initial recording sessions and a series of exclusive photographs of their various activities. So much stuff, in fact, that I was featuring them in every issue.

Once The Beatles began to achieve worldwide success, Brian became a celebrity in his own right and set about building a show-business empire, moving his offices to London. He'd signed up a number of other Liverpool acts who were successful in the wake of The Beatles: Gerry and The Pacemakers, Billy J. Kramer, Cilla Black, The Fourmost, although it was becoming apparent that he was not only taking too much on but did not have the gift of developing talent that he'd imagined. The Big Three were a tough, exciting group who pre-dated The Cream. Brian had them dress in mohair suits and record songs such as Mitch Murray's 'By The Way': the wrong material, the wrong image — they told him so and left him. So did The Chants and other acts. He continued signing artists: Tommy Quickly, The Silkie, Michael Haslam, Cliff Bennett and The Rebel Rousers — and although they had hits, their record successes were with Lennon and McCartney songs; without Beatle material the acts just faded out of the limelight. Brian began to have more failures than successes.

His book *A Cellarful Of Noise* was published and he conducted a number of TV interviews for an American network. His organization, NEMS Enterprises, employed a number of his personal friends from Liverpool: Peter Brown, Alistair Taylor, Geoffrey Ellis — and he bought the Saville Theatre and appointed Tony Bramwell as manager.

He was wealthy, successful, owned several houses, but was ultimately unhappy. It has been suggested that he was fearful of losing The Beatles, that they wouldn't re-sign with him when their contract was due for renewal. It was also suggested that he attempted to commit suicide.

NEMS hadn't become the great show-business empire he'd dreamed about and a lot of the acts he'd signed up just hadn't happened, so he brought Robert Stigwood into the organization to discover new acts — and Stigwood brought in The Cream and The Bee Gees.

Time was running out for Brian. One weekend in August 1967, he invited his friends Peter Brown and Geoffrey Ellis to his house in Kingsley Hill, Surrey, to join him for the weekend. However, he drove back to London and locked himself in his room. His butler and maid, fearing the worse, called in a doctor who broke down the door to Brian's room. He was already dead. The date was August 17th. A Coroner's Court recorded a verdict of accidental death due to an overdose of Carbitral and his memorial service was held, appropriately, at the New London Synagogue in Abbey Road, St John's Wood, on October 17th.

The Beatles were stunned by the news. Brian was never replaced. Peter Brown attempted to fit into his shoes for a while and Paul McCartney tried to interest the rest of the group in various activities — but with the death of Brian, some of the heart seemed to have gone from the group and within a few years they had disbanded.

The Chants I received a phone call from Bob Wooler one day urging me to come down to the Cavern immediately. He sounded so excited that I took his advice. On arriving he introduced me to The Chants, a five-piece vocal harmony group, one of Liverpool's first all-black bands. They had previously appeared at Stanley House in Upper Parliament Street as The Shades. Leader Joe Ankrah always wanted to form an American-style vocal group and The Chants were his third attempt. Apart from Joey they comprised Edmond Ankrah, Nat Smeda, Alan Harding and Eddie Amoo, together with a reserve singer, Peter Chang.

The Beatles also became excited by the group, who made their Cavern début on November 21st, 1962. At first The Chants did not have a regular backing band, so The Beatles offered to back them at the Cavern. Brian Epstein was furious and told them they mustn't do it, but they argued with him and won. Brian was later to manage the group for a short time in 1963. Their first disc was released by Pye Records on September 17th, 1963: 'I Could Write A Book' c/w 'A Thousand Stars'. Their other releases included 'Sweet Was The Wine' c/w 'One Star' (a tribute to Stanley House) and 'She's Mine' c/w 'Then I'll Be Home'.

Freda Kelly The Beatles' longest-lasting fan club secretary. Freda, who was born in Ireland and brought to Liverpool when she was 13, worked in an office in the city centre and was a troglodyte (a Cavern dweller) when her friend Bobbie Brown became engaged early in 1963. Freda then took over the reins of The Beatles Fan Club, which was then a small branch based in Liverpool. As the club grew and the HQ was moved to London, Freda turned down the offer of a London job, preferring to stay where her friends were. She became joint national secretary of the club in October 1966. Freda was one of those stout 'Cavernites' who went down fighting when the Cavern was due to be demolished and on February 28th, 1966 was involved in the sit-in at the Cavern, entertained by The Hideaways group, who kept on playing when the barricades were torn down by the police.

At one time, when *Mersey Beat* offices moved to larger premises in Hackin's Hey, I shared an office with Freda. Each morning huge tea chests would arrive, packed with presents for The Beatles from fans in different countries throughout the world. They ranged from intricate drawings to tea services, from teddy bears to knitted mittens. If a Beatle mentioned he liked something, fans from the four corners would send it to them. Ringo mentioned that he liked science fiction and thousands of books poured into the office. Freda was in charge of seeing that everything was distributed to the family.

She married a Liverpool guitarist Brian Norris and has now settled down to a family life on Merseyside.

Alistair Taylor A friend of Brian Epstein's who worked on the record counter of NEMS store in Liverpool and became Brian's first personal assistant. He accompanied him on his first visit to the Cavern and also witnessed the signing of the management contract between Brian and The Beatles. He moved to London with the organization to become general manager of NEMS. After Brian's death he was employed at Apple as 'Office Manager and Chief Fixer'. He was one of the numerous people with a long association with The Beatles who was fired by Allen Klein. He remained in the south of England but no longer worked in the music business. He auctioned a number of items from his personal collection of memorabilia at the special 'Rock 'n' Roll And Advertising Art' sale at Sotheby's in Belgravia, London on December 22nd, 1981.

When Paul McCartney designed a poster inviting new talent to contact Apple Music in Baker Street, Alistair was featured on the poster as a one-man-band.

Bobbie Brown Girl who formed the first official Beatles fan club in Liverpool in May 1962. She passed over the running of the club to her friend Freda Kelly when she got engaged early in 1963.

Terry Doran One of the long-time members of The Beatles camp. He first met Brian Epstein in a Liverpool pub in 1959 and was one of several close

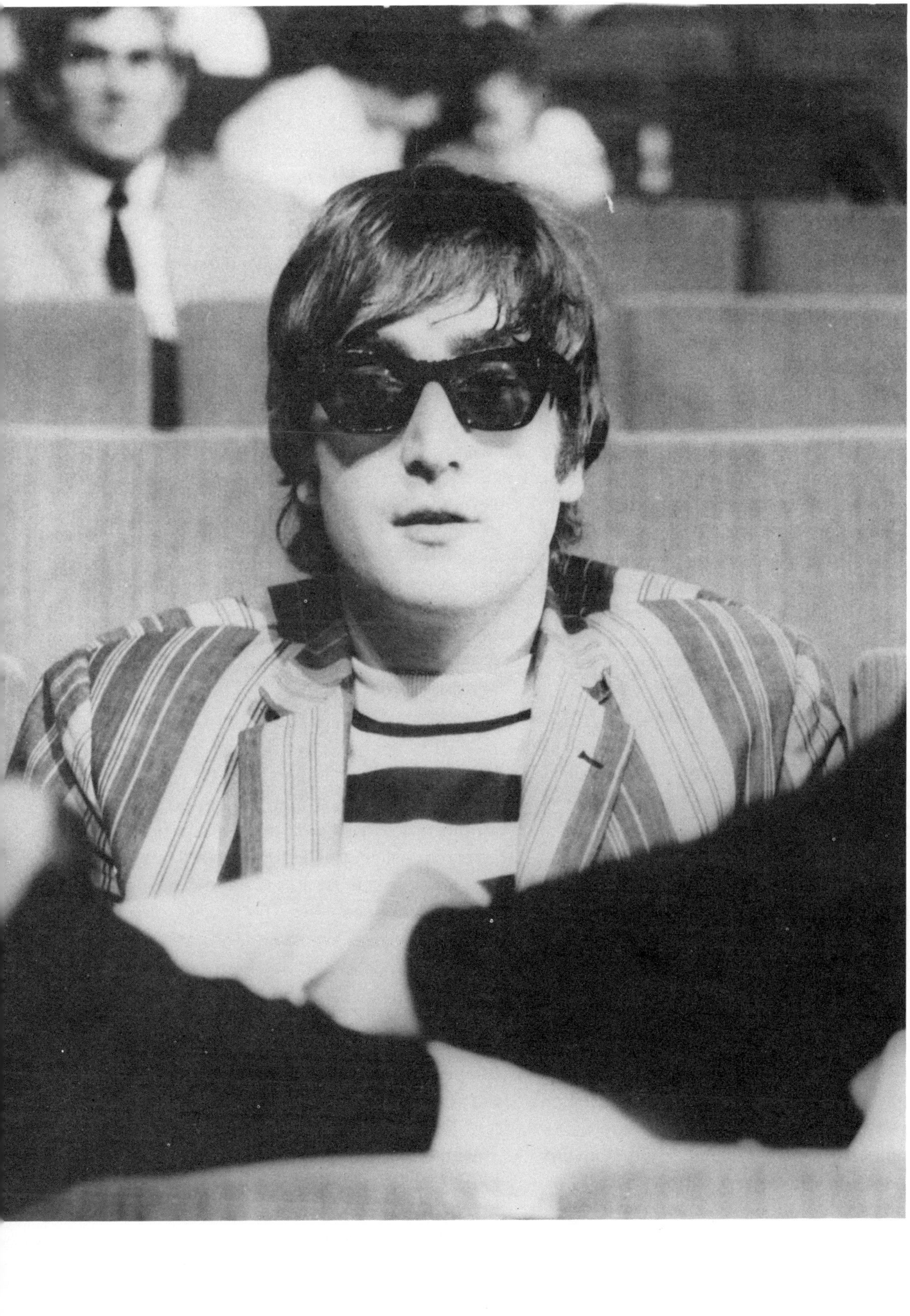

friends who Brian brought into his organization when The Beatles became a success. Terry had been a car salesman and Brian thought that most of his successful artists would need to buy cars, so he set Terry up in his own business, with himself as a silent partner. The combination of the two names resulted in Brydor Cars. Later, after Brian's death, when The Beatles set up Apple, Terry was appointed head of Apple Music in September 1967. He continued his association with the individual members after the split and has acted as a personal assistant to George Harrison.

Mal Evans A gentle giant of a man, Mal was a telecommunications engineer when, at the age of 26, he first dropped round to the Cavern. The visit was to change his life and he became a regular 'cave dweller', making friends with George Harrison who recommended that he work on the door of the club where his size (6ft 2ins) and bulk would make him an ideal 'bouncer'. Together with people like Tony Buck, Sean Connelly and Pat Delaney, the Cavern bouncers towered over the tiny entrance, looking like giants. He'd been working there for three months when, in 1963, Brian Epstein offered him the job of roadie with The Beatles. Neil Aspinall had previously been in the position but it was decided that he should no longer be a 'humper' (the lowest in the pecking order of road managers — the one who humps the gear around, unloading it from the vans and setting it up). He then began to work under Neil and the two of them travelled the world with the group, Mal often writing columns on his adventures for publications such as *Beatles Monthly*. He also did guest spots in most of their films.

After three years of globetrotting with the Fab Four he was given a job as one of their personal assistants when they ceased touring. In 1968 he was appointed an executive at Apple and took an interest in the recording activities there, discovering a group called The Iveys. He produced their record, 'No Matter What'. They later changed their name to Badfinger. He also helped to co-produce a record by Jackie Lomax. With the dissolution of Apple he moved to America but had so involved himself with The Beatles that he found himself at a loose end when he no longer associated with them. He'd also become estranged from his wife and two children. He began to write a book of his experiences with The Beatles and then the tragedy happened, on January 6th, 1976. Mal was in Los Angeles living with a woman and her four-year-old daughter. When he seemed in a depressed and desperate state, she rang the police. Mal was locked in an adjoining room and had an air pistol. When two policemen burst into the room they saw the pistol and fired six shots into him. A terribly violent end for a man who had such a gentle nature.

The American touring party

Tony Bramwell A childhood friend of George Harrison who became an office boy at NEMS in Liverpool after Brian Epstein had signed The Beatles. From office boy he graduated to doing various assignments and soon became one of those close friends they always had around who was also capable of doing a good job of work. He travelled to America with them and wrote reports of their activities for various publications, including the *Beatles Monthly*. Brian Epstein appointed him stage manager at the Saville Theatre and after Brian's death he joined Apple, involving himself in a number of tasks including record production and the film company Subafilms. He was also Apple's chief plugger and proved particularly adept at getting radio plays and TV spots for the Apple signings. Tony was a dab hand with the camera and many of his photographs of Apple acts, such as Mary Hopkins, were syndicated throughout the world. Following the collapse of Apple he worked for Harry Saltzman's music publishing company, then produced a Big Three album and became an independent promotions man. By the end of the seventies he was ensconsed in an executive position at Polydor Records, retaining his independence and continuing to maintain his reputation as one of the best 'pluggers' in the business.

The former NEMS office boy also became one of London's most eligible bachelors, dating an assortment of Miss Worlds, celebrities such as Christine Keeler and, for a number of years, lived with the stunning Swedish actress Julie Ege.

Tony Barrow When Tony Barrow moved from Liverpool to work in London he began writing album notes for artists in the Decca Records group. In addition, he produced a weekly record review column for the *Liverpool Echo* under the pseudonym 'Disker'. When Brian Epstein took over The Beatles and was seeking every avenue of promotion, he wrote to Disker via the *Echo*, asking if the columnist would include a plug for a local group, The Beatles, in his column. The letter was passed on to Tony in London and he wrote back stating that his column was concerned mainly with recording acts and that should The Beatles secure a recording contract he would be happy to give them a plug. Now aware that Tony worked for Decca, Brian visited him in London with an acetate and asked if he could help him in any way. Tony contacted the marketing side of Decca, rather than the A & R Department, because he was aware that NEMS was an important retailer in the north-west and the marketing managers would be interested in doing him a favour. Eventually, Decca agreed to give The Beatles their audition and Mike Smith was pleased with the result, although they were given the thumbs down by Dick Rowe. When Brian secured a Parlophone deal he contacted Tony for further advice and Tony agreed to prepare a press kit on The Beatles, although this was distributed by two show-biz PRs, Tony Calder and Andrew Oldham.

As The Beatles' success began to take off, Brian needed a full-time PR and as Andrew Oldham turned down the job, he asked Tony if he would be interested. Initially he was reluctant to surrender a secure position with a major record company to gamble on a career with an impresario from the provinces but on May 1st, 1963, he became full-time PR

On another leg of their world tour – this time in Japan

for The Beatles and NEMS Enterprises and moved into some small offices in Monmouth Street, London. As the organization grew he graduated to plush offices in Argyle Street, next to the London Palladium and as The Beatles were more or less a full-time account, he concentrated on the other NEMS artists while Brian employed various people such as Brian Somerville and Derek Taylor to look after The Beatles' career, although Tony did continue to handle their press activities from time to time. He also continued to write prolifically: a book about the Cavern for Souvenir Press, various record sleeves and regular articles about The Beatles' activities for *Beatles Monthly*. In many cases he had to use a pseudonym. Although he wasn't earning a great deal from NEMS Enterprises, his contract stated that any proceeds from freelance writing using his own name would have to be shared with the company, therefore Tony used the name Allistair Griffin for his Cavern book and Frederick James for his *Beatles Monthly* articles.

After Brian's death he set up his own PR company — Tony Barrow International — retaining artists such as Cilla Black and expanding his activities until he had a roster of star names. Unfortunately, ill health caused him to retire in the late seventies and he moved to Morecambe. In 1980 he had recovered sufficiently to begin freelance writing and by 1981 had become prolific in his output with regular features in *Beatles Monthly* (this time under his own name)

Tony Barrow conducts a Beatles press reception

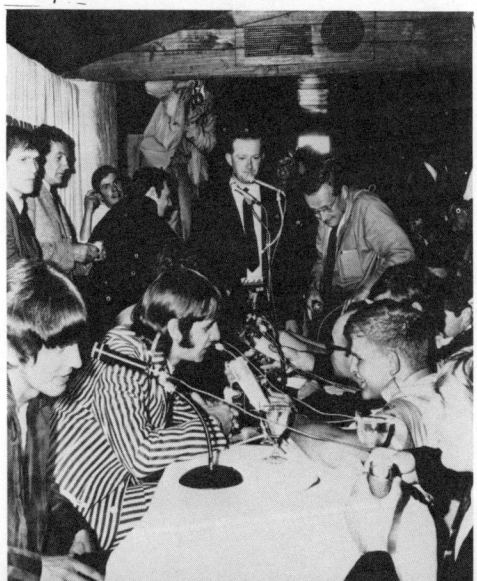

and syndicated columns in provincial publications, in addition to numerous commissions for record sleeves. He also sought out personalities with former Beatles associations in order to ghost their 'stories' for the national press; Angie McCartney was the subject of one of his series in the *Daily Star.* In 1982 he wrote a book on The Beatles which was published by Mirror Books.

The Koobas Liverpool band, originally formed in April 1963 as The Kubas, who performed at all the major Merseyside venues, appeared in Hamburg and were signed to Brian Epstein for a short time. They also appeared in the film *Ferry 'cross The Mersey* in 1965 and toured Britain with The Beatles from December 3rd to December 12th, 1965. There were occasional changes in personnel, but the basic line-up was Keith Ellis (bass guitar), Stu Leithwood (rhythm guitar), Tony O'Reilly (drums) and Roy Morris (lead). They later signed with Tony Stratton-Smith and had minor-record success.

Peter Brown Born in Bebington on Merseyside, Peter worked for a time in one of the large stores in Liverpool's city centre, Henderson's, before his appointment as manager of the record department in another store, Lewis's. A close personal friend of Brian Epstein, he was invited by Brian to manage the Charlotte Street branch of the record store chain when Brian moved to the new shop in Whitechapel. In 1965, having established himself in London, Brian contacted Peter in Liverpool and asked him if he would like to become his personal assistant, which he did. He was the ideal right-hand man to Brian and they were similar in many ways: sartorial, polite, at home at social functions and dinner parties. After Brian's death he was hired by The Beatles as an executive for Apple and in some ways filled the gap that Brian had left in their lives. There was a system at Apple in which the directors resigned each year and were then automatically reappointed. Allen Klein ensured that when Peter's resignation came in it was not renewed. Peter simply left to take up a far more challenging post within the Robert Stigwood Organization in America and has written a book of his experiences with Brian and The Beatles.

Cilla Black Born on May 27th, 1943, Cilla was the only girl singer from Liverpool to achieve major success during the Mersey Beat years.

I used to bump into Cilla and her mate

Derek Taylor and Peter Brown in the Apple offices

Pat Davis whenever I visited the various Liverpool clubs in 1960, whether it was the Jacaranda, the Cassanova or the Cavern. When I began *Mersey Beat* I asked Cilla if she could contribute a fashion column. She wrote one piece for me which I published. Naturally, I was keen to write about her when the paper first came out as, although she worked in an office, she sang occasionally at night with various groups including Faron's Flamingoes and Kingsize Taylor and The Dominoes. The first piece I wrote about her was headlined 'Swinging Cilla' and I mentioned an offer she'd received to audition for Kenny Ball's Jazzband, but she'd been too frightened to turn up. Since I had such a heavy workload in those days I often misspelt or mixed up people's names and I mistakenly put down Cilla Black instead of her real name of Priscilla White, but she preferred the 'Black' and continued to call herself by that name. The type of numbers she sang in those days included 'Fever', 'Always', 'Boys' and 'Summertime' and she told me that she wanted to become a jazz singer. Once The Beatles began to achieve national success she asked me if I'd become her manager. I had too much work on with the running of the newspaper to consider such a task but she continued to pop into the office to persuade me, telling me she'd like a jazz trio to back her. One night when Cilla was down at the Blue Angel I noticed that Brian Epstein was present. I asked Cilla if she'd get up and sing, and arranged for the group on stage to back her performing the number 'Boys'. Then I asked Brian to listen to her and when she'd finished the song I brought her over and introduced her to him, then left the two of them together to have a chat. A few days later she phoned me to say that Brian had signed her up.

It was an easy job for Brian to place her with George Martin on the Parlophone label and she made her début with the Lennon/McCartney number 'Love Of The Loved'. The single was released on February 27th, 1963, on Parlophone R5065 but didn't achieve the anticipated success, reaching only as high as No. 35 in the charts. Brian then changed her image, dressed her in sophisticated fashions and achieved a No. 1 British hit with her second release, a cover of Bacharach and David's 'Anyone Who Had A Heart', a US chart topper for Dionne Warwick. Issued on Parlophone R5101, it achieved its hit status in February 1964. Her second American cover 'You're My World', issued on Parlophone R5133 also hit the top spot in the UK. She then recorded another Lennon/McCartney number — 'It's For You' — released in Britain on Parlophone R5162 on July 31st, 1964, where it reached the No. 7 position. It was issued in America on Capitol 5258 on August 17th, 1964.

Cilla became a major middle-of-the-road artist in Britain with her own BBC television series which ran for several seasons. She also appeared in a guest spot in the film *Ferry 'cross The Mersey* and made her acting début opposite David Warner in the movie *Work Is A Four Letter Word*. For her TV shows in the sixties she used a Lennon/McCartney number 'Step Inside Love' as her theme tune. The song was issued in Britain on Parlophone R5674 on March 8th, 1968, where it reached the No. 8 position. The American release on Bell 726 was issued on May 6th, 1968.

Throughout the seventies Cilla consolidated her position as an established British all-round show-biz personality on television and comedy shows and in cabaret and summer seasons at holiday resorts and has earned the tag 'a pocket Gracie Fields'.

She married her long-standing boyfriend Bobby Willis and during the eighties reduced the number of her live appearances in order to concentrate on bringing up her sons.

Little Richard One of the legendary rock-and-roll singers, born in 1932, who had a string of enduring hits in the fifties, including 'Long Tall Sally', 'Rip It Up', 'Good Golly Miss Molly' and 'Keep A-Knockin''. The Beatles were great fans of his and first met him during one of their Hamburg stints. He appeared at the Odeon, Liverpool and then Brian Epstein decided to book him on some gigs for NEMS Enterprises, the most ambitious of which was at the Tower Ballroom, New Brighton on Friday October 12th, 1962. The Beatles were second on the bill and nine other Mersey Beat bands performed on the five-and-a-half-hour show which was compered by Bob Wooler.

Mike Smith A&R man for Decca Records who originally conducted a recording audition with The Beatles.

Shortly after Brian Epstein signed the group in Liverpool he approached Merseyside writer Tony Barrow who reviewed records for the *Liverpool Echo*

Little Richard at the Tower Ballroom surrounded by four fans

under the pseudonym 'Disker' and also wrote biographies for Decca Records' artists. Tony contacted the company and impressed upon them the importance of Brian as a local retailer. Their Artists and Repertoire Department sent executive Mike Smith to Liverpool to see the boys perform at the Cavern and he was favourably impressed and arranged a recording audition at Decca's West Hampstead studios on January 1st, 1962. The group recorded approximately 15 numbers, including: 'To Know Her Is To Love Her'; 'Memphis, Tennessee'; 'Love Of The Loved'; 'Hello Little Girl'; 'Money'; 'Three Cool Cats'; 'Till There Was You'; 'Please Mr Postman'; 'Red Sails In The Sunset'; 'Like Dreamers Do'; 'The Shiek Of Araby'; 'What'd I Say'. It has been suggested that Brian requested them not to perform any of their own numbers, but 'Love Of The Loved' and the inclusion of 'Hello Little Girl' doesn't bear this out.

Mike Smith was very enthusiastic about the session and would have liked to have signed the group to Decca. However, his superior, Dick Rowe, returned from a trip to America and decided to turn the band down. Brian was able to obtain the tapes to use as a selling point with other companies but they were rejected by several of them, including Pye Records.

Dick Rowe Decca recording manager who came under a black cloud in the sixties because he turned down The Beatles. The group had been visited in Liverpool by Rowe's assistant, Mike Smith, at the Cavern and Smith was impressed enough to book them for a recording audition on January 1st, 1962. Also auditioning that day were a Dagenham group, Brian Poole and The Tremeloes. By all accounts it seems that Smith preferred The Beatles but he was overruled by his boss when Rowe returned from America. Rowe decided to take The Tremeloes, possibly because Dagenham was closer than Liverpool and would thus be more convenient.

The stigma would probably have been attached to Dick Rowe for the rest of his life were it not for a stroke of good fortune in which The Beatles were connected. Rowe was judging a beat contest at the Philharmonic Hall in Liverpool when George Harrison began to chat to him, George mentioned that The Beatles had been very impressed by an unknown London band they had seen in Richmond called The Rolling Stones. Rowe rushed pell mell from the hall, made his way to London and immediately signed The Stones — thus bringing Decca the world's second biggest group, which went some way to reducing the loss they had suffered by his rejection of The Beatles. He is writing a book called *The Man Who Turned Down The Beatles.*

Brian Poole and The Tremeloes
Dagenham group who auditioned for Decca on January 1st, 1962 on the same day as The Beatles. Dick Rowe decided to sign The Tremeloes rather than the Mersey band but their initial releases didn't meet with much success. Then, with the success of The Beatles, they began to play in the Mersey Beat style and recorded 'Twist and Shout', which reached No. 4 in the charts in 1964. They then enjoyed a regular series of hits throughout the sixties. They comprised Brian Poole (vocals) Ricky West (lead guitar), Alan Blakely (rhythm guitar), Alan Howard (bass guitar) and Dave Munden (drums).

Ted Huntley A link in the chain of events leading to The Beatles' recording contract. In 1962 Ted was working at the HMV shop in Oxford Street, London, in charge of cutting discs for customers. When Brian Epstein came into the shop to have acetates made of some Beatles numbers, Ted, a former engineer at EMI studios, was impressed by the group's sound: something which several A&R men with different record companies had not been. After a chat with Brian he discovered that the group did not have a publishing contract so he phoned Syd Coleman of EMI's publishing company, Ardmore and Beechwod, who was in the same building and recommended that he meet Brian. Syd was also impressed with the material and called George Martin's office. In his autobiography, Martin mentions that Ted Huntley now runs a hotel in Jersey.

Sid Coleman Another link in the chain which led to The Beatles' first major recording contract. When Brian Epstein was attempting to interest record companies in The Beatles in 1962, several of them rejected the group. Armed with some tapes they had made for a Decca audition, Brian went to the HMC centre on Oxford Street to have the tapes put onto acetate, which would be more convenient for carrying on his trips around the London show business scene. One of the engineers listened to the recordings and contacted Coleman on the floor above. He was then manager of Ardmore and Beechwood, EMI's publishing company. Sid immediately sat down with Epstein and listened to the numbers. He was impressed and offered to publish 'Love Of The Loved' and 'Hello Little Girl'. He then phoned George Martin, A&R head of Parlophone Records and arranged a meeting for Brian via George's secretary. The rest is history — although Sid didn't even get the publishing he'd hoped for: that went to Dick James. Sid's assistant at Ardmore & Beechwood, Kim Bennett, was one of the people responsible for promoting records, one of which was to be 'Love Me Do'.

George Martin The Beatles recording manager whose knowledge of the technical side of music played a part in the development of their sound on record.

Another person who has been tagged 'The fifth Beatle', Martin was born in 1926. In his early teens he formed a band called The Four Tune Tellers and at the age of 17 joined the Fleet Air Arm. After the war he studied for a time at the Guildhall School of Music before spending a short period working at the BBC Music Library. He joined EMI records in 1950 and recorded a wide variety of people including Johnny Dankworth, The Goons, Judy Garland, Tommy Steele, Stan Getz, Michael Flanders and Donald Swann and Peter Sellers. In April 1962 Syd Coleman of Ardmore and Beechwood, EMI's publishing company, phoned Martin's secretary and arranged for an appointment with Brian Epstein. Brian had already been touting The Beatles tapes around for some months and had been turned down by most record companies, including Philips, Pye, Decca — and EMI itself. Martin arranged for the first recording audition to take place at Abbey Road No. 3 studio on June 6th, 1962 where he met The Beatles for the first time. He mentions in his autobiography that he took to The Beatles immediately, although various other sources suggest that he accepted them on sufferance.

The Beatles returned to London in September 1962 with their new drummer Ringo Starr to cut their first Parlophone record, although George had by then hired a session drummer, Andy White. Following the success of The Beatles, Brian brought George a succession of artists, including Gerry and The Pacemakers, Billy J. Kramer and Cilla Black.

Numerous other hits followed and in August 1965, he left EMI to set up AIR (Associated Independent Recording) with Ron Richards and John Burgess. Despite his break with EMI, caused by the pittance he was receiving in relation to the financial success his recordings were bringing the company, he continued to record The Beatles, one of his greatest achievements being the recording of *Sergeant Pepper's Lonely Hearts Club Band*, arguably the best rock album ever produced. George was later to make a deal with Chrysalis Records regarding financial control of AIR, leaving him with artistic control of the company and he even set up a recording studio in the idyllic setting of the Caribbean island of Montserrat. He was to involve himself, over the years, in various recordings with his own George Martin Orchestra and a number of his albums were treatments of Beatles songs. They included *Off The Beatle Track* which contained the numbers 'All My Loving'; 'Don't Bother Me'; 'Can't Buy Me Love'; 'All I've Got To Do'; 'I Saw Her Standing There'; 'She Loves You'; 'From Me To You'; 'There's A Place'; 'This Boy'; 'Please Please Me'; 'Little Child'; 'I Want To Hold Your Hand'. The LP which also sported a sleeve note by John Lennon was first issued on Parlophone PCS 3057 on July 10th, 1964 and in the US on United Artists UAS 6377 on August 3rd. The album was reissued in Britain on Charly Records in March 1982.

The album *The Beatle Girls* contained the tracks 'Girls'; 'Eleanor Rigby'; 'She Said She Said'; 'I'm Only Sleeping'; 'Anna (Go To Him)'; 'Michelle'; 'Got To Get You Into My Life'; 'Woman'; 'Yellow Submarine'; 'Here There And Everywhere'; 'And Your Bird Can Sing' and 'Good Day Sunshine'. It was issued in America on United Artists UAS 6539 on November 12th, 1966 and the following year in Britain on United Artists SULP 1157 on March 3rd. He produced, in addition to the original soundtracks, albums of music from *A Hard Day's Night* and *Help* and his singles included 'All My Loving' c/w 'I Saw Her Standing There'; 'Ringo's Theme' c/w 'And I Love Her'; 'I Should Have Known Better' c/w 'A Hard Day's Night'; 'I Feel Fine' c/w 'Niagra Theme'; 'Yesterday' c/w 'Another Girl'. He also arranged Paul McCartney's tune 'Love In The Open Air' for the film *The Family Way* and, in addition to the single, issued a soundtrack album of the movie. Paul called on his services again to record 'Live and Let Die' for the James Bond film and George also produced the soundtrack album. Another soundtrack album he was responsible for was *Yellow Submarine* which contained the tracks 'Pepperland'; 'Sea Of Time'; 'Sea Of Holes'; 'Sea Of Monsters'; 'March Of The Meanies'; 'Pepperland Laid Waste' and 'Yellow Submarine In Pepperland'. It was issued in the US on January 13th, 1969 on Apple SW 153 and in Britain a few days later on January 17th on Apple PCS 7070. His next album, issued on December 11th, 1970, issued in Britain on Sunset SLS 50182, was called *By George!*. Other projects over the years included a *Beatles Concerto* album and

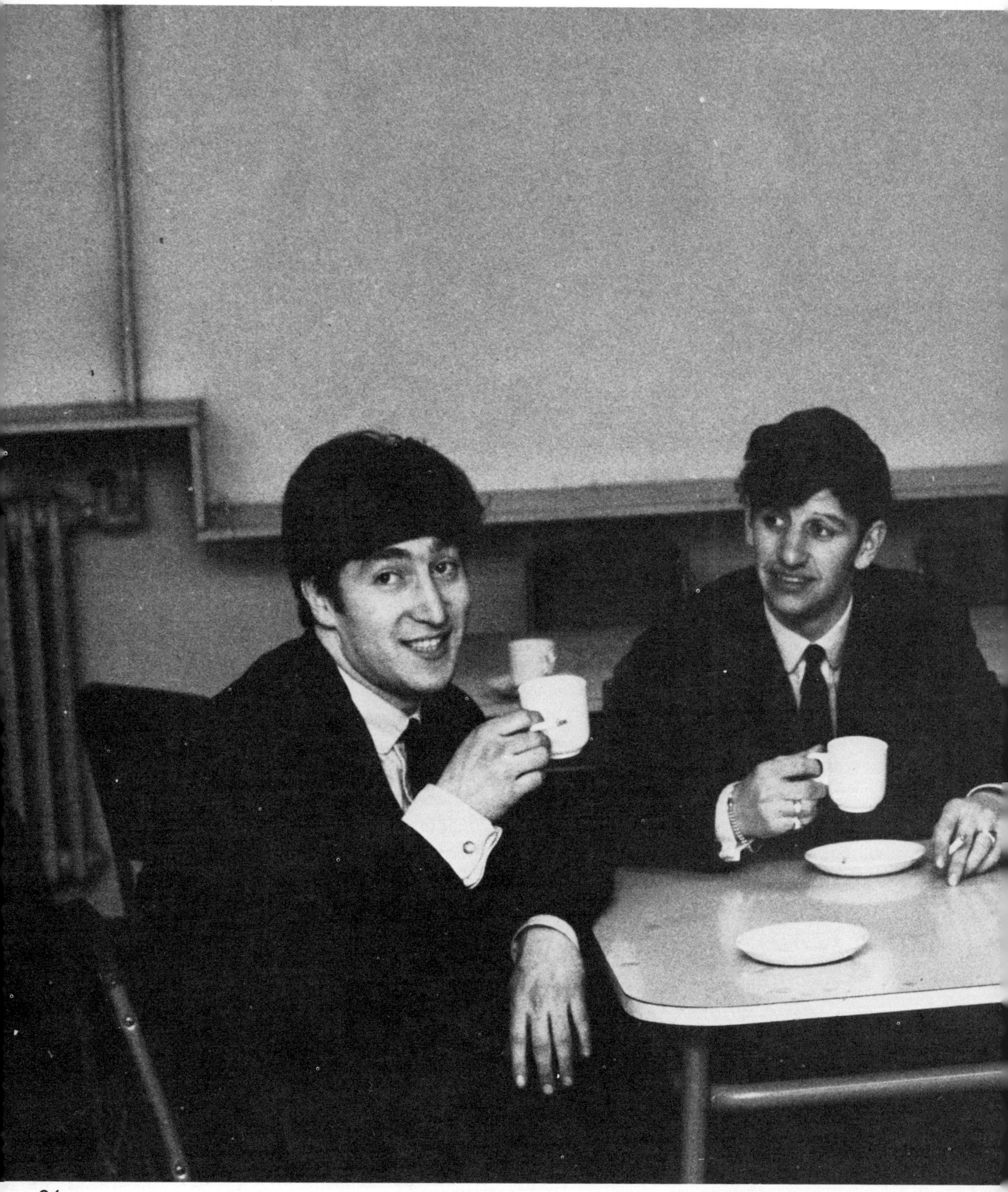

The Beatles share a cuppa with George Martin at the recording studio canteen

the music for the Robert Stigwood film, *Sergeant Pepper's Lonely Hearts Club Band*.

Along with Mickie Most, he is Britain's most famous record producer and was the subject of a *This Is Your Life* programme in 1980. He was also the subject of a television documentary *A Little Help From My Friends*, which also featured Ringo Starr and was screened on British television on December 24th, 1969. His autobiography *All You Need Is Ears* was published in 1979.

Norman Smith The Beatles' recording engineer. Norman was born in Edmonton, North London and was a versatile musician, playing several instruments, until he served in the RAF. He left the Air Force in 1947 and, unable to make a career as a musician, eventually became an engineer at EMI. George Martin used him for the Beatles sessions, including their first-ever EMI recording stint. John used to call him 'Normal Smith'. He also engineered sessions for various bands in the sixties, including Billy J. Kramer and The Dakotas, Freddie and The Dreamers and Cliff Bennett and The Rebel Rousers. Norman found success in his own right as a recording artist, using the name Whispering Smith. After several hits he retired to the country to breed horses.

Dick James Born in 1920 in the East End of London, Richard Leon Vapnick became a professional singer at the age of 17 in 1937 when he joined Al Berlin and His Band who were resident at the Cricklewood Palais. During the war he joined the Medical Corps and continued to play in a band and in 1942 he made his first record with Primo Scala's Accordian Band. In 1945 he changed his name to Dick James. He recorded the number 'Robin Hood' for George Martin on the Parlophone label in 1955 and the number became the theme tune for the TV series starring Richard Green and reached No. 9 in the charts. He ceased singing professionally in 1959 and worked as an assistant to Sidney Bron until he formed his own music publishing company in September 1961. He approached George Martin with the number 'How Do You Do It'. He met Brian Epstein and The Beatles on July 1st, 1962 and discussed the possibility of obtaining the publishing rights to 'Please Please Me'. He arranged for The Beatles to have their first nationwide TV spot on *Thank Your Lucky Stars* via Phillip Jones of ATV. The grateful Brian Epstein then agreed that Dick should become their publisher and booking agent and was thrilled when it was suggested that a special company called Northern Songs

Dick James, who built a publishing empire on the foundation of Lennon and McCartney songs

should be formed. Dick James had a larger share in the company than either Brian or John or Paul.

During the days of Beatlemania, Dick decided to record again and went into the studio to warble a Beatles medley which was issued on Parlophone R5212 on January 1st, 1965 under the title 'Sing A Song Of Beatles' and comprised a medley of 'From Me To You'; 'I Want To Hold Your Hand'; 'She Loves You'; 'All My Loving'; 'I Should Have Known Better' and 'Can't Buy Me Love'.

John Lennon and Paul McCartney felt that he betrayed them when he sold his shares in Northern Songs to Sir Lew Grade, becoming a millionaire in the process. The deal meant that John and Paul found themselves unable to gain control of the company publishing their songs.

Dick continued to flourish, virtually creating his own music empire with superstars such as Elton John and today runs his thriving business from James House in London.

Clive Epstein Brian Epstein's younger brother. When Brian launched NEMS Enterprises in 1962 it was a business supported by his family and he wanted Clive to become active in it. Although Clive was a major shareholder, he concentrated on the Liverpool end of the family concern: the shops. Four days after Brian died, Clive became chairman of NEMS with 90% of the shares. He was never really happy taking charge of such a large concern in London, feeling much more at ease in his native Liverpool. He suggested to The Beatles that they involve themselves in a commercial activity, apart from their musical career, to offset the huge amount of money they'd have to pay in tax. Clive's idea was that The Beatles should buy shops. They took his advice but formed Apple instead. Clive eventually decided to sell NEMS to The Beatles, but the deal became complicated with the appearance of Allen Klein and he sold the majority shares to Triumph Investments. He continued to work in Liverpool, primarily in the property business and then set up an agency-management company with Joe Flannery, called the Carlton-Brooke Agency, to handle local talent. Twelve years after he originally retired from show-business, Sid Bernstein contacted him and suggested they become co-managers of a group. The Anglo-American partnership was launched in 1981 with a Liverpool quartet called Motion Pictures.

John Charles Julian Lennon
John's first son, born in Sefton General Hospital on April 8th, 1963. When Cynthia discovered that she was pregnant, John decided that they should get married, although the fact that they were wed was hushed up for some time. One of Julian's drawings was used as the design for the cover of the fan club record *Christmastime Is Here Again* in December 1967 and another of Julian's drawings of a girl called Lucy inspired John to write 'Lucy In the Sky With Diamonds'. With the estrangement and divorce, John saw little of his son during the years that followed and Julian was brought up in Ruthin, Wales for a number of years by Cynthia and her third husband, John Twist. In the latter part of the seventies, Julian had the opportunity of meeting his father again following some trips to New York but before any real closeness could develop, John was murdered. After the killing, Cynthia began touring the States with her paintings

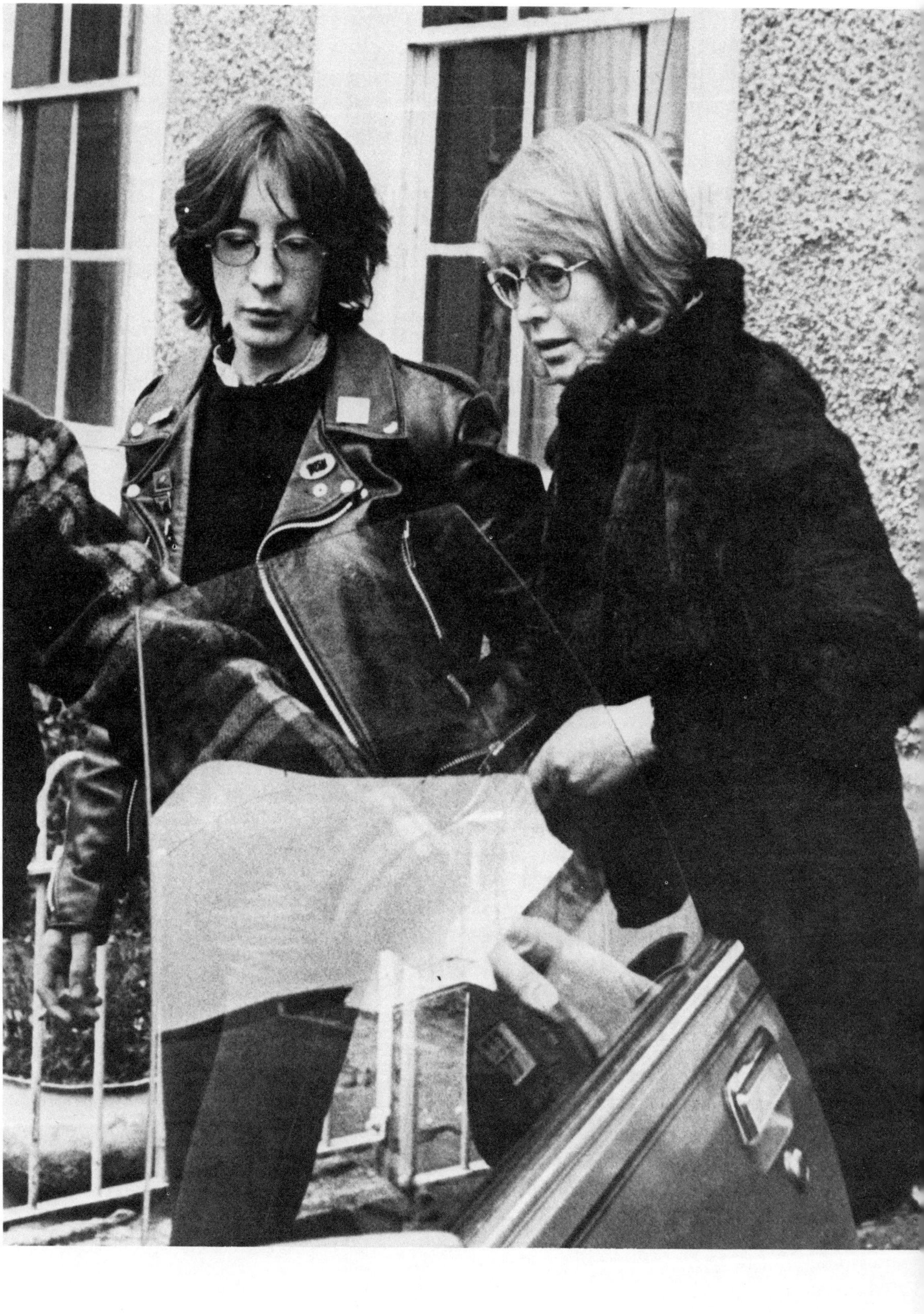

and Julian moved to London where his antics in fashionable nightclubs with starlets, strippers and models as his companions were frequently reported in the press.

Arthur Howes Major British promoter of the early and mid-sixties. He first 'tested' The Beatles by including them on a bill topped by Frank Ifield at the Embassy Theatre, Peterborough. Their two appearances at the theatre were not particularly well received, but Arthur decided that he liked the group personally and engaged them for their first-ever British tour, supporting Helen Shapiro. Other acts on the bill included vocalists Danny Williams and Kenny Lynch, vocal group The Kestrels and the Red Price Orchestra. The 15-date tour opened at the Gaumont, Bradford on February 2nd, 1963 and the venues were mainly on the stages of cinemas. Their reception this time was encouraging and Arthur immediately placed them on another tour, headlined by two American singers: Chris Montez and Tommy Roe. The tour opened at the Granada, East Ham on March 9th, 1963. Howes then decided that they deserved to top the bill of the next tour and although Roy Orbison was a major American act with a string of hits in Britain, The Beatles were engaged to close the show on a tour which opened at the Granada, Slough on May 18th. Gerry and The Pacemakers were also on the bill. Howes continued to promote Beatles tours in Britain during the next few years.

Don Howarth BBC producer who made a 30-minute documentary in 1963 called *The Mersey Sound*. At the time he said:

'I visited Liverpool several months ago to see if the city was a good subject for a programme. I saw Bill Harry, Brian Epstein and several of the leading lights in the beat scene and visited several clubs including the Cavern and the Iron Door. Within two days I knew that there was such atmosphere and excitement on the Mersey scene that I just had to use it in the programme.

'When I brought the production unit down in August I decided to let the people of Merseyside make their own comments on the scene and allowed the people who were interviewed to talk freely. In that way a truer picture of the scene could be formed.'

The Beatles were strongly featured in the documentary and were filmed performing 'Love Me Do', 'Twist and Shout' and 'She Loves You' on stage at the Odeon, Southport. Group One performed 'Pretend' at the Iron Door Club and The Undertakers played their début single 'Mashed Potatoes'. Musician, Dave Williams, talked of group members on the dole, promoter Les Ackerley about a local protection racket and Stan Gutteridge from Rushworth's about the boom in guitar sales. Not unnaturally, The Beatles were the stars of the programme and George discussed their early appearances in Hamburg while Ringo enacted a scene in a ladies' hairdressing salon where, sartorially dressed, he walked down a bank of hairdriers greeting his clients: this was in reference to his statement that he hoped to make enough money out of The Beatles to be able to open his own hairdressing salon.

Gay Byrne Irish television presenter who worked for Granada television in the early sixties, hosting a programme called *People And Places*, concerned with people and events in the north-west of England. He presented The Beatles on their television début when they performed 'Love Me Do' for the show on November 7th, 1962. The Beatles received a fee of £35. The programme was to change its name to *Scene At 6.30* and Gay later returned to Ireland where he is a major television personality.

Johnny Hamp Producer at Granada television studios which covers the north-west of England. He first booked The Beatles on his *People And Places* programme on December 17th, 1962 and used the group regularly. A few years later he was to comment: 'I first saw The Beatles in a club in Hamburg. They were very scruffy characters but they had a beat in their music which I liked.' Coincidentally, it was on December 17th (in 1965 this time), that Johnny produced his most ambitious Beatles enterprise, a major TV special on the music of Lennon & McCartney. This included Paul singing 'Yesterday' with Marianne Faithful and various other artists who performed the duo's songs included Cilla Black ('It's For You'); Peter and Gordon ('World Without Love'); Billy J. Kramer and The Dakotas ('Bad To Me'); Lulu ('I Saw Him Standing There'); Esther Phillips ('And I Love Him'); Richard Anthony ('All My Loving'); The George Martin Orchestra ('I Feel Fine', 'Another Girl'); The Liverpool Philharmonic Orchestra ('She Loves You'); Alan Haven ('A Hard Day's Night') and Peter Sellers ('A Hard Day's Night').

Andy White Session drummer who was booked by George Martin to play drums on the 'Love Me Do' recording. At the time he was married to Lyn Cornell, a singer who had been a member of the Liverpool female vocal group The Vernon Girls.

Andrew Loog Oldham For a short period of time early in 1963 he was employed as publicist to The Beatles. Brian Epstein offered him the position of Press Officer for the entire NEMS Enterprises operation but he turned it down. Fortunately for him because he became manager of The Rolling Stones shortly afterwards.

Roger Stinton Acted as press agent for The Beatles for a short period before becoming a personal representative of Billy J. Kramer on behalf of Brian Epstein.

Russell Jamieson One of The Beatles' most ardent Merseyside fans. Affectionately called 'Russell Beatle', he was four years old in 1963 when the

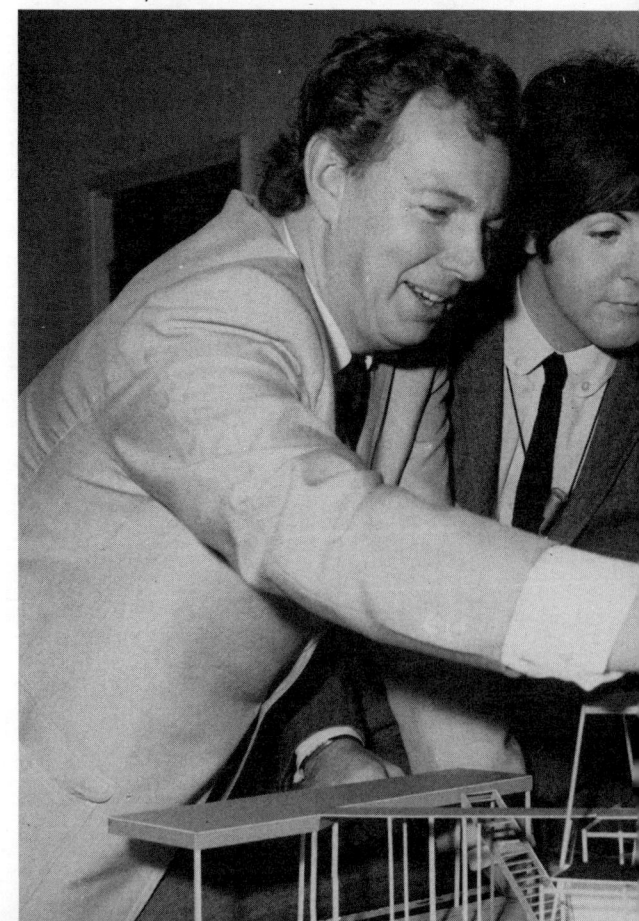

Brian Epstein with Andrew Oldham, former Beatles P.R. man who became manager of The Rolling Stones

press took numerous photographs of him dancing to Beatles records and wearing Beatles-style clothes. His devotion was such that he was made an honorary member of their fan club.

George Harrison Columnist with the *Liverpool Echo*. When Brian Epstein took over The Beatles, *Mersey Beat* was the only publication reporting on the group's activities. Brian particularly sought the prestige of *Echo* coverage and George Harrison obliged with items in his 'Over The Mersey Wall' column. As their fame grew he became the main writer providing *Echo* coverage on the group and travelled to America with them. Some of his reports are contained in *Around The World With the Beatles*, a souvenir book produced by the *Liverpool Echo* at Christmas 1964.

Derek Taylor I first met Derek Taylor in Manchester in 1963. The occasion was the showing of Don Howarth's documentary *The Mersey Sound* at the BBC's office in Peter Square. He worked for the Manchester office of the *Daily Express* and had his own column 'Taylor On Saturday'. He was keen to write an article on The Beatles but as every other journalist in the country had the same thing in mind he wondered if I could give him an angle which had not been used before. I told him to go to Hamburg, describing the scene there and providing him with a list of contacts.

It proved to be a far more rewarding trip than he'd anticipated and developed into a series which ran daily in the paper for a week. After that, Derek was the Beatles' expert on the *Daily Express* and when they arranged for George Harrison to provide them with a column, Derek was elected to ghost it. He travelled with The Beatles to Paris and soon became one of their close friends. Within a matter of months he'd received an offer from Brian Epstein and became his personal assistant. He spent

Granada TV's Johnny Hamp shows Paul and John a scale model of the set for The Music Of Lennon And McCartney

GREAT NEWS !!!

THE CAVERN

BRITAIN'S No. 1 BEAT BASEMENT

NOW HAS AN EXCITING NEW 30 MINUTE RADIO PROGRAMME ALL ABOUT ITS

GALS, GUYS, GROOVES AND GROUPS

EACH SUNDAY AT

10-30 p.m. on Radio Luxembourg

"SUNDAY NIGHT AT THE CAVERN"

YOU MUST NOT MISS IT !! "Tune in to the trend at 10-30" TELL YOUR FRIENDS !!

THE HOME OF THE BEATLES

ALL REQUESTS FOR POSSIBLE INCLUSION IN THIS PROGRAMME TO BE SENT TO: BOB WOOLER, D.J. COMPERE, THE CAVERN, 10 MATHEW STREET, LIVERPOOL, 2. CENtral 1591.

a few weeks ghosting Brian's autobiography *A Cellarful Of Noise* and was then appointed press officer to The Beatles. He resigned at the end of the 1964 American tour following some arguments with Brian and remained in the States, taking up the offer of Radio KRLA in Los Angeles who hired him as their press officer. The job didn't last very long and he opened offices in Sunset Boulevard as a PR consultant, his first clients being The Byrds. He became very successful but when Apple was launched The Beatles asked Derek to join them; as his family were becoming homesick he returned to England and headed Apple's Press Division, originally from 95 Wigmore Street and later from the plush offices in Saville Row.

Derek's reminiscences are to be found in his entertaining autobiography *As Time Goes By*, first published in 1973. His idyll at Apple ended when he was fired by Allen Klein and he moved to WEA Records as Director of Special Projects. Since leaving WEA he has been involved with various projects in the music world.

Helen Shapiro British singer who found fame at the age of 15 with a string of hits, including 'Don't Treat Me Like A Child', and 'Walking Back To Happiness'. She topped the bill of The Beatles' first tour for Arthur Howes, a 15-date cinema tour which began at the Gaumont, Bradford on February 2nd, 1963. The show was filmed by ABC TV and excerpts were featured on *Thank Your Lucky Stars*.

The Kestrels Vocal group who first toured with The Beatles on the cinema tour headlined by Helen Shapiro which began on February 22nd, 1963. They also accompanied The Beatles on a six-week tour of England and Ireland starting on November 1st. The Kestrels recorded the Lennon and McCartney song 'There's A Place'.

Chris Montez American singer who had just had a big chart hit with 'Let's Dance' when he co-headlined a British tour in 1963 with fellow American, Tommy Roe. The Beatles supported them on the bill and Montez commented: 'Who are these guys The Beatles? I try to keep up to date with the British scene, but I don't know their work.'

Tommy Roe American singer whose hits 'Sheila' and 'Susie Darlin'' led him to co-star on an Arthur Howes promoted tour of Britain in 1963 with fellow American Chris Montez. The Beatles were also on the bill. Tommy next appeared with them at the Coliseum concert in Washington DC on February 11th, 1962, along with The Chiffons and The Caravelles.

Peter Jay and The Jaywalkers Band from East Anglia comprising Peter Jay (drums), Pete Miller (lead guitar), Tony Webster (rhythm guitar), Mac McIntyre (tenor sax/flute), Lloyd Baker (piano, baritone sax), Geoff Moss (acoustic bass) and Johnny Larke (bass guitar). The group toured with The Beatles from November 1st until December 13th, 1963. During their tour they had several jam sessions with The Beatles and the Brook Brothers, some of which were taped.

Bob Bain British comedian/compere, popular on the cabaret circuit, who appeared with The Beatles on their fifth British tour.

Roy Orbison Texan singer known as 'The Big O' who had 16 chart hits in Britain. He was booked to headline a British concert tour, promoted by Arthur Howes, in May 1963. Howes then decided that The Beatles were becoming very hot and placed them top of the bill. Orbison didn't complain and commented, 'Mark my words, those boys will be tremendous in America.'

Mary Wells Tamla had always been a highly-regarded label in Liverpool ever since Oriole-American first made releases available. When Mary Wells made her début appearance on a British tour it was on the bill with The Beatles at the Gaumont, Bradford on October 9th — the start of a four-week tour. I went backstage to interview her at the Apollo, Manchester. Although she'd had five singles in the American Top Five, she'd only become known recently in Britain for her hit 'My Guy'. She told me: 'I first heard that I'd be touring with The Beatles in September and I thought it

John Lennon enjoying himself at Roy Orbison's birthday party

Back home at Liverpool Town Hall The Beatles are given a civic reception

was wonderful. I admire them very much and as far as I'm concerned they're the best.' She added, 'I'd just love to record a number by John and Paul and I think I'll ask them about it.' I saw John later that evening and mentioned it to him and he said, 'We've got a number which we think will be really suitable for her', but I heard no more, although she appeared on their TV show *Around The Beatles*. She did pay tribute, though, with her album *Love Songs To The Beatles*, which featured: 'He Loves You'; 'All My Loving'; 'Please, Please Me'; 'Do You Want To Know A Secret'; 'Can't Buy Me Love'; 'I Should Have Known Better'; 'Help!'; 'Eight Days A Week'; 'And I Love Him'; 'Ticket To Ride'; 'Yesterday' and 'I Saw Him Standing There'.

Mitch Murray British songwriter who specialized in lightweight pop songs. Dick James gave George Martin the Murray composition 'How Do You Do It', which Martin wanted The Beatles to record. They didn't like it and told him so. He challenged them to come up with a better song, which they did: 'Please, Please Me'. But they still recorded 'How Do You Do It', although their version has never been officially released. Martin was right about the song being commercial, it gave Gerry and The Pacemakers their first No. 1 hit. Brian Epstein used another Mitch Murray composition 'By The Way', for The Big Three, but

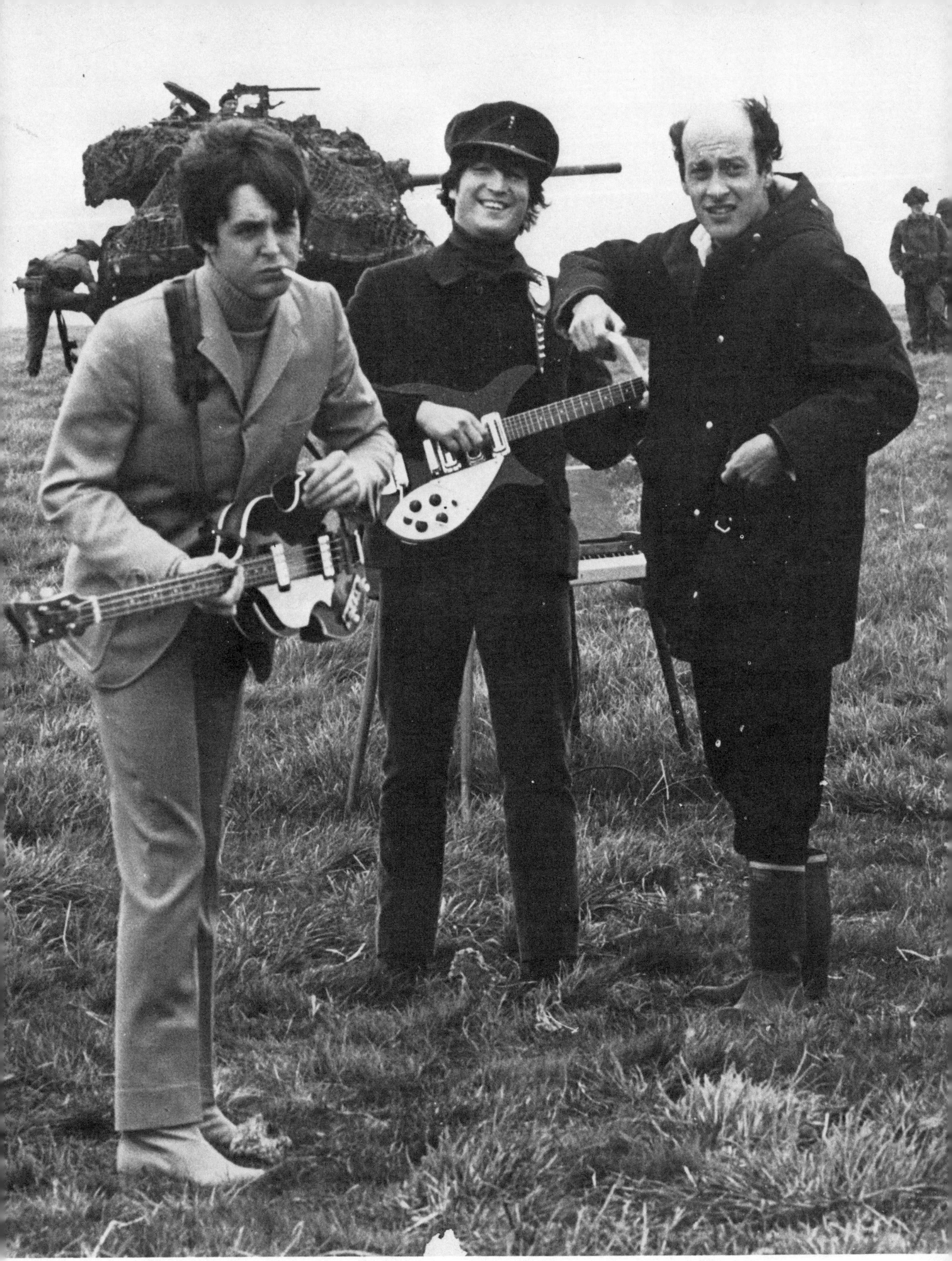

although it was a minor hit, as in the case of The Beatles, it was the wrong song for the wrong group: The Big Three were a hard-driving aggressive-sounding rock band. Murray teamed up with Peter Callendar and continued to produce a string of pop hits, including 'Bonnie and Clyde' and 'The Night Chicago Died' and his songs on record have sold over 100,000,000 copies. He went into tax exile in Holland for a while, then moved to the Isle of Man, which also provided a tax haven and from there, in the eighties, began to concentrate on writing jingles.

The Trends Liverpool band comprising Mike Kelly, Frank Bowen, Freddie Self and Johnny Hayes who had a minor hit with the Lennon/McCartney song 'All My Loving'.

The Scaffold Liverpool trio who gained prominence in the mid-sixties with comedy hits such as 'Thank U Very Much' and 'Lily The Pink'. Comprising Mike McGear, Roger McGough and John Gorman, the trio teamed up with several other poets and musicians to appear in an outfit called Grimms during the seventies. The Scaffold were revived during 1974 when Paul McCartney produced and wrote a single for them: 'Liverpool Lou' c/w 'Ten Years After On Strawberry Jam'. The single (Warner Brothers K16400) was released on May 24th, 1974 and reached No. II in the British charts. It was also issued in America (Warner Brothers 8001) on July 29th, 1974.

The Vernons Girls Originally formed

On location on Salisbury Plain with director Dick Lester

On tour with Mary Wells, one of their favourite singers

in December 1961 and sponsored by the Liverpool football pools firm, Vernons. There were various personnel changes during the career of the group whose major hit was 'Lover Please'. The group survived as a trio for some years and appeared with The Beatles on a special Merseyside edition of the TV programme *Thank Your Lucky Stars* on December 22nd, 1963 with fellow Liverpudlians Cilla Black, The Searchers, Billy J. Kramer and Gerry and The Pacemakers. The Vernons Girls also appeared on a five-week British tour with the Fab Four and recorded a number called 'We Want The Beatles'.

Dick Lester American producer/director who was born in Philadelphia in 1932. As a musician, Lester had toured the world playing guitar and piano in various bars and clubs. During his last

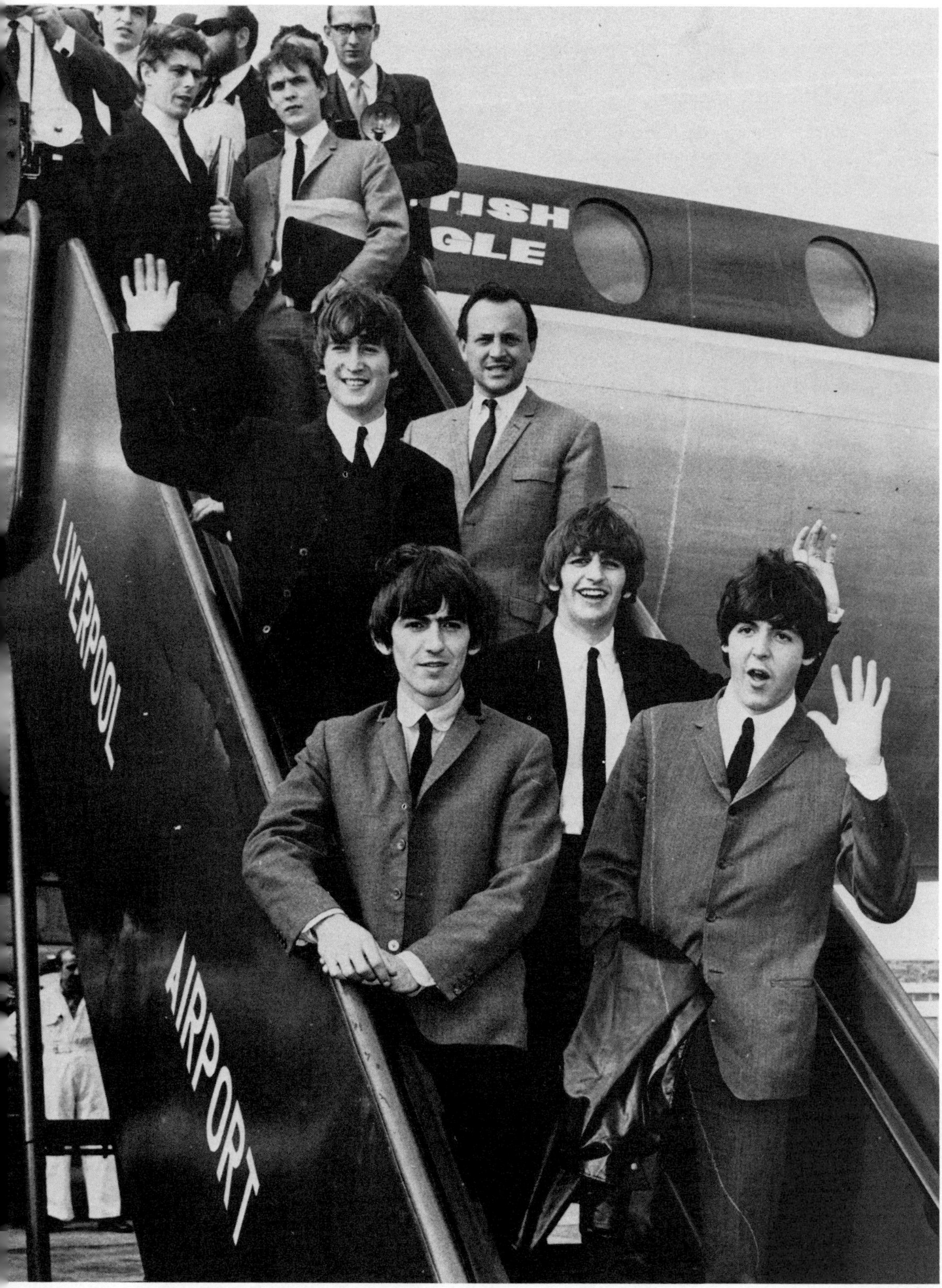
TISH
GLE
LIVERPOOL
AIRPORT

year at university he formed a vocal group which made regular appearances on local television in America. He became a stage hand at the studios and eventually a director. he then moved to Britain where he made his first film, *The Running, Jumping, Standing Still Film*, in 1959. He made his first pop film, *It's Trad, Dad*, in 1962. Lester directed two Beatles films, *A Hard Day's Night* (1964) and *Help!* (1967). He also signed John Lennon for his solo film début as Private Gripweed in the 1967 film *How I Won The War*. His other movie credits include *Petulia, Juggernaut, The Three Musketeers* and *Superman II*.

Walter Shenson San Francisco-born film producer, educated at Stanford University. He became a press officer at Columbia Pictures before moving to Britain where he produced the films *The Mouse That Roared* and *Mouse On The Moon*. He was approached by United Artists to produce The Beatles' début film and he selected Dick Lester as director. A clause in his contract stated that the rights to the film would revert back to him after a 15-year period. He also produced *Help!* (with the same contractual clause) and was odds-on to make a third Beatles film. However, a satisfactory script proved difficult to find and Shenson even asked John Lennon at one point whether he'd care to write a script himself. Jo Orton's 'Up Against It' was turned down, perhaps it was too controversial, then another of Shenson's suggestions, Richard Condon's 'A Talent For Loving' was considered but rejected because of Condon's script. The Beatles were also dissatisfied with 'Shades Of Personality', a script which showed four sides of one man's personality — the idea being that all four would play the same man. So much time had elapsed that The Beatles had cooled in their attitude to making another movie and later were involved themselves in *Let It Be*.

Shenson remained in Britain producing numerous films, including *Thirty Is A Dangerous Age, Cynthia; Don't Raise The Bridge, Lower The River* and *Digby, The Biggest Dog In The World*. When the rights of *A Hard Day's Night* reverted back to him in 1981 he re-released it with a Dolby stereo soundtrack and did the same with *Help!* the following year.

Alun Owen Liverpool Welshman who was one of Britain's major playwrights for television in the sixties, responsible for some gripping dramas with Liverpool settings, such as *No Trams To Lime Street*. When discussions about The Beatles' début film, tentatively entitled 'Beatlemania' and later to become *A Hard Day's Night*, were taking place, Alun's name was put forward and he was commissioned to provide the script. He travelled to Ireland to spend two days with the Fab Four on their Irish tour and Walter Shenson also took him to visit them in Paris while they were staying at the George V Hotel. Everyone loved the screenplay, which was nominated for an Oscar and John Lennon commented: 'He wrote the whole thing based on our characters then: me, witty; Ringo, dumb and cute; George, this; Paul, that.'

Alun had taken notes of their conversations and with his remarkable ear for dialogue had perfectly captured their Scouse humour. He also introduced several of the Liverpool expressions such as 'fab', 'wack' and 'gear', which became popular almost overnight when the film was released. In one scene he has George using the expression 'grotty' when commenting on some shirts shown to him by a trendy advertising firm. 'I wouldn't be seen dead in them. They're dead grotty', he says, explaining that the word is an abbreviation of grotesque. One scene featured a press reception which was particularly true to life.

At the time, Alun had recently settled in St Dogmaels, a small Welsh village near to Cardigan, but often travelled to Liverpool to listen to the dialogue and take note of it for use in his plays. His musical *Maggie May* was premiered in Manchester in August 1964. It was set in contemporary Liverpool and presented scenes at the pier head, inside a beat club, on the Mersey Ferry, in New Brighton Fairground and at the docks. Various Liverpool artists were featured in the musical, including singer Diane Quiseekay, The Nocturnes and Geoff Hughes.

Wilfred Brambell British character actor noted for his portrayal of the grizzled rag-and-bone man, Steptoe, in the long-running BBC TV series *Steptoe and Son*. He co-starred with The Beatles in *A Hard Day's Night* as John McCart-

Horsing around in a field on the set of A Hard Day's Night

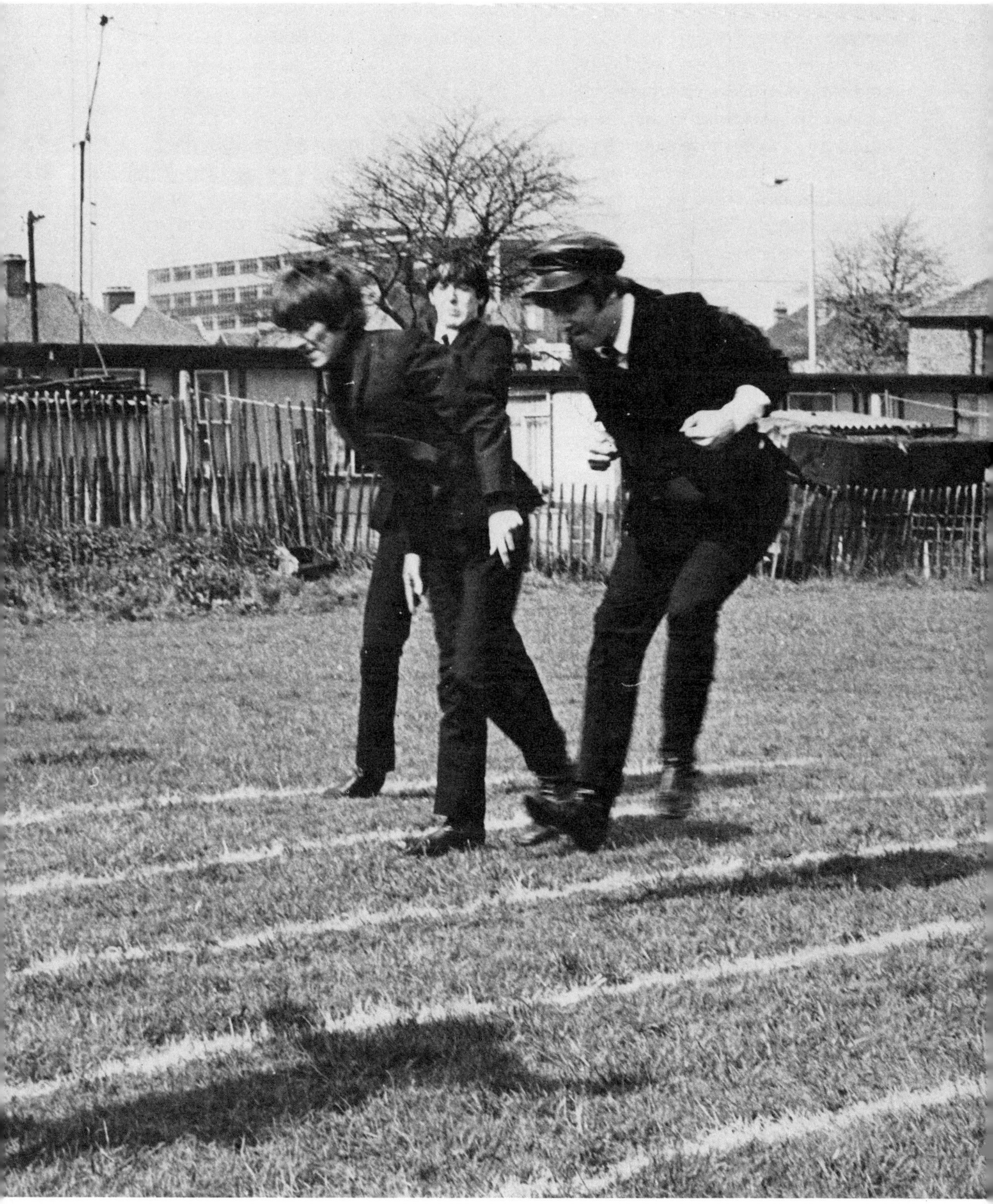

ney, Paul's eccentric grandfather, who travels down to London with them and causes chaos wherever he goes. At the time of the filming he commented: 'I was worried about how someone like myself would fit in with these Beatles. I liked their music but I was no expert and I felt the whole thing could easily become a fiasco. Instead, they positively amazed me with their cool and professional approach.'

Norman Rossington Liverpool-born character actor who appeared as Norm, one of The Beatles' road managers in *A Hard Day's Night*. The character he portrayed was based on Neil Aspinall. He also portrayed Arthur Babcock in *Double Trouble*, the Elvis Presley movie, and has thus appeared in films with the two greatest rock sensations of all time.

John Junkin British comedian/character actor who portrayed a road manager called Shake, a Mal Evans type, in *A Hard Day's Night*.

Victor Spinetti Welsh actor who became a close friend of The Beatles, holidaying with John and Cynthia Lennon in North Africa in 1968. Victor's first association with the Fab Four came when he portrayed the panicky television director in *A Hard Day's Night*. He next appeared as the mad scientist in *Help!* attempting to divest Ringo of his sacrificial ring by the use of lasers. In *Magical Mystery Tour* he portrayed an army recruiting sergeant in a scene with Paul McCartney, perhaps his best cameo in all three films. Spinetti also appeared with John Lennon in *How I Won The War* and co-authored *In His Own Write — The Lennon Play* with John Lennon and American dramatist Adrienne Kennedy. This was a one-act play based on two of John's books, *In His Own Write* and *A Spaniard In The Works*. Sir Laurence Olivier approved a Sunday evening production of the play in the summer of 1968 as part of the National Theatre repertoire and it opened at the Old Vic, London as a National Theatre production on June 18th, 1968. Using a character called Me, based on Lennon, the play developed John's pieces from the books in a structure attacking the Establishment. As well as co-writing the play, Spinetti appeared in it and a book of the play was published by Jonathan Cape in 1968.

Patti Boyd Patti, born Patricia Anne Boyd on March 17th, 1944, first came to London to be a model in 1962 and was brought to the attention of the British public via her series of television commercials for Smith's Crisps in the early sixties. The commercials were produced by Dick Lester and when he was commissioned to direct the Beatles' début movie *A Hard Day's Night*, he booked Patti for the part of one of the schoolgirls who meet The Beatles on a train travelling from Liverpool to London. George Harrison was enchanted by her (she reminded him of his favourite film star Brigitte Bardot) and their romance blossomed. She moved into his bungalow, Kinfauns, in Esher and he proposed to her on Christmas Day 1965. The couple were wed at Epsom Register Office, Surrey on January 21st, 1966 and Paul McCartney was in attendance. Whilst George was heavily involved in touring it was Patti who became interested in spiritual matters and she was the first member of The Beatles' circle to join the

George and Patti on holiday

Maharishi's Spiritual Regeneration movement and encouraged the others to attend his lecture at the Hilton Hotel, London on August 24th, 1967.

Her vivacity and beauty made headlines — she was an ideal Beatles bride in the eyes of the media. Over the years, however, the couple drifted apart. When they were ensconced at Friar Park in Henley-on-Thames, Patti was not unaware of the interest George's best friend, Eric Clapton, showed in her. In an effort to revive George's interest, or to make him jealous, she began to flirt with Eric and soon Eric realized he had fallen deeply in love with Patti. He wrote a number declaring his love, which he based on a Persian book called *Layla and Majnun*. The song 'Layla' was included on an album Eric made under the pseudonym Derek and The Dominoes — and George was invited to play on it. The number entered the Top Ten in 1972 and again in 1982.

Dezo Hoffman setting up one of his famous photo sessions which were later to be included in a book of his work

Patti left George to join Eric on his American tour but the couple were briefly reconciled before the final split when Patti went to live with Clapton. George commented: 'I'd rather she was with him than some dope.' Patti was divorced from George in 1977 and married Eric in 1979. George was a guest at the reception.

Rosemary Frankland An ex-Miss World who appeared as a glamorous showgirl in *A Hard Day's Night*.

John Burke Prolific British writer of 'novelizations' of film scripts. He is the author of the novel *A Hard Day's Night*, which was based on the Alun Owen screenplay and published by Pan Books

The cast of The Beatles Christmas Show. *The Fab Four with Cilla Black, Billy J. Kramer and The Dakotas, The Fourmost and Rolf Harris*

in 1964. The paperback was illustrated with 12 photographs from the film.

Peter Jones Professional music journalist who wrote the first-ever Beatles paperback book, *The True Story Of The Beatles*, under the name Billy Shepherd. During his term as editor of *Record Mirror* he became the first journalist on a national music paper to interview The Beatles, in August 1962. An account of the interview is given in the November 1978 issue of *The Beatles Book*. Peter interviewed the Fab Four on numerous occasions and was a regular contributor to *Beatles Monthly*.

Maureen Cleave A major writer for London's *Evening Standard* newspaper in the sixties. In February 1963 she interviewed The Beatles and thus provided them with their first write-up in a British national paper. In the March 4th, 1966 issue of the *Standard* her interview with John Lennon appeared in which he made the reference to The Beatles being more popular than Christ. This led to a fierce anti-Beatles campaign in America, particularly in the 'Bible belt' and in the south where the Ku Klux Klan burnt their photographs and records. She left full-time employment with the *Standard* but began to contribute interviews on a freelance basis in the eighties and is invariably commissioned to review Beatles books for their pages.

Dezo Hoffman Photographer based in London who took hundreds of photographs of The Beatles between the years 1963 and 1964. A book of these photographs, entitled *The Beatles: Photos by Dezo Hoffman* was published in Japan.

Peter Yolland Producer hired by Brian Epstein to present The Beatles Christmas shows. Yolland devised a number of humourous sketches for The Beatles to appear in and the first show was presented at the Astoria, Finsbury Park on Christmas Eve 1963 and ran until January 11th, 1964. Artists on the bill supporting The Beatles were Tommy Quickly, Cilla Black, The Fourmost, Billy J. Kramer and The Dakotas and Rolf Harris. The following year he devised and produced the Christmas show at the Hammersmith Odeon which ran from December 24th, 1964 until January 16th, 1955 and starred The Beatles with support from Jimmy Saville, Ray Fell, The Mike Cotton Sound, Freddie and The Dreamers, Sounds Incorporated, Elkie Brooks and Mike Haslam. The same year, Peter also produced a similar venture for Gerry and the Pacemakers: *Gerry's Christmas Cracker*, which opened in Liverpool and then moved on to two other northern cities.

Ricky Gleason and The Top Spots Liverpool group comprising Ricky Gleason (vocals), Graham Little (rhythm), Tony Limb (drums), Keith Dodd (lead) and Kenny Rees (bass). They hit the headlines when they went to London to see *The Beatles Christmas Show* at Finsbury Park Astoria, London in December 1963. The band turned up outside the theatre on a lorry, complete with amps and equipment and began to play. They were mobbed by the 2,000 youngsters in the crowd and the police had to be called. An inspector moved them on. Ricky commented: 'We wanted to show people that the Mersey groups are proud of The Beatles and are in no way envious of their success. It was a tribute to The Beatles and, we're pleased to say, enjoyed by all.'

The Moody Blues Birmingham group who became close friends of The Beatles. They sent a parcel of kippers to the Fab Four when The Beatles were appearing on *Blackpool Night Out* and toured with them in December, 1965. Moody singer Denny Laine was later to become one of the mainstays of Wings.

The Rolling Stones At one time regarded as The Beatles' closest rivals, The Rolling Stones were, in fact, good friends of the Fab Four. It was originally on George Harrison's recommendation that Dick Rowe went rushing to Richmond to sign them up for Decca and The Beatles gave the group a Lennon/McCartney number 'I Wanna Be Your Man' which took The Stones to No. 12 in the charts in December 1963 on Decca F 11764. They socialized and went to clubs such as the Ad Lib and the Scotch of St James together; Paul and Ringo

The Rolling Stones, signed by Decca on the recommendation of The Beatles – and a great face-saver for Dick Rowe

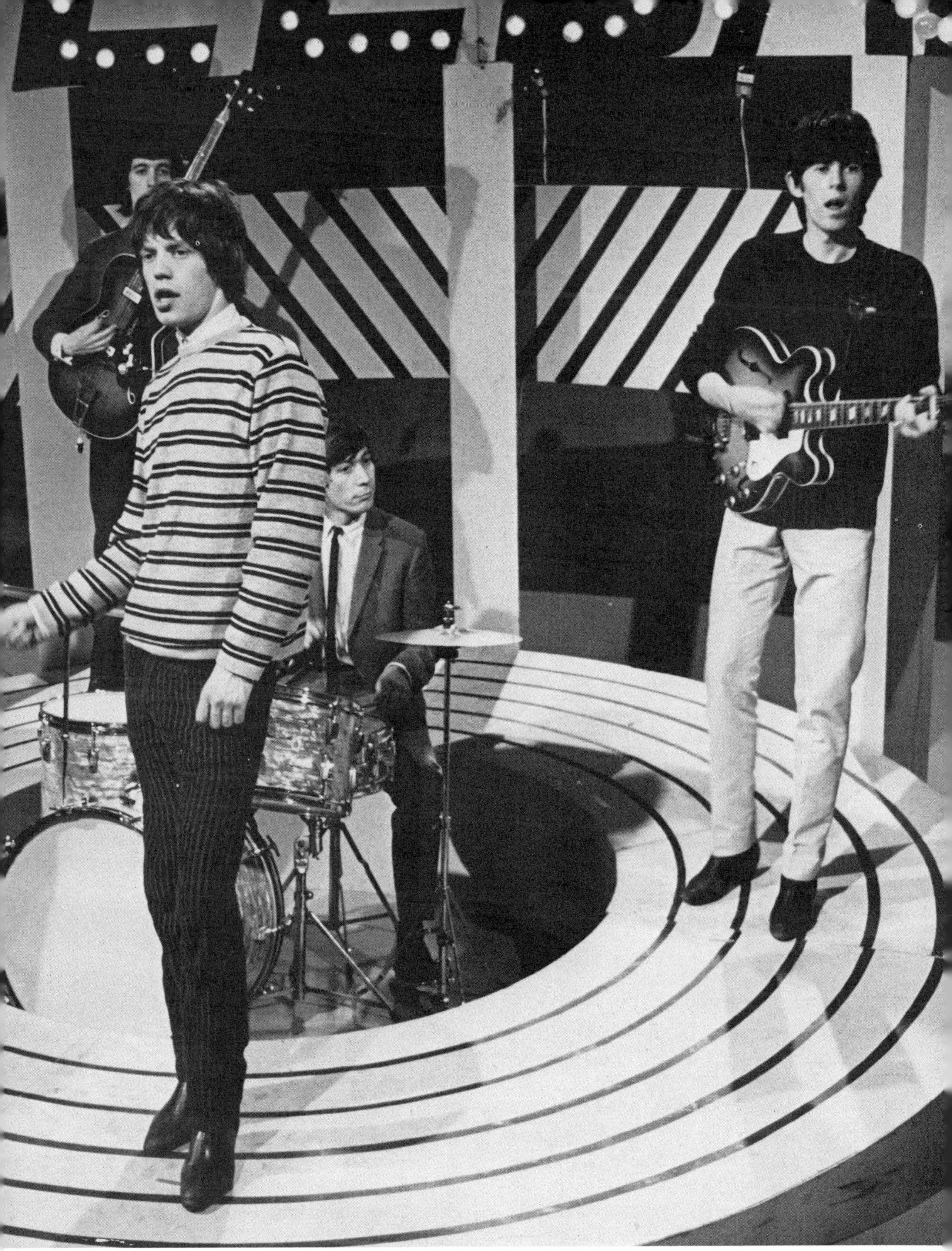

attended Mick Jagger's wedding and Mick joined them on their famous satellite TV appearance *Our World*. There was often talk of their teaming up for joint business ventures and in October 1967 Mick discussed their joint ownership of a recording studio, but plans fell through. When Allen Klein acted as financial adviser to The Rolling Stones and was able to increase their royalties and obtain £3 million for the group, Mick strongly recommended that they take Allen Klein on themselves. Later when The Stones realized that Klein's involvement was not as straightforward as they'd first imagined, Mick Jagger went to visit The Beatles to warn them. Unfortunately, Klein arrived before Mick could venture his opinion.

Peter and Gordon Duo comprising Peter Asher and Gordon Waller who had a number of chart hits with Lennon/McCartney material. Their first major success was 'World Without Love' (Columbia DB 7225 in the UK and Capitol 5175 in the US). The British single was issued on February 28th, 1964 and the American on April 27th, 1964. It stayed in the British charts for 9 weeks where it reached the No. 1 position. The next Lennon/McCartney composition by the duo was 'Nobody I Know', issued in Britain on May 29th of the same year (Columbia DB 7292) and in the States on June 15th (Capitol 5211). Five weeks in the British charts, its highest position was No. 10. Their third and final Lennon/McCartney song was 'I Don't Want To See You Again', released September 11th, 1964 in Britain (Columbia DB 7356) and in America on September 21st, 1964 (Capitol 5272) — 2 weeks in the British charts this time, with a position of No. 16. Their only other Beatle-associated single was 'Woman', which Paul McCartney wrote for them under a pseudonym. It was released in Britain on February 11th, 1966 (Columbia DB 7834) and in the States on January 10th, 1966 (Capitol 5579). Five weeks in the British charts, it reached the No. 14 position. The duo disbanded in 1968.

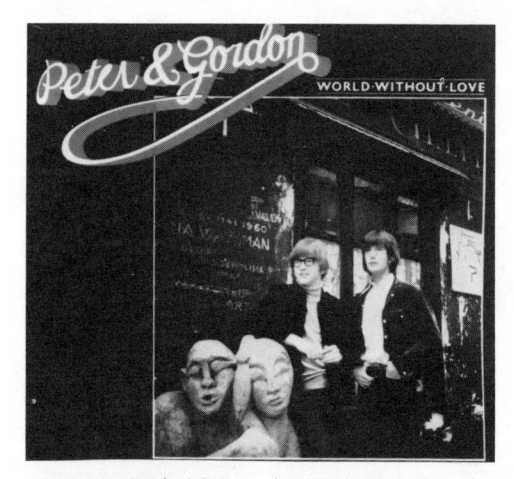

David and Jonathan British duo who had a six-week chart residency with the Lennon/McCartney number 'Michelle'. Issued on Columbia DB 7800 on January 13th, 1966 it entered the charts on January 29th and reached No. 11. The two singers were actually a British songwriting team, Roger Cook and Roger Greenaway who later had a number of hits in their own right.

The Overlanders British folk trio (Paul Arnold, Laurie Mason, Peter

Bartholomew) who hit the No. 1 spot in the British charts with their version of the Lennon/McCartney composition 'Michelle'. Released on Pye 7N 17034 on January 13th, 1966 it entered the charts on January 22nd and remained there for ten weeks. The trio also featured the number on an album and an EP.

Cliff Bennett and The Rebel Rousers British band, originally formed in 1961, who were to make many friends among the Liverpool bands when they appeared regularly in Hamburg. Respected for their music, they nevertheless remained unsuccessful in the recording world until 1964 when they had a hit with 'One Way Love'. Then Paul McCartney produced them, performing the *Revolver* album number 'Got To Get You Into My Life'. Issued on Parlophone 5489 on August 5th, 1966 in Britain and on ABC 10842 in America on August 29th, 1966, the record reached the No. 6. position in the UK charts. Paul also produced their *Got To Get You Into My Life* album, issued by Parlophone (PCS 7017) on Januarty 27th, 1967 in Britain. The group were never to achieve recording success again and disbanded in 1969. Cliff went on to form a few more bands, including Toe Fat and Shanghai before retiring from the music scene.

The Hollies Northern group comprising Allan Clarke (vocals), Tony Hicks (lead guitar), Graham Nash (rhythm guitar), Eric Haydock (bass guitar) and Bobby Elliott (drums), who had their first hit in May 1963 with '(Ain't It) Just Like Me' and became one of Britain's major international groups with a distinctive sound based on their vocal harmony, particularly with the voice of Allan Clarke and Graham Nash. Initially they were tagged 'Manchester's Beatles' and they reacted to this by telling me, 'Our sound is entirely different and the comparison has probably been made because we wear leather pants. The reason why we wear leather is because it's more serviceable and you can do anything with leather and it still stays the same. If you analyse the Beatles sound you will find it's entirely different from ours — and we hope people will stop associating our name with theirs.'

The Hollies had numerous major hits over the years, including 'Searchin' '; 'Stay'; 'Just One Look'; 'Here I Go Again'; 'Yes I Will'; 'I'm Alive' and 'Look Through Any Window'. Probably their least successful single in their heyday was their first and only cover of a Beatles number, George Harrison's composition 'If I Needed Someone' which was on the *Rubber Soul* album. The Hollies single was issued on Parlophone R 5392 and entered the charts in December 1965 where its highest position was No. 20.

The Applejacks The group from Solihull in Warwickshire comprised Al Jackson (vocals), Martin Baggott (lead), Phil Cash (rhythm), Don Gould (organ), Megan Davies (bass) and Gary Freeman (drums). Their first single 'Tell Me When' reached No. 7 in the British charts and their follow-up was the Lennon/McCartney composition 'Like Dreamers Do', issued on Decca F 11916 on June 5th, 1964 in the UK and on London 9681 on July 6th in the States. The record reached No. 20 in the British charts.

Sounds Incorporated British instrumental group from Kent, originally formed in 1961. They comprised Alan Holmes (flute/sax), Griff West (sax), John St John (guitar), Barrie Cameron (keyboards), Wes Hunter (bass guitar) and Tony Newman (drums). Brian Epstein signed the group to a management contract and they appeared on The Beatles' autumn tour of Britain in 1964 and on their Christmas show in London in December of the same year. In 1965 they appeared on The Beatles' American tour.

St Louis Union R & B band who made their recording début with the Lennon & McCartney number 'Girl' on Decca in January 1966. The flip side of the disc was 'Respect'. The line-up comprised Tony Cassidy (vocals); Keith Miller (guitar); Alex Kirby (tenor sax); David Tomlinson (organ); John Nichols (bass); and Dave Webb (drums).

Marmalade Scottish group that took the Lennon/McCartney number 'Ob La Di Ob La Da' to No. 1 in the British charts. Their version of the song, released on December 4th, 1968, on CBS 3891, entered the charts on December 21st and remained there for 10 weeks. Their line-up at the time was: Dean Ford (vocals), Junior Campbell (lead guitar), Pat Fairlie (rhythm guitar), Graham Knight (bass guitar) and Raymond Duffy (drums).

Eric Idle Former member of Monty Python's Flying Circus. A friend of George Harrison, Eric appeared as Dirk McQuickly in the TV satire The Rutles, in which George also made an appearance. When the Monty Python team found themselves left without a backer for Life of Brian after EMI pulled out of the deal, Eric approached George who chipped in two-and-a-half million pounds. The film was a major success and George joined Eric in Handmade Films, whose next project was The Time Bandits, for which George wrote the title music.

William Marshall Prominent feature writer with one of Britain's biggest-selling daily newspapers, the Daily Mirror. Bill was based in Liverpool in the early sixties, witnessing the heyday of Mersey Beat, during which he wrote several articles on the local scene. In the seventies he co-authored, with Allan Williams, a book called The Man Who Gave The Beatles Away.

Tommy Quickly Young, wide-eyed, freckle-faced young singer from West

Tommy Quickly, one of Brian Epstein's failures. Note Tommy's cute toy dog, part of his stage act

Derby, Liverpool. Brian Epstein picked him from a Mersey band and decided to manage him as a solo artist. Unfortunately, after his initial success with The Beatles, Gerry, Cilla and The Fourmost, Brian was finding it increasingly difficult to get his new signings off the ground. He tried everything with Tommy, including an association with The Beatles, hoping that some of their fame would rub off. Tommy was given one of Liverpool's best group of musicians, The Remo Four, as his backing band and a Lennon and McCartney number 'Tip Of My Tongue' to record. This was issued in Britain on Piccadilly 7N 35137 on July 30th, 1963, with 'Heaven Only Knows' on the flip side. He joined *The Beatles Christmas Show* which opened at the Gaumont, Bradford, on December 21st, 1963, moved to the Empire, Liverpool, on December 22nd and then began a short season at the Astoria, Finsbury Park, London, from December 4th until January 11th, 1964. Tommy performed 'Winter Wonderland' and 'Kiss Me Now'. He was also booked to appear on The Beatles' fifth British tour which ran from October 9th until November 11th, 1964. He was an engaging personality and included a toy dog that moved and opened and closed its jaws in his act. Other records followed including 'Wild Side Of Life' c/w 'Forget The Other Guy' and 'Humpty Dumpty' c/w 'I Go Crazy', but they all failed to register in the charts. He recorded a number called 'No Reply', but Piccadilly decided not to release it.

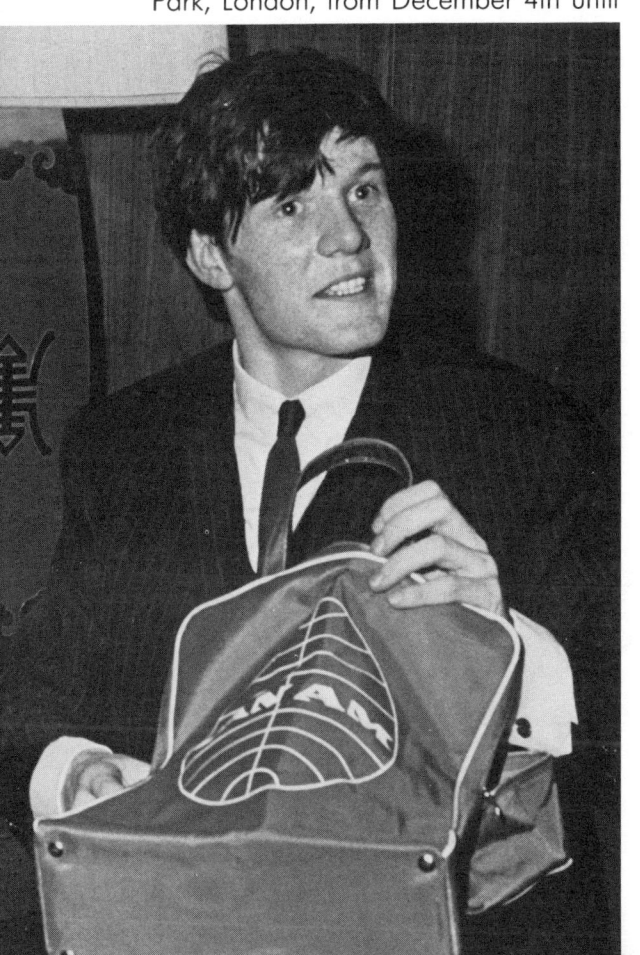

I remember seeing Tommy in the Blue Angel one night, crawling on the floor and howling like a dog. I was told he had a breakdown soon after and his success proved to be short-lived.

The Rutles Group created for a television parody of *The Beatles Story*. An inspired production which had its origins in the Eric Idle television series *Rutland Weekend Television*. An initial sketch in the series during which Neil Innes's Beatles spoof song 'I Must Be In Love' was featured, eventually led to an extravagant Beatles TV satire *The Rutles*, screened on BBC 2 on Easter Monday, 1978 and repeated on May 27th in the same year. It was shown in the States on March 22nd. To coincide with the programme, WEA Records released a lavish album, together with a 20-page colour booklet. The visual images of the television programme were so faithful to the source upon which they were based that the actual show was almost believable as a genuine Beatles history. Somewhat weak on satire, it was nevertheless steeped in nostalgia and the adventures of the 'Prefab Four': Dirk McQuickly (Eric Idle), Ron Nasty (Neil Innes), Stig

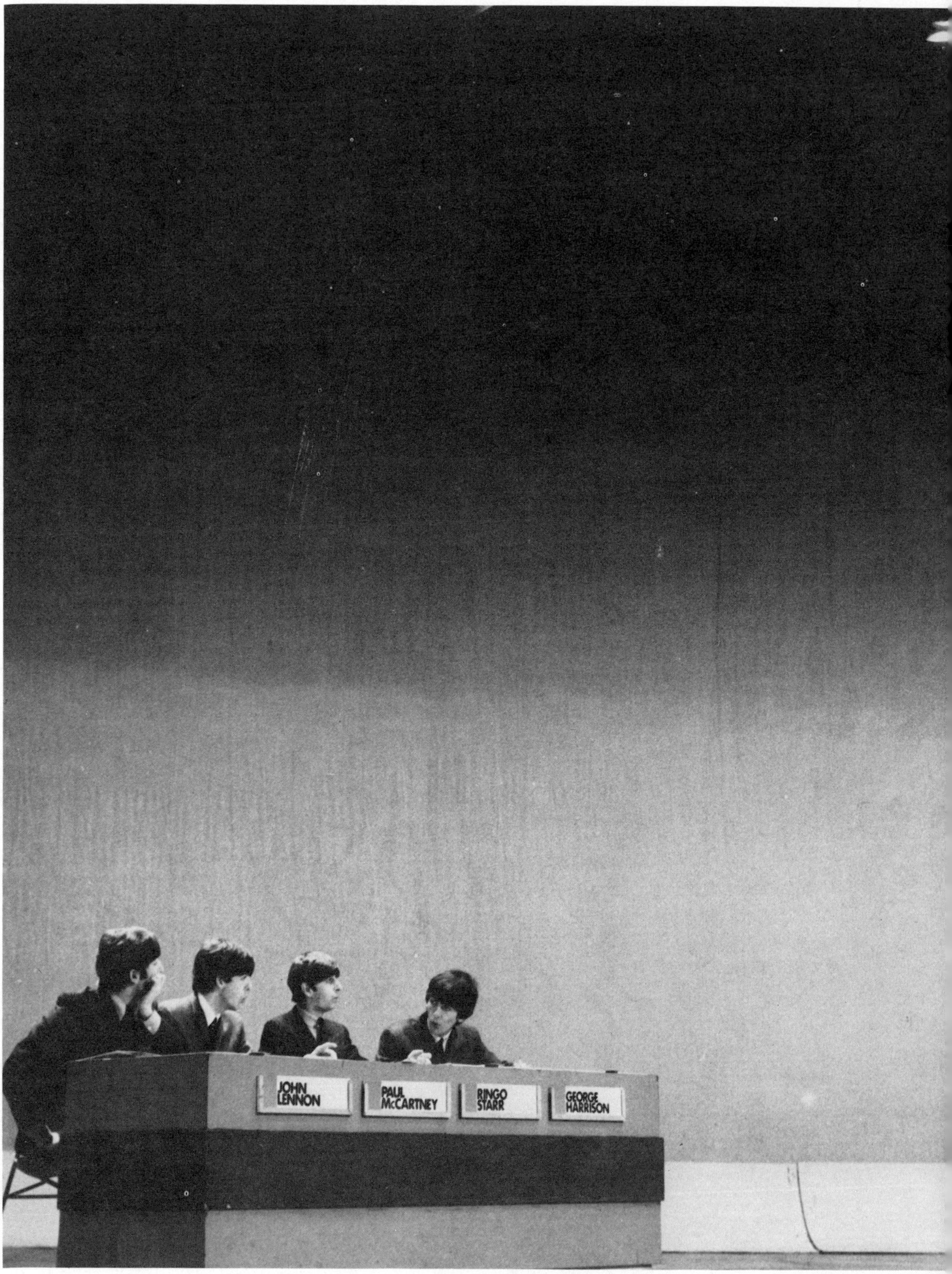
JOHN LENNON
PAUL McCARTNEY
RINGO STARR
GEORGE HARRISON

O'Hara (Rikki Fataar) and Barry Wom (John Halsey) eventually turned into a tribute to The Beatles' career.

Guest stars in the show included Mick and Bianca Jagger, Paul Simon — and George Harrison as an interviewer. The album's booklet, a superb production, contains scores of photographs of The Rutles in familiar Beatles poses. The album *All You Need Is Cash*, also sports a cover which faithfully lampoons the covers of the *Meet The Beatles, Magical Mystery Tour, Sergeant Pepper's Lonely Hearts Club Band* and *Let It Be* albums. The LP tracks, all composed by Neil Innes, are also faithful to the sound of the Fab Four and include: 'Hold Me Hand'; 'Number One'; 'With A Girl Like You'; 'I Must Be In Love'; 'Ouch!'; 'Living In Hope'; 'Love Life'; 'Nevertheless'; 'Good Times Roll'; 'Doubleback Alley'; 'Cheese And Onions'; 'Another Day';

The all-Beatle panel of Juke Box Jury, *hosted by David Jacobs*

'Piggy In The Middle'; and 'Let's Be Natural'.

The Silkie A folk group, formed at Hull University, that comprised Sylvia Tatler (vocals); Mike Ramsden (guitar/vocals); Ivor Aylesbury (guitar/vocals) and Kevin Cunningham (double bass). Brian Epstein became their manager and they made their recording début in June 1965 on the Fontana label with 'Blood River' c/w 'Close The Door Gently'. They entered the Top 30 with their second release, the Lennon/McCartney number 'You've Got To Hide Your Love Away' c/w 'City Winds', issued in October 1965 and actually produced by John Lennon and Paul McCartney. The track was featured on an album of the same name, released in America on November 22nd, 1965, on Fontana SRF 67548. Their other releases were 'Keys To My Soul' c/w 'Leave Me To Cry', issued in February 1966 and 'Born To Be With You' c/w 'So Sorry Now', issued in June of the same year. They also issued an album in October 1965 entitled *The Silkie Sing The Songs Of Bob Dylan*.

Michael Haslam Lancashire singer, aged 24 in 1964 when Brian Epstein signed him to a management contract. Despite exposure on the sell-out Beatles tour in October 1964 and his appearance on their Christmas show at the Hammersmith Odeon in December of that year, he did not achieve the success Brian Epstein predicted he would have.

Henry Higgins A British bullfighter whom Brian Epstein signed up during the sixties. Born in Columbia of a British father and a Mexican mother, he was brought up in Woking, Surrey. Brian supported his ambition to be a bullfighter and Henry became the first Englishman to be made a full Matador in Spain. He retired from the bullring in 1974 to become a businessman in Spain. Tragically, he died in August 1978 at the age of 34 when he broke his neck gliding, a sport he had only taken up two months previously.

David Jacobs Prominent show-business lawyer, based in London. When Brian Epstein moved NEMS Enterprises down south, David became his solicitor and was responsible for advising on many of the business contracts that were signed, including one that gave a company called Seltaeb the merchandising rights to The Beatles, a controversial deal in which Seltaeb took 90 per cent and The Beatles and their company only received 10 per cent. A matter of weeks after Brian Epstein's death, Jacobs was found hanging in his garage and a verdict of suicide was given. In his book *Shout! The True Story Of The Beatles*, Philip Norman hints that there may have been a conspiracy by a powerful organization in America to kill both men because of the legal action they had taken regarding the Seltaeb deal.

Brian Sommerville Yet another of Brian Epstein's friends who found himself assured of a position in the ever-growing NEMS empire. Brian, an ex-Naval officer was employed as press officer to The Beatles in November 1963. Although he had never had any experience in the field before, he was able to bring a certain disciplined approach to the task which enabled him to cope with the endless streams of agitated reporters. However, the strain began to tell and there were many upsetting incidents, particularly as individual members of the group seemed to delight in playing pranks on him, as can be gleaned by details of his ordeals at the hands of The Beatles in Michael Braun's book *Love Me Do*. Brian eventually exploded at George Harrison's insulting behaviour towards him and left their employ to set up his own PR business in July 1964.

Mike and Bernie Winters A popular comedy double-act who now no longer appear as a team. The Beatles were their guests at the ABC Theatre, Blackpool, in July 1964 when the duo hosted a television show called *Blackpool Night Out*. I went along to the rehearsals of the show and Brian Epstein, Neil Aspinall and Mal Evans were there talking to Liverpool comedian Johnny Hackett. Jimmy Edwards and Frank Berry kept coming out with jokes that weren't in the script and John Lennon told me: 'They'll use different jokes on the actual programme because they want to keep the musicians in the pit laughing.' Apart from performing numbers such as 'A Hard Day's Night' and 'Long Tall Sally', The Beatles appeared in several sketches, joined by Mike and Bernie. In one, Ringo was a patient awaiting an operation and in another they were a crew of dustmen.

Sean O'Mahony Enterprising publisher who launched *Beat Instrumental*, a magazine devoted to beat groups with a feature on The Beatles in each issue, in March 1963. He approached Brian Epstein with the offer of publishing a monthly magazine about the group which would help relieve the pressure on the fan club which was receiving tens of thousands of letters per day. Sean negotiated a deal with Brian and *Beatles Monthly* was launched, with a print run of 80,000 copies for the first issue which grew to 350,000 at its peak. The first issue was published in August 1963 and the series ended in 1969 before reaching its 80th issue. Six years later, interest in The Beatles had grown to such an extent that Sean launched a series of reprints, adding a bonus of new material and photographs. This series came to an end in late 1982 when Sean continued the publication with completely new editorial material. His other ventures concerning other groups, such as *Gerry and The Pacemakers Monthly*, were short-lived. He currently runs several other publications, including *Record Collector*, which regularly contains Beatles features.

Leslie Bryce Official photographer for *The Beatles Book* enabling him to travel around the world with The Beatles and take literally thousands of photographs of them. Leslie had previously worked under renowned photographers such as Baron and Lord Snowdon and passed many tips to The Beatles, who were very interested in photography. One of the many people who were given the tag 'the fifth Beatle'.

Bettina Rose Blond-haired girl from Surrey who joined the London branch of The Beatles Fan Club to help run the southern area and later became a national secretary.

Duggie Millins London tailor, based in the Soho district, who specialized in show-business clientele. He became tailor for The Beatles after completing their suits for *A Hard Day's Night* and he also made the outfits for the original Madame Tussaud's Beatles waxworks.

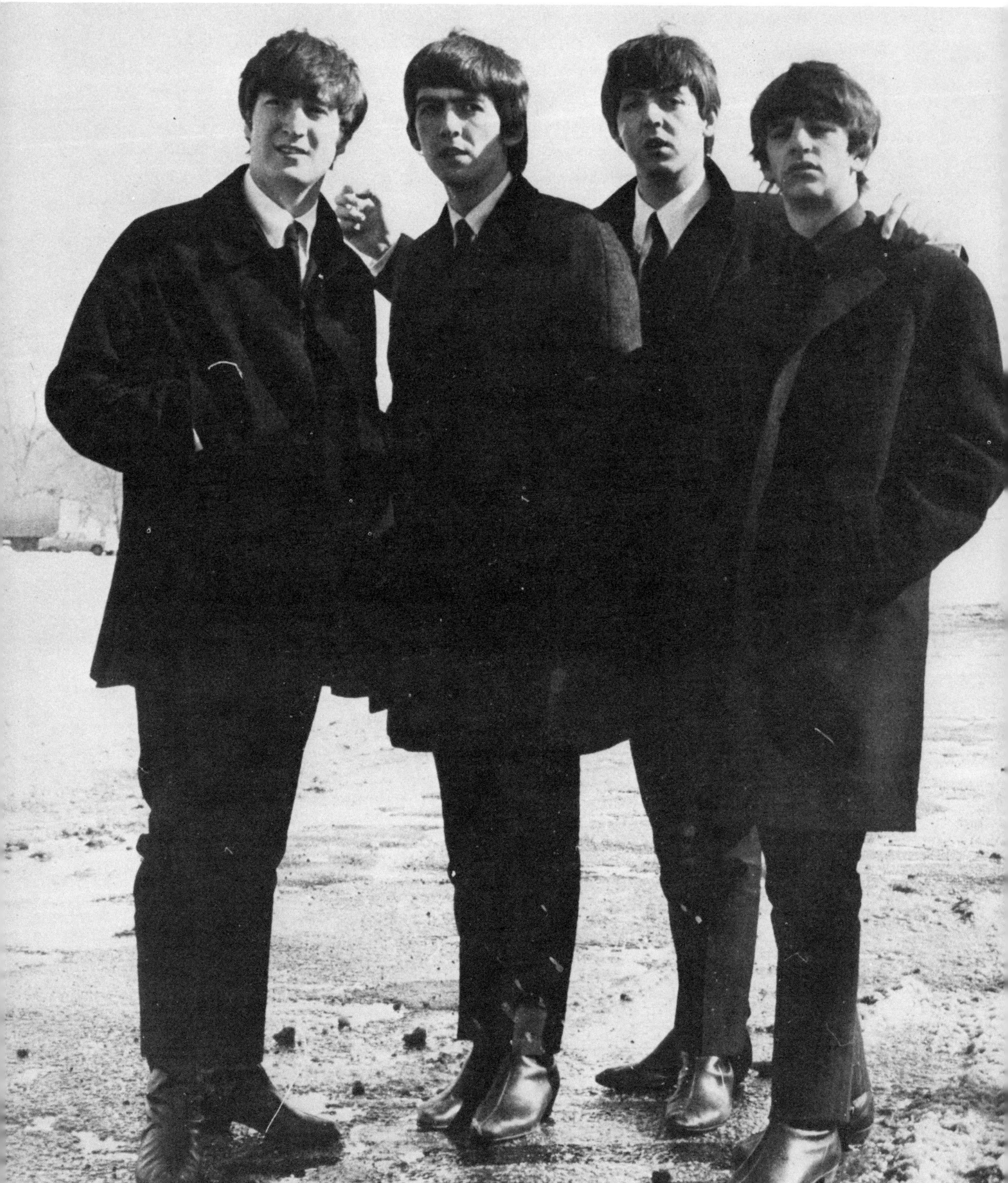

Peter Sellers The late Peter Sellers was one of Britain's major screen comedians and much remembered in the UK for his early career on radio as a member of The Goons. He proved to be a talking point when The Beatles first socialized with George Martin as George had previously produced a successful album with the comedian called *Songs For Swinging Sellers*. Peter appeared as a guest on Granada's popular TV spectacular *The Music Of Lennon and McCartney* during which he dressed as Richard III and performed a hilarious rendition of 'A Hard Day's Night'. His single of the performance was issued on Parlophone R 5393 and reached No. 14 in the British charts in December 1965. Ringo Starr portrayed his adopted son Youngman Grand in the film *The Magic Christian*, based on a book by Terry Southern who wrote *Candy*. *The Magic Christian* was produced by Dennis O'Dell. On May 4th, 1969, Peter and Ringo held a joint party at the fashionable Les Ambassadeurs in London and John and Yoko and Paul and Linda McCartney attended, along with a host of film stars who included George Peppard, Michael Caine, Roger Moore, Richard Harris, Sean Connery, Christopher Lee, Spike Milligan and Stanley Baker. Later that month Sellers joined Ringo, John, George and their respective wives on the QE2, heading for New York. His version of 'She Loves You', originally recorded in 1965, was finally released in 1981.

Spike Milligan Zany British comedian, humorist and author, former member of The Goons, who were very popular with the British public in the fifties due to their radio series. John Lennon contributed a review of Spike's book *The Goon Show Scripts* to the September 30th, 1973 issue of the *New York Times* Book Review. George Martin produced Spike's single 'Purple Aeroplane' (Parlophone R 5513) which was a parody of 'Yellow Submarine'.

Del Shannon Michigan-born singer whose major hits included 'Runaway', 'Hats Off To Larry', 'Swiss Maid' and 'Little Town Flirt'. He recorded 'From Me To You' in 1963 and became the first American artist to cover a Beatles song. He also appeared with the group in 1963.

Ed Sullivan Legendary American chat-show host who died in the seventies. *The Ed Sullivan Show* was one of the most influential showcases on American television and helped to boost the careers of Elvis Presley and The Beatles. Sullivan had originally been reluctant to have Elvis on his show in 1958 but the Memphis singer had received such publicity on a rival network that Sullivan signed him and found himself with one of the biggest TV audiences ever recorded. He had no hesitation in securing The Beatles and booked them for three consecutive shows for the relatively minor sum of $10,000. There were over 60,000 requests from viewers wishing tickets for the live show, which had an audience of 729 in CBS TV's Studio 50 in New York. Screened live on February 9th, 1964, there were 73 million people watching — the largest-ever audience for such a show, once again. A telegram from Elvis to The Beatles was read out and the group performed 'All My Loving', ''Til There Was You', 'She Loves

The Beatles made a major impact with appearances on The Ed Sullivan Show

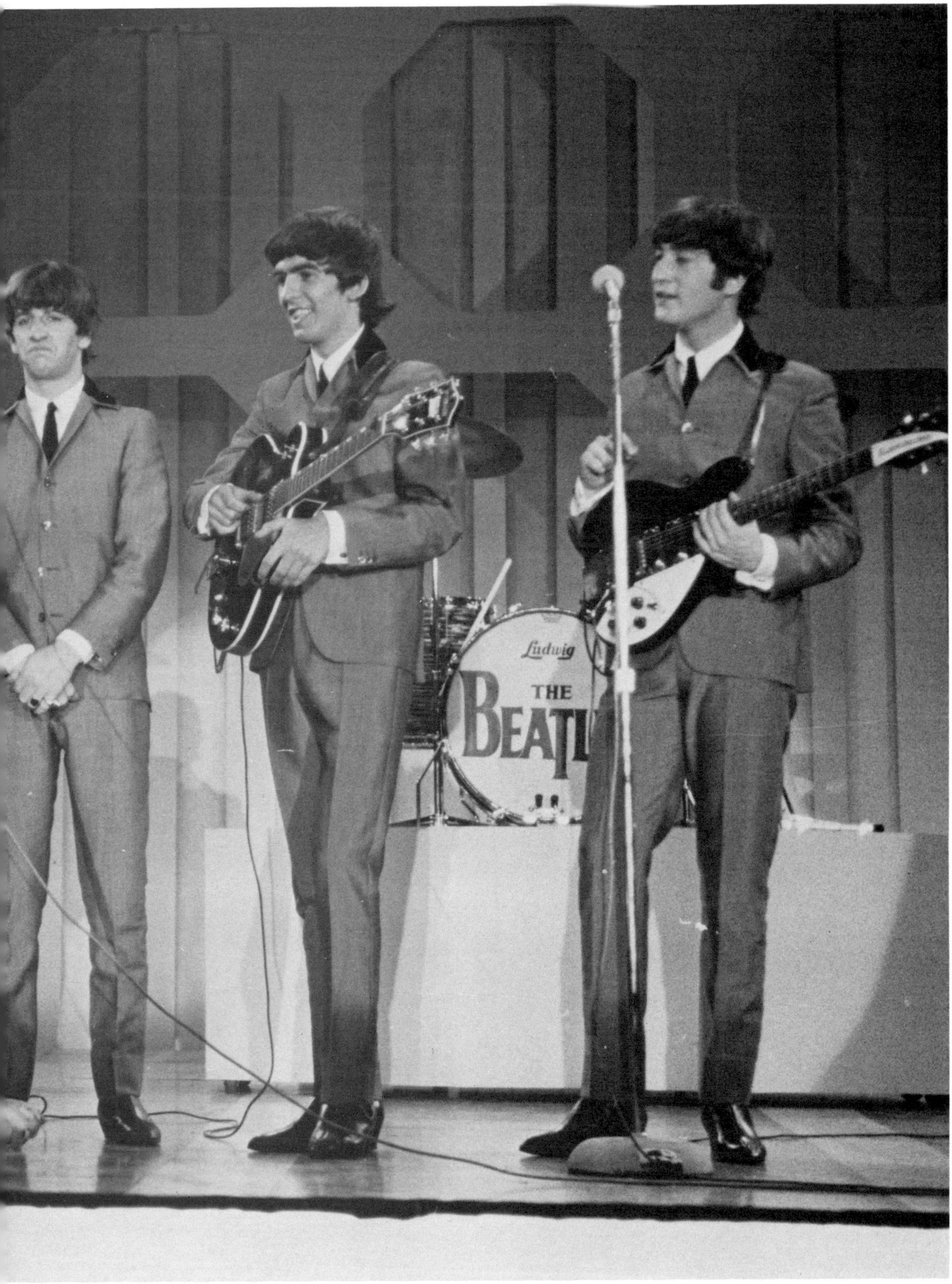
Ludwig
THE
BEATL

You', 'I Saw Her Standing There' and 'I Want To Hold Your Hand'. Their second appearance took place on February 15th at the Deauville Hotel, Miami and was watched by an even bigger audience than the first: 75 million. Their third appearance, on February 23rd, was filmed as the group had returned to England. During the following years, Sullivan presented many promotional film clips of the group on his show.

On August 15th, 1965, Ed Sullivan introduced their concert at the Shea Stadium where they appeared before 56,000 fans. The concern was also filmed.

The famous Shea Stadium appearance

Murray The K Disc jockey from the New York station WINS who switched on to The Beatles when they arrived in New York on their first visit and never let go. He'd actually begun playing 'She Loves You' in October 1963 at the request of a listener on his weekly record contest show, but it aroused no great interest. When they booked into the Plaza Hotel, Murray (real name Murray Kaufmann) contacted them and conducted a radio interview with them 'live' over the telephone. This tickled their interest and they didn't object when he turned up at the hotel (although Brian Epstein later objected to him calling himself 'the fifth Beatle'). Soon he was almost running their social life, taking them to New York nightclubs to meet starlets such as Tuesday Weld and Stella Stevens, visiting the Playboy Club, and conducting interviews. When the group moved on to the Deauville Hotel, Miami, to record another *Ed Sullivan Show*, Murray flew to Florida and bunked down in George's room. He continued taking them to nightspots, such as The Peppermint Lounge.

Over the years, Murray kept in touch, visiting them in London where he interviewed them during the filming of *A Hard Day's Night*. He also travelled to the Queen Elizabeth Hotel, Montreal, some years later when John and Yoko had a ten-day bed-in and was one of the celebrities present (including Petula Clark and Timothy Leary) who provided the background clapping on the 'Give Peace A Chance' recording.

His interviews from New York, Miami, London and Washington were contained on an EP: *The Beatles And Murray The K As It Happened* on Fairway 526, which also contained the songs 'She Loves You' and 'Shout'. The interviews he recorded in 1965 are to be found on bootleg albums such as *Soldier Of Love* and *Murray The K Fan Club*. He compered the *Around The Beatles* TV show which was first shown on May 6th, 1964, and also featured Millie, Cilla Black, Long John Baldry and P. J. Proby. Murray also wrote a book of his experiences in 1966 called *Murray The K Tells It Like It Is, Baby,* which had an introduction by George Harrison. He played himself in the film *I Want To Hold Your Hand,* released in 1978, which concerned the adventures of a group of American youngsters attempting to see The Beatles on their first American visit. He also participated in a major Beatles festival held in the Californian town of Knotts in 1980. Tragically, Murray died of cancer on February 2nd, 1982.

Louise Harrison George Harrison's elder sister who studied at a training college in Liverpool before marrying an American, Gordon Caldwell in 1954 and moving to St Louis. George made his first-ever trip to America early in 1963 when he went to visit them. On The Beatles' first tour of the States, Louise visited George at the Plaza Hotel and nursed him when he had a sore throat. She became in demand for interviews on American radio shows and in 1965, Recar Records (2012) issued *All About The Beatles*, a compilation of her interviews with five American radio stations:

WMEX Boston, WNDR Norfolk, WHK Cleveland, WKNR Detroit and KIMN Denver.

Jack Paar American television personality who was the first person to show The Beatles on US television when he introduced a segment from a film recorded on November 16th, 1963, in England of the lads performing 'She Loves You' on his 'The Jack Paar Show' on January 3rd, 1964.

Ed Rudy Journalist and radio announcer who was the only American reporter allowed to cover the entire first stateside tour by The Beatles. It resulted in an interview album The Beatles American

The Beatles were star guests at the British Embassy in Washington

Tour With Ed Rudy which entered the American album charts and reached its highest position of No. 20 in July 1964. There are several bootlegs of the LP which, when released, contained in the blurb: 'The Beatles call Ed Rudy "the fifth Beatle"'.

Sid Bernstein The promoter who brought The Beatles to the Carnegie Hall and Shea Stadium. Sid worked for a major agency, GAC and he realized the huge potential of the British group. He left the agency and raised $6,500 which he offered to Brian Epstein for two Beatles appearances at the Carnegie Hall on February 12th, 1964. He next presented them at the famous New York baseball arena, Shea Stadium, attracting the biggest-ever audience of fans at a concert to that date: 55,600. The gate brought in a collosal $204,000 gross, although Bernstein only received $7,000 for the promotion, which was filmed. The group performed 12 numbers and were introduced on stage by Ed Sullivan. Fan fervour was so intense that the group had to be driven away from the gig in a Wells Fargo armoured van. Sid presented them at Shea Stadium the following year during their last American tour on August 23rd.

Once established as an impresario, Sid began to expand his operations and took on the management of a number of American acts. However, he still saw the fantastic potential that The Beatles continued to generate following their break-up and tried to get them together to perform a concert. In 1976 he conceived the 'Simulcast' which would be a concert during which The Beatles could raise $200 million with ticket sales, movie rights and a double-live album. Sid took out full-page advertisements in some American papers outlining his plan and suggested that the money raised could be used for the education of orphan children of needy natives. The only response he received was a polite enquiry from John Lennon's secretary. He tried again in 1979 and George Harrison was to say: 'It was cute the way the ad in the [New York] Times tried to put the responsibility for saving the world on our shoulders.'

In 1981, Sid teamed up with Clive Epstein to manage a talented Liverpool band called Motion Pictures.

Sir David Ormsby-Gore Later to become Lord Harlech. He was the British Ambassador to America when The Beatles made their first US tour and played host to the group at the British Embassy in Washington on February 11th, 1964, following their first-ever concert appearance in the States at the Washington Coliseum. They were cordially greeted by the Ambassador but didn't enjoy the treatment they received from ill-mannered guests who pushed and shoved them around, demanded autographs and made the party uncomfortable for the boys by their attitude. One young lady took out a pair of nail scissors and hacked at Ringo's hair. John left early but the others saw the evening out.

Charles O'Finley Kansas City baseball promoter who kept his promise to local citizens that he would stage a Beatles concert at the local municipal stadium during the group's first tour of America in 1964. Although Kansas City was not on the schedule of the tour, Finlay travelled to San Fransico to make Brian Epstein the offer of $150,000 for the appearance, an unprecedented figure at the time. His slogan was 'Today's Beatles fans are tomorrow's baseball fans' and The Beatles duly appeared there on September 17th. Also on the bill were The Bill Black Combo and Jackie De Shannon.

Elvis Presley An important musical influence on the lives of the early Beatles and the major figure in rock music prior to their emergence. When they first arrived in America, Elvis sent them a telegram, which was read to them on the *Ed Sullivan Show*. It read: 'Congratulations on your appearance on the *Ed Sullivan Show* and your visit to America. We hope your engagement will be a successful one and your visit pleasant.' The two greatest names in rock had their historic meeting on August 27th, 1965, at Elvis's Bel Air mansion where they spent three hours together in conversation.

Al Aronowitz Among the many journalists from around the world whom I guided round the Liverpool scene was an animated, intriguing writer from the *Saturday Evening Post* called Alfred G. Aronowitz. Al was responsible for getting The Beatles switched on to Bob Dylan. He wrote a major feature on The Beatles for the *Saturday Evening Post* and interviewed the group on several occasions. As a going-away present when he reluctantly left Liverpool he presented me with a tiny packet of marijuana which I deposited in a dustbin.

Muhammed Ali Three times World Heavyweight Champion and 'The Beatles of the boxing world'. During their first trip to America, when they went to Florida to record an *Ed Sullivan Show*, The Beatles visited Ali at his training camp in Miami on February 18th, 1964. It was a few days before his fight with Sonny Liston which was to make him World Heavyweight Champion Of The World for the first time and he was still known as Cassius Clay. There were many jovial photos taken of the champ feinting at The Beatles' chins and pics of the Fab Four on the canvas in the KO position.

Jeanne Dixon Prominent American psychic who was reputed to have forecast the death of President Kennedy. She was also accused of predicting that The Beatles would be killed in an air crash but denied it, saying: 'The boys are an inspiration for the good to our teenagers'.

Rev. David A. Noebel Author of two anti-Beatles booklets published in America in 1968. Their titles were *The Beatles: A Study In Drugs, Sex And Revolution* and *Communism, Hypnotism, And The Beatles*.

Art Kane American photographer of repute who produced a pictorial portfolio for *Life* magazine on The Beatles songs. He said, 'I listened to most of their lyrics and then flew to London because The Beatles' images are intrinsically English. Part of their establishment is totally unlike ours. It's an older nation with a pomp and circumstance, for instance, that does not exist in the United States.' A selection of photographs illustrating such songs as 'Eleanor Rigby', 'A Day In The Life', 'Strawberry Fields', 'When I'm Sixty Four' and 'Lady Madonna' are to be found in his book *Art Kane: The Persuasive Image*, together with the glaring boob: 'Kane knew Strawberry Fields was the name of an orphanage where Beatle John Lennon had lived.'

The Chipmunks Experimenting with various recording speeds until he found a novelty sound which reminded him of chipmunks caused Ross Bagdasarian, professionally known as David Seville, to create The Chipmunks in 1958. The fictitious chipmunks were named Alvin, Theodore and Simon and Seville's productions of Chipmunks records went on to sell over 30 million copies before his death in 1972. Of particular interest is his album *The Chipmunks Sing The Beatles Hits* which was issued in America on August 24th, 1964, on Liberty LST 7388 and in Britain on February 19th, 1965, on Liberty LBY 1218. Tracks were: 'All My Loving'; 'Do You Want To Know A Secret'; 'She Loves You'; 'From Me To You'; 'Love Me Do'; 'Twist And Shout'; 'A Hard Day's Night'; 'P.S. I Love You'; 'I Saw Her Standing There'; 'Can't Buy Me Love'; 'Please, Please Me' and 'I Want To Hold Your Hand'. Singles and albums from this session have been released on various occasions since.

Screaming Lord Sutch Outrageous British rock-and-roll singer who, during the early sixties, campaigned for a seat in Parliament. In 1964 he stood as National Teenage Candidate in the Huyton constituency of Liverpool as opponent to Harold Wilson. His platform consisted of obtaining a knighthood for The Beatles, licences for cats and road tax on bicycles. He lost his deposit.

David Frost Internationally famous British chat-show host who first rose to fame on the satirical sixties show *That Was The Week That Was*. He became a globe-trotting superstar in his own right and featured members of The Beatles on several of his shows, a number of which have been taped and feature on bootleg albums. The group performed 'Hey

Taking a break on a ranch during their American tour

Jude' on *Frost On Sunday*, screened by London Weekend Television on September 4th, 1968. For some years he hosted *The David Frost Show* on which Ringo performed 'Sentimental Journey' on March 29th, 1970. John and Yoko were guests on the January 13th, 1972, show and George Harrison appeared live for an interview in December 1972.

Jane Asher Red-haired British actress and former fiancée of Paul McCartney. Born on April 5th, 1946. Her father was a doctor, her mother a musician. She has a younger sister Clare and her brother Peter Asher is now a leading show-business impresario on the west coast of America and was formerly one half of the singing duo Peter and Gordon. Jane made her film début at the age of 5 in *Mandy* and continued her career as an actress on the stage, television and in films.

She first met Paul McCartney on May 9th, 1963, when asked to write an interview on The Beatles for the *Radio Times*. She met the group at the Court Hotel in Sloane Street and joined them at the flat of NME news editor Chris Hutchins where she conducted the interview. Paul made a date with her and for the following five years they were almost inseparable, attending the theatre and clubs together and holidaying in Portugal, Switzerland, Kenya, Scotland and America. During their relationship she continued her career as an actress, appearing in films such as *Alfie* and *Masque Of The Red Death* and touring

VOX!
went the BEATLES USA

Congratulations ... Beatles, on your overwhelming success in the United States ... and thanks for phoning your appreciation of the new VOX Amps featured in your fine performances.
The Beatles, like Britain's other Top Radio, T.V. and Recording Stars, feature Vox Sound Equipment.

VOX Amplifiers featured by the Beatles:
Two — A.C. 50 watt Models
One — A.C. 100 watt Model

JENNINGS MUSICAL INDUSTRIES LIMITED
DARTFORD ROAD · DARTFORD · KENT

America with the Bristol Old Vic in *Romeo And Juliet*. The couple became formally engaged on Christmas Day 1967 when Paul bought her an emerald and diamond ring. During their years together Paul had announced to the press on several occasions his intention of marrying her. Their relationship deteriorated during 1968 and on July 20th of that year Jane announced during an interview on the television programme *Dee Time* that the engagement was over.

She lived with British cartoonist Gerald Scarfe for several years. The couple then married and have a daughter, Kate. Jane returned to acting in the eighties, portraying Peter Pan on the London stage and starring in a number of major television presentations, including *Brideshead Revisited* and *Voyage Round My Father*.

John Bratby British painter who was fashionable in the late fifties and early sixties. His exhibition at the Zwemmer Gallery in London, which opened on November 7th, 1967, featured three portraits of Paul McCartney.

Jimmy Nicol When Ringo Starr collapsed in a photographer's studio and tonsilitis was diagnosed on June 3rd, 1964, The Beatles were about to embark on a world tour. Emergency plans went into operation and by the next day John, Paul and George were rehearsing with a young drummer, Jimmy Nicol, a former member of Georgie Fame's Blue Flames. He made his début with them at the Tivoli Gardens, Amsterdam, then travelled to Holland where he appeared at the Exhibition Hall, Blokker on June 6th. In between the actual gigs there were various radio and TV spots and the

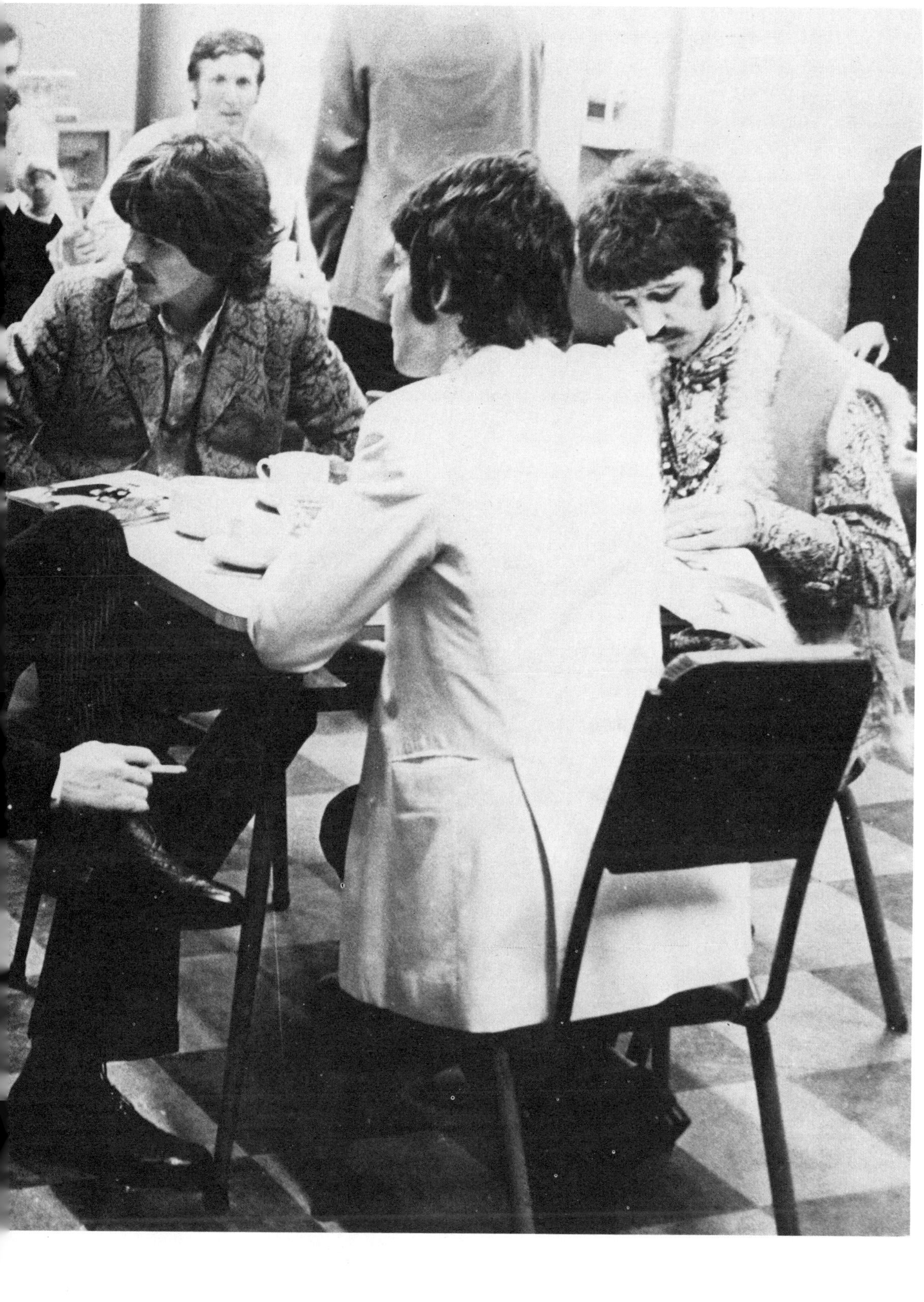

group left Holland for London where they boarded a plane on the first leg of their journey to Hong Kong where they did two shows at the Princess Theatre on June 10th. Ringo had recovered sufficiently to fly to Australia to rejoin them and watch Jimmy perform with the group at the Centennial Hall, Adelaide. Ringo then took over his drum seat for the Festival Hall, Melbourne, appearance on June 16th. Jimmy's relatively short spell in the limelight gave him enough impetus to form and become leader of a band of his own, The Shubdubs. Unfortunately, they were not successful and Jimmy soon faded from the limelight.

Alan Aldridge Prominent self-taught British designer/illustrator whose first book was *The Penguin Book Of Comics*. He became interested in the possibility of visual images illustrating Beatles lyrics and produced *The Beatles Illustrated Lyrics* in 1969. It proved so popular that he followed it up with a further book in which he gathered together some of the most famous artists, designers and photographers in the world, including Ethan Russell, Art Kane, David Hockney, David Bailey, Adrian George, Allen Jones, Eduardo Paolozzi and Ralph Steadman.

George Kelly Man hired by Paul McCartney as a butler in 1966. His departure from the McCartney payroll was not an amicable one and he sold an 'exposé' of stories of wild parties at Paul's house to a newspaper.

Robert Freeman Photographer/designer who became one of the several photographers favoured by The Beatles for a certain span of time. He once acted in an 'official' capacity, photographing special Beatles events such as the marriage between Ringo Starr and Maureen Cox. He designed the titles for the film *A Hard Day's Night* and his photographs were used on the covers of several albums and EPs, including *A Hard Day's Night*, *Help!* and *Rubber Soul*. He also designed both of John's books, *In His Own Write* and *A Spaniard In The Works* and produced a book of his own called *Beatles Limited*.

Bob Adams British road manager, reputed to be the first in the business, who retired in 1981 after 21 years as a 'roadie', having worked for numerous bands including Cliff Richard and The Shadows, the Everly Brothers and Bo Diddley. He was hired for a time by The Beatles, who called him 'Old Bob'. John Lennon presented him with a signed photograph from 'The Beaters' as initially he could never remember their name. He also worked for Paul McCartney and Wings.

Maureen Cox Pretty, dark-haired Liverpool girl who achieved a fan's ultimate ambition — to marry her idol. Maureen was born in a similar working-class district to that of Ringo and was one of the many fans to support the group at their Cavern appearances. She claims that the first time she met Ringo, she was going to an evening class on hairdressing when she noticed him getting out of a car and got his autograph. One night at the Cavern, she waited for The Beatles to come off stage and, for a dare, kissed both Paul and Ringo. Ringo later asked her for a dance, dropped her off at her home and began to date her.

Maureen, a hairdresser, finally married Ringo at Caxton Hall in London on February 11th, 1965. The ceremony took place at 8 a.m. as the hall had opened two hours early for them in order to avoid the expected crowds. The best man was Brian Epstein. Also present were Ringo's mother and stepfather, Maureen's parents, John and Cynthia Lennon, and George Harrison — who arrived at the hall on a bicycle. Maureen was 18 years old at the time and Ringo was 24. The couple's wedding breakfast took place at Brian Epstein's London house and they then travelled to Hove on the south coast for their honeymoon.

Their first baby, Zak, was born at 8 a.m. on September 13th, 1965, their next son Jason at 3.25 p.m. on August 19th, 1967 and their daughter, Lee, on November 15th, 1970. The couple were eventually divorced in July 1975 when Maureen sued for adultery, citing American model Nancy Andrews as co-respondent. Following their divorce, Ringo gave Maureen and the children the Tittenhurst Park estate in Ascot which he'd bought from John. Later, he bought them another estate nearby.

A happy Jimmy Nicol, deputising for Ringo Starr

Brian Epstein with Ringo and Maureen at their wedding ceremony

Zak Starkey The first child of Maureen and Ringo Starkey, born in Queen Charlotte's Hospital, Hammersmith, London on September 13th, 1965. If a girl, the baby would have been called Lee. Ringo admitted that Zak was a name he'd always wished he'd been called when he was a boy. Zak has followed in his father's footsteps and has become a drummer in a rock band called The Next.

Jason Starkey Maureen and Ringo Starr's second child, born at 3.25 p.m. on Saturday, August 19th, 1967 at Queen Charlotte's Maternity Hospital, Hammersmith. He weighed 8lb 5½oz and his name was chosen by Maureen.

Geoffrey Ellis Another of Brian Epstein's close group of friends, that included Peter Brown and Terry Doran, who were to share the fruits of his success. One of Brian's boyhood friends, he studied law at Oxford and after graduating worked for several years in New York and also for the Royal Liverpool Insurance Company. Brian brought him into the NEMS London office as a senior executive in October 1964 and the next year he was appointed a director. His speciality was contract work. Later he was to move to publisher Dick James's organization and then on to John Reid Enterprises.

Nathan Weiss New York attorney who had once represented British impresario Larry Parnes. This proved a talking point when Brian Epstein was introduced to him at a party and Brian happened to be seeking an attorney to represent him in America at the time. Thus began a relationship that lasted until Brian's death. Weiss formed an artist management company with Epstein called Nemperor Artists and took over the management of a group called The Randells. John Lennon suggested that they change their name to The Cyrcle and the group had a major American hit with 'Red Rubber Ball'. The group appeared with The Beatles on their American tour in 1966.

Maharishi Mahesh Yogi Born Mahesh Prasad Varma in India in 1918, the Maharishi graduated from Allahabad University with a degree in physics in 1942. For 13 years he studied with prominent Indian religious teachers and spent a period of two years in seclusion in the Himalayas where he developed his system of Transcendental Meditation. He toured India in 1956 and established the International Meditation Society in London in 1959. The Beatles were impressed with his teachings in 1967 when they heard him lecture at a London hotel. All four Beatles studied TM, together with their wives, girlfriends and associates. There is no doubt that they brought the system into the world spotlight and established it as the most popular form of meditation in the West. The Beatles and their party, together with various personalities such as film star Mia Farrow, also studied at the Maharishi's ashram (place where meditation is taught) in Rishikesh, India. The group were present with the Maharishi in Wales when news of Brian Epstein's death was brought to them. The Beatles eventually severed relations with the Maharishi after accusing him of being too materially oriented.

Mia Farrow British-born actress, once married to Frank Sinatra, whose most famous role was in the film *Rosemary's Baby*. She was one of the celebrities present at the Rishikesh ashram in February 1968. Alexis Mardas hinted to John Lennon and George Harrison that the Maharishi had made sexual advances to Mia and the two of them, without substantiating the rumour, departed from Rishikesh leaving the Maharishi without an explanation for their behaviour. John was so furious at the idea of the sage committing indiscretions with Mia Farrow that he wrote a song about it, but was advised not to use the Maharishi's name, so he called it 'Sexy Sadie'.

Prudence Farrow Sister of film star Mia Farrow. Prudence was among the 70 people taking a course in Transcendental Meditation at the Maharishi's ashram in Rishikesh, India in 1968. The Beatles, The Beach Boys, Donovan, Mia Farrow, Jane Asher and others were also in attendance. 'Dear Prudence' was one of 15 numbers John Lennon wrote at the ashram and he wrote the song after he'd noticed that Prudence spent such a long time indoors, meditat-

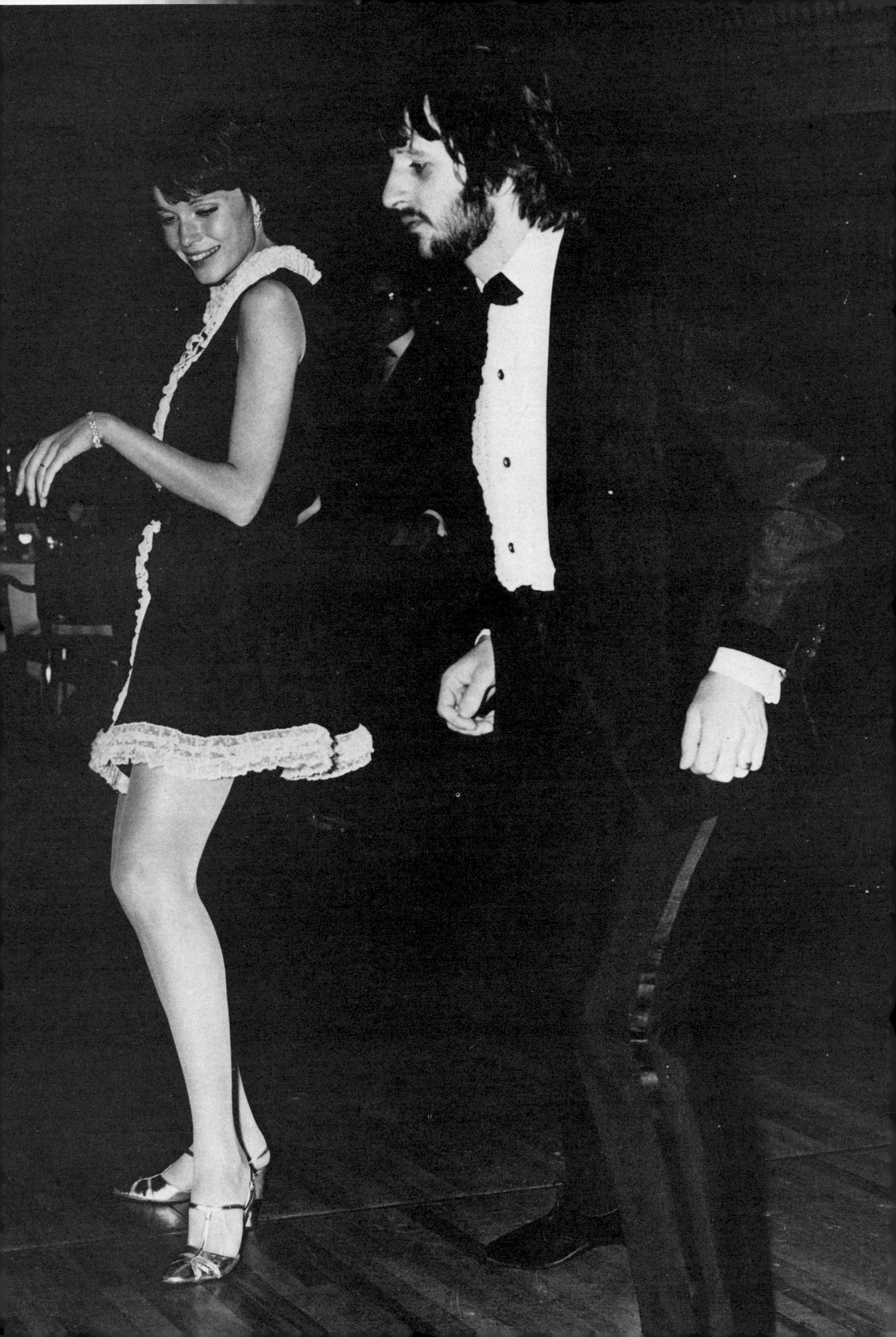

ing. The number was featured on *The White Album*.

Jenny Boyd Younger sister of Patti, who became a model for a time and then worked in the Apple Boutique. She was among the members of The Beatles party who flew to Rishikesh in February 1968. Following the collapse of the Apple Boutique, she and her sister went into the antique business with a stall called Juniper in Chelsea market, but they closed it at the beginning of 1969 because it entailed getting up early in the morning. For a time she lived with Alexis 'Magic Alex' Mardas and then married Mick Fleetwood and went to live in America. They divorced, were reconciled, then split up again.

Ravi Shankar Born on April 7th, 1920 in Benares, India, Ravi Shankar studied music in India and Europe and from the age of 18 spent seven years studying the sitar in the Ustad Allaudin Khan. The sitar is an Indian 21-string instrument which is plucked with a wire plectrum: George Harrison first became aware of the instrument when on the set of the film *Help!* He later introduced a sitar sound on 'Norwegian Wood' and met Ravi Shankar at a friend's house in June 1966 and invited him to his own home in Esher. Together with tabla player Alla Rakha, Ravi gave George his first sitar lesson and later George and Patti joined him for two months in Bombay where further instruction on the playing of the sitar was given.

For the next two years, following the trip to India, George listened to Indian music and both he and Patti became interested in mysticism, meditation and even Krishna chanting, as is evidenced by the number 'Within You, Without You' on the *Sergeant Pepper* album, which was made with sitar and tabla accompaniment. In 1968 George wrote 'The Inner Light' using Indian musicians and by the summer of 1969 was recording several chant numbers with London's Radha Krishna Temple. However, Shankar remained his true guru and George produced a film about him called *Raga*, the soundtrack of which was issued as an album in America on December 7th, 1971 on Apple SWAD 3384. Other Ravi Shankar records produced by George included *In Concert, 1972* recorded live at New York's Philharmonic Hall on April 8th, 1972. This featured: Ravi Shankar, sitar; Ali Akbar Khan, sarod; Alla Rakha, tabla; Ashoka Susan, tambouras. The double-album set was issued in America on January 22nd, 1973 on Apple SAPDO 1002. Another album produced by George was *Shankar Family And Friends*, issued in Britain on George's own label, Dark Horse AMLH 22002, on September 20th, 1974 and in America on October 7th on Dark Horse SP 22002.

Their most fruitful association occurred following Ravi's concern about the heartbreaking conditions in Bangladesh. He considered the idea of holding a concert in order to raise some money for the starving children. He had in mind a fairly modest amount of approximately $25,000 and put forward the idea to George when they were together in California recording the soundtrack for the film *Raga*. George immediately took the situation in hand and contacted Ringo Starr and Leon Russell. Within a matter of weeks the

Ringo bruising the dance-floor with actress Mia Farrow

The Indian musician Ravi Shankar brought a new direction to George's music

concert had been organized, a number of musicians had shown a willingness to offer their services to the cause and the event took place before a crowd of 40,000 at Madison Square Garden on August 1st, 1971. The concert raised $243,418.50 on the night and a cheque for that amount was sent to the United Nation's Children's Fund For Relief To Refugee Children Of Bangladesh on December 12th of that year.

The other money-spinning off-shoots of the concert were a film and boxed record set. The film, entitled *The Concert For Bangladesh* was released the following year. It was directed by Saul Swimmer and produced by George Harrison and Allen Klein. The film ran for 99 minutes and featured George, Ravi,

Eric Clapton, Bob Dylan, Billy Preston, Leon Russell, Ringo Starr, Klaus Voorman and Badfinger. The three-album boxed set on Apple STCX 3385 was issued on January 8th, 1972. The box also contained a handsome souvenir book with 100 colour photographs of the event. The tracks were: side one 'Bangla Dhun', Ravi Shankar; side two 'Wah-Wah', 'My Sweet Lord', 'Awaiting On You All', George Harrison; 'That's The Way God Planned It', Billy Preston; side three 'It Don't Come Easy', Ringo Starr; 'Beware Of Darkness', George Harrison, Leon Russell; 'While My Guitar Gently Weeps', George Harrison, Eric Clapton; side four 'Jumpin' Jack Flash', 'Youngblood', Leon Russell; 'Here Comes The Sun', George Harrison; side five 'A Hard Rain's Gonna Fall', 'It Takes A Lot To Laugh, It Takes A Train To Cry', 'Blowin In The Wind', 'Mr Tambourine Man', 'Just Like A Woman', Bob Dylan; side six 'Something', 'Bangladesh', George Harrison.

Alexis Mardas Blond-haired Greek inventor, called Magic Alex, who insinuated his way into The Beatles' burgeoning business to become head of Apple Electronics. Despite all the gimmicks he produced, he never completed some of the main ventures, such as a 72-track studio. Mardas travelled to Rishikesh with The Beatles and it was his unsubstantiated comments about the Maharishi and Mia Farrow that caused John Lennon and George Harrison to confront their TM mentor and leave the ashram. It was also Mardas who was delegated to travel to Italy where Cynthia was on holiday with her son and her mother to tell her that John would be divorcing her and taking Julian away from her.

Harold Wilson British prime minister of the sixties who put forward The Beatles' names for the Honours List in which they received their MBE's. He also attended the re-opening of the Cavern Club on July 23rd 1966. His constituency was in the Huyton district of Liverpool.

Hunter Davies British journalist-turned-novelist, author of several novels, including *Here We Go Round The Mulberry Bush*, as well as non-fiction books, the most famous of which is *The Beatles — The Authorised Biography*, first published in hardback on September 14th, 1960 with a cover by Alan Aldridge. Davies dedicated the book to Brian Epstein. He has written the obituaries of the individual Beatles for *The Times* newspaper.

Robert Stigwood Australian impresario who had been in Britain for several years promoting, managing, signing up new bands. In 1967 Brian Epstein brought him in as co-director of NEMS. Brian's judgement in seeking new talent had not been fruitful for a number of years and Stigwood was to bring fresh blood into the organization, with acts such as The Cream and The Bee Gees. On Brian's death, Clive took over the running of the organization, although Stigwood had had the option of stepping into Brian's shoes. He declined because the NEMS artists, particularly The Beatles and Cilla Black, would never agree to his management. He found success with his own bands and in 1975 sponsored the West End production of Willie Russell's *John, George, Paul, Ringo And Bert* which had previously only been seen at the Everyman Theatre in Liverpool. He moved to America where his success blossomed,

The Fabs and their ladies, happily ensconced at a première

particularly in the film world with movies such as *Saturday Night Fever* and *Grease*. Not so successful was his film of *Sergeant Pepper's Lonely Hearts Club Band* which starred The Bee Gees and Peter Frampton. Brian Epstein's personal assistant, Peter Brown, went to work for him when the organization moved to America.

Jo Orton British playwright who was murdered on August 9th, 1967. Orton had written successful plays such as *Loot* and *Entertaining Mr Sloane*. During dinner with Brian Epstein and Paul McCartney one evening they discussed a film follow-up to *A Hard Day's Night* and *Help!* Orton agreed to write a script and submitted a draft of *Up Against It* to Epstein, who turned it down because he found it too controversial, particularly its homosexual undertones.

Of his meeting with McCartney, Orton wrote: 'He was just as the photographs, only he'd grown a moustache. His hair was shorter, too. He was playing the latest Beatles record, "Penny Lane". I liked it very much. Then he played the other side — Strawberry something. I didn't like this as much.'

Although his script had been turned down as a project for The Beatles, Orton rewrote it and was due to discuss the filming of *Up Against It* with Dick Lester when he was murdered by Kenneth Halliwell.

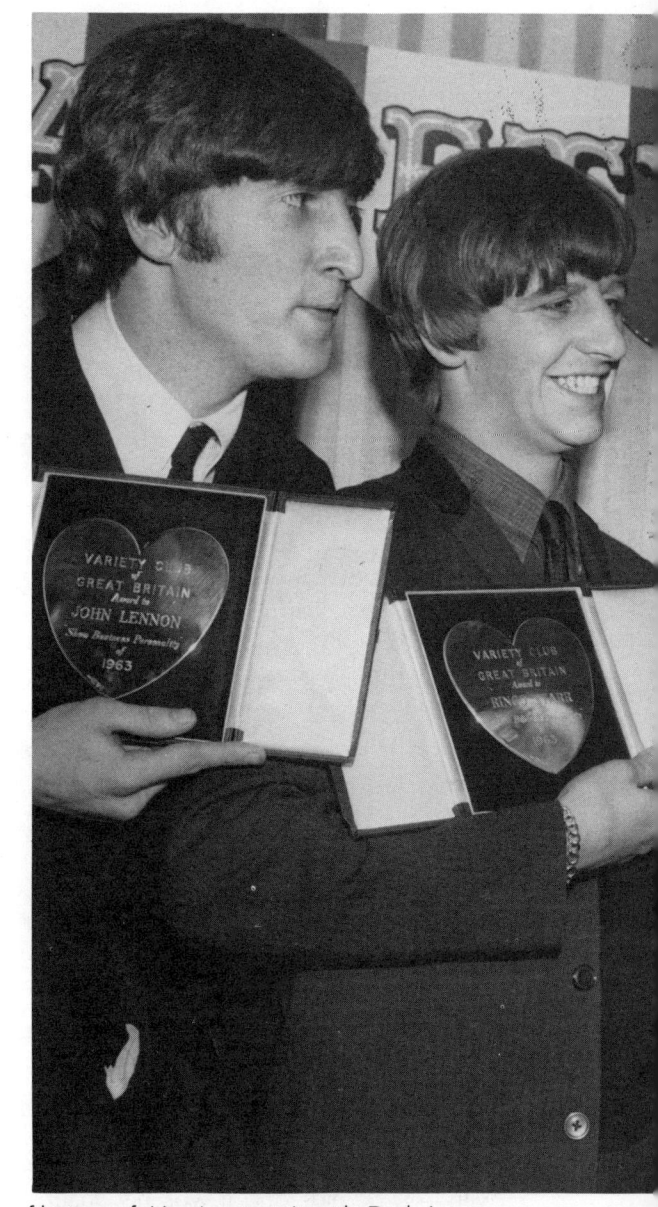

Jack Good British TV producer, born in London in 1931, who was to produce numerous rock-and-roll programmes for television, including *6.5 Special*, *Oh Boy!*, *Boy Meets Girl* and *Wham!*. In 1964 he produced *Around The Beatles*,

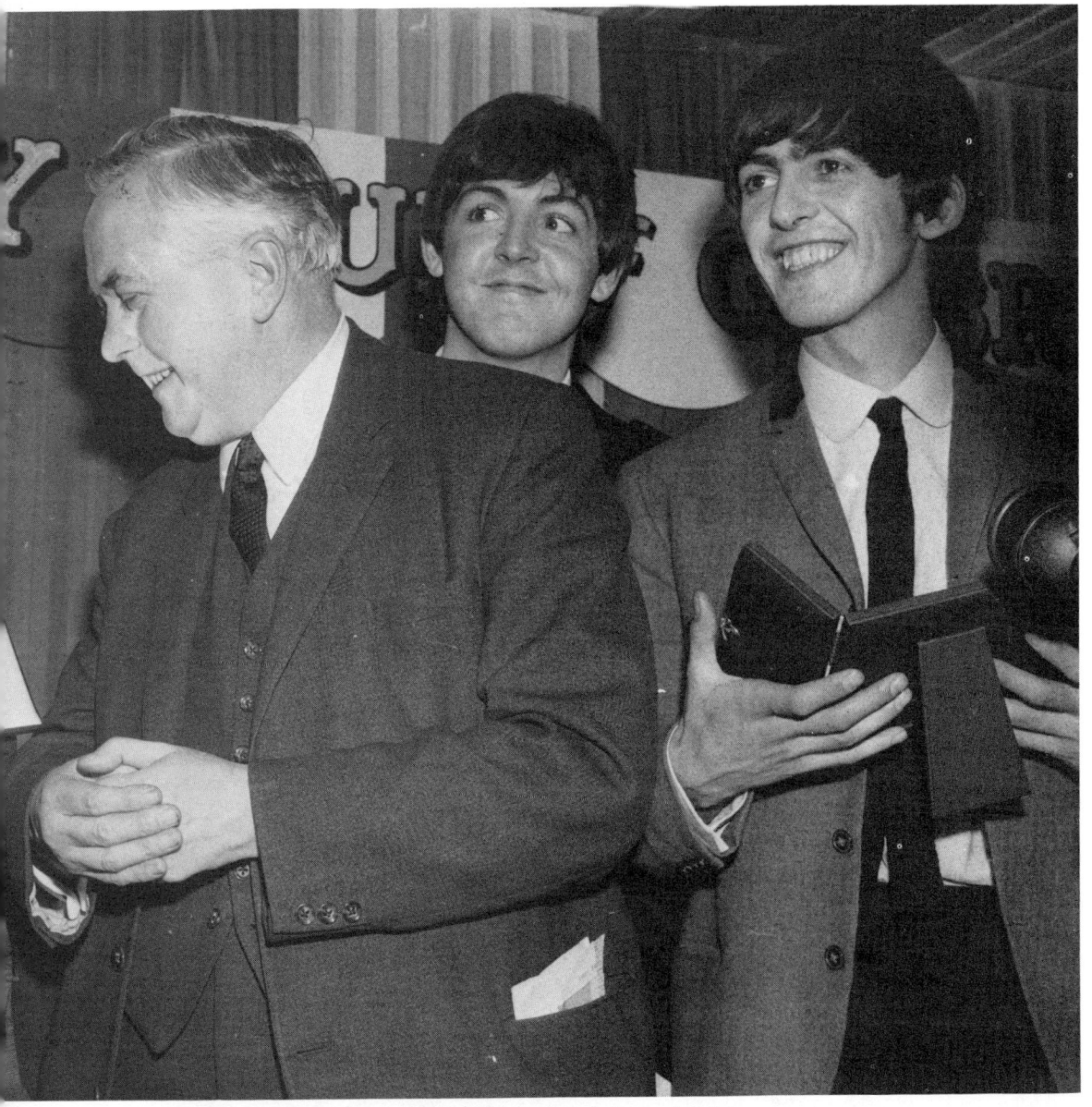

The Beatles with Harold Wilson, then British Prime Minister

an hour-long show featuring the group performing 'She Loves You', 'I Want To Hold Your Hand', 'Can't Buy Me Love', 'Twist And Shout', 'Roll Over Beethoven', 'I Wanna Be Your Man', 'Long Tall Sally' and 'Shout'. They also sang a medley: 'Love Me Do'/'Please, Please Me'/'From Me To You' and presented an excerpt from Shakespeare's *A Midsummer Night's Dream* with John as Thisbe, Paul as Pyramus, George as Moonshine and Ringo as the Lion. The show was first screened in Britain on May 6th, 1964 and repeated on June 8th of the same year. An edited version was screened by ABC TV in America on

May 24th, 1964. Good had spent most of his time in America during an eight-year period from 1962 and presented a show called *Shindig* there. In 1964 he returned to London to film a British edition of the show to be screened in the States in October. The programme was filmed at the Granville Theatre, Waltham Green, Fulham. The Beatles were featured performing 'Kansas City', 'I'm A Loser' and 'Boys'. Other acts on the show were Sandie Shaw, Sounds Incorporated, P.J. Proby and Lyn Cornell.

Good continued to present rock shows and during the seventies revived *Oh Boy!* on British TV.

Tommy Charles Manager of WAQY, a C&W radio station in Birmingham, Alabama who, on July 31st, 1966 announced that the station wouldn't play any more Beatles records and asked listeners to burn records and photographs of the group because of John Lennon's alleged statement that The Beatles were bigger than Jesus. Other stations followed suit.

Ewa Aulin Blond, Swedish actress who made her movie début in the 1969 film *Candy* in which Ringo Starr appeared in a cameo role as Emmanuel, a Mexican gardener who, like the rest of the male cast, manages to seduce the heroine. Ewa gave Ringo his first screen kiss, filmed on Wednesday, 13th December, 1967.

Alan Smith Merseyside journalist who, under the pseudonym George Jones, wrote several articles on The Beatles for *Mersey Beat*. He continued

John enjoying a Shakespearian role on the Around The Beatles *show*

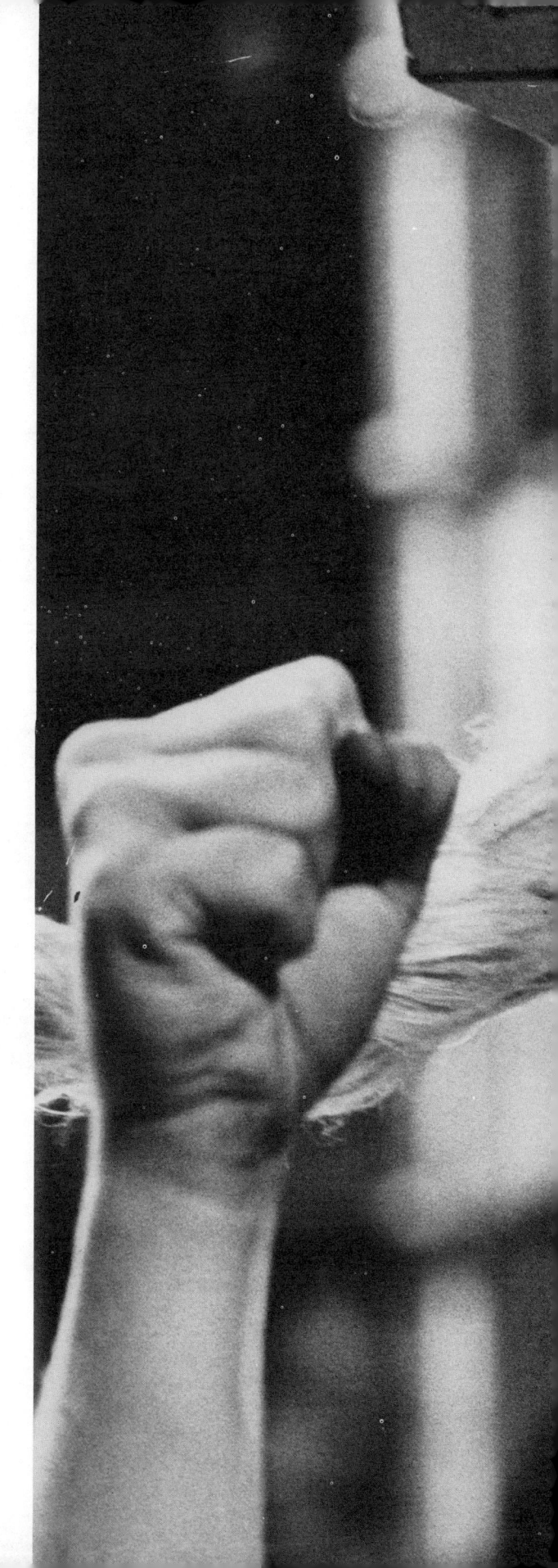

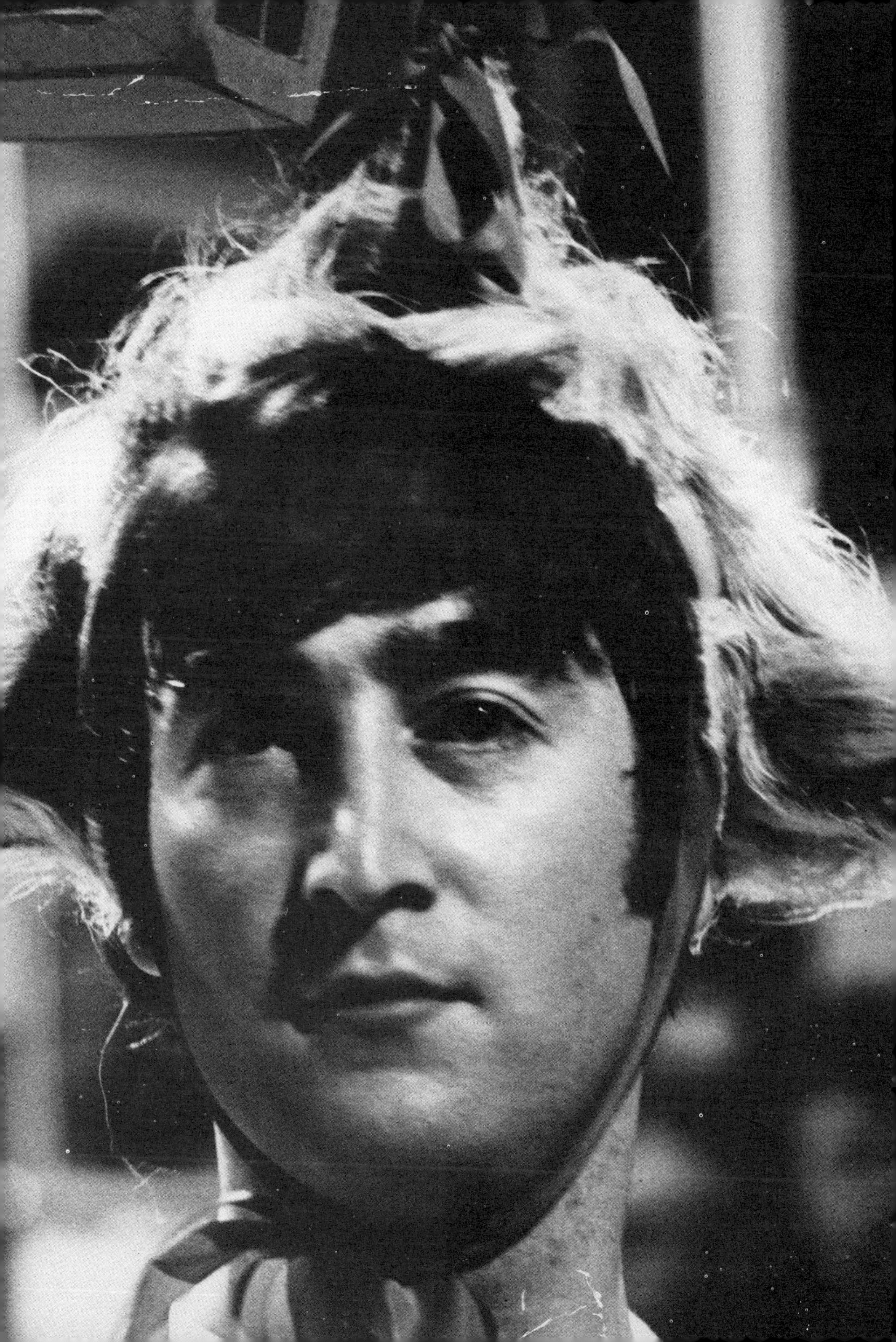

interviewing The Beatles in his capacity as writer with the New Musical Express and was later to become that publication's editor. His wife Mavis, a show business PR, worked for a time in the press office at Apple.

George Tremlett Originally a journalist with the Coventry Evening Telegraph in the fifties, George became a music journalist and interviewed The Beatles on many occasions. Together with his research team he scoured Liverpool in the mid-sixties, interviewing numerous friends who had been associated with The Beatles and collecting various items of memorabilia. He wrote a series of biographies of leading pop stars and groups for Futura Books during the seventies, which included The Paul McCartney Story and The John Lennon Story. He turned to politics and became a prominent member of the Conservative administration in London, specializing in the area of housing. His work showed such attention to detail that it was a pity he never completed books on George Harrison and Ringo Starr. He prepared a Beatles Almanack in the mid-seventies but this was turned down by publishers.

Paddy, Klaus and Gibson Trio comprising Gibson Kemp (drums), Klaus Voorman (bass) and Paddy Chambers (lead guitar/vocals). Gibson was a top Liverpool drummer who replaced Ringo in Rory Storm and The Hurricanes and later married Astrid Kirchnerr. Paddy Chambers was previously with Faron's Flamingoes and The Big Three and Klaus had always wanted to join a group from the moment he first saw The Beatles in Hamburg. They were originally managed by Tony Stratton-Smith, a London-based journalist who had signed several Liverpool acts, including Beryl Marsden and The Koobas. Brian Epstein showed interest in the group so Tony agreed to the management change and they signed with Brian on August 13th, 1965. However, as with almost every act signed by Brian Epstein following his initial handful of Liverpool successes, they vanished without a trace. Paddy returned to Liverpool to manage the Wooky Hollow club for a time; Gibson became a prominent record executive, first in Hamburg, then London and finally in Australia and Klaus continued his association with The Beatles and appeared on many of their solo projects.

Ron Kass American record executive who formerly ran Liberty Records in the States. When The Beatles launched Apple they appointed Kass head of the music division in charge of both the Apple and Zapple labels. Zapple was to be the company's outlet for experimental music. Kass, who is married to British film star Joan Collins, was one of the first to be discharged when Allen Klein took over representation of The Beatles' business interests.

Dennis O'Dell Irish-born head of Apple Films. When Apple Films was originally formed in February 1968 he was appointed a director, together with all four Beatles and Neil Aspinall. He was also a director of Apple Publicity. He was involved in the productions of Magical Mystery Tour, Let It Be and The Concert For Bangladesh.

Chris O'Dell Girl from Tucson, Arizona who moved to Hollywood where she

Ringo with his Candy *co-star Ewa Aulin*

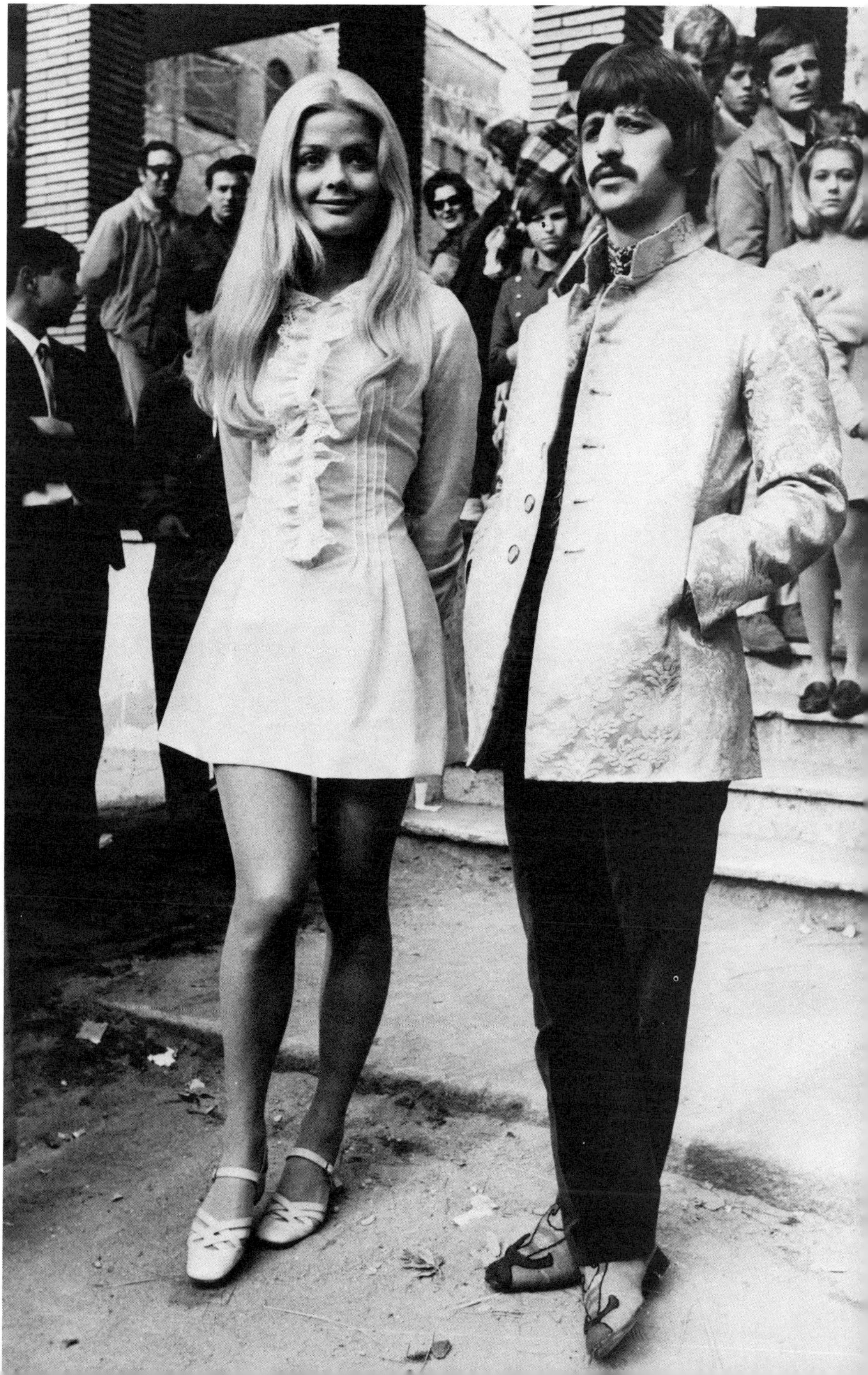

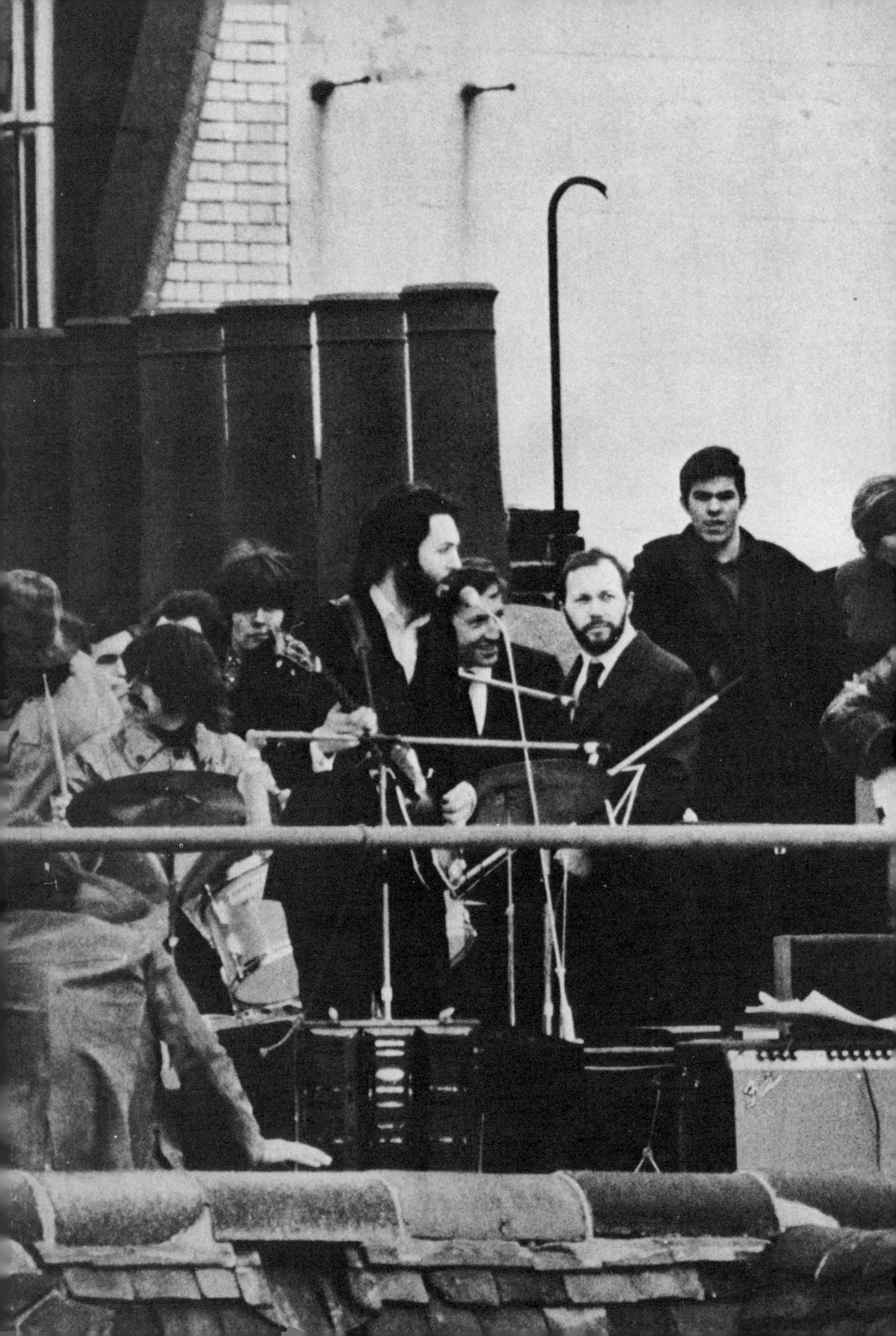

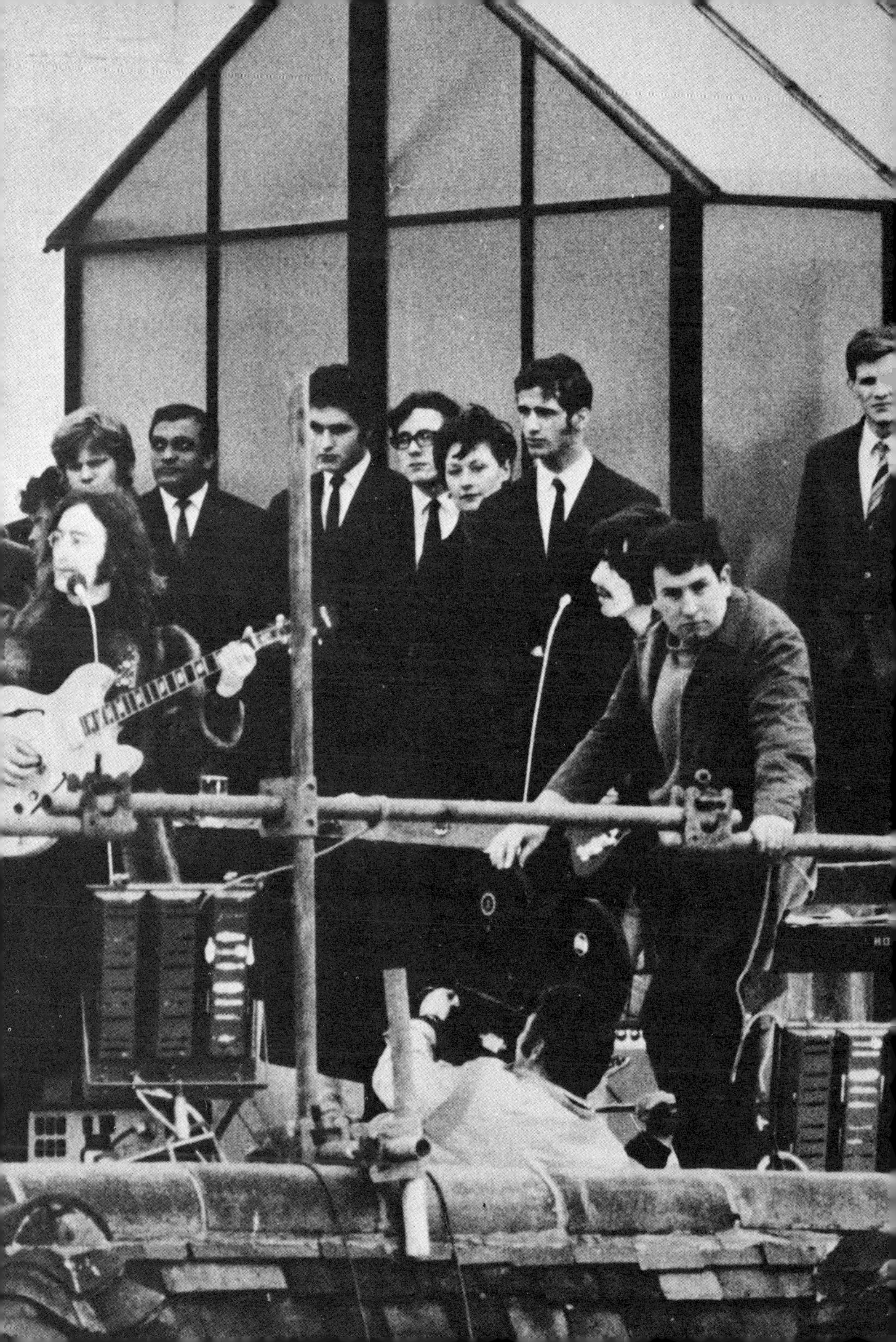

was given a letter of introduction to Peter Asher. She came to London and Asher fixed her up with a job in Apple and, shortly after, she became Asher's secretary. George Harrison wrote his song 'Miss O'Dell' in honour of her.

Richard Di Lello New Yorker, born on September 28th, 1945, who became acquainted with Derek Taylor in San Francisco. He arrived in Britain in November, 1967, then left for North Africa for four months before returning to London and asking Derek Taylor for a job. Derek was able to provide him with a post as assistant press officer to himself, after 'fixing up' Richard with a work permit in his own inimitable way. Richard, who became known as 'the House Hippie', became photographer and chronicler of the Apple days as he documented the day-to-day life in the Saville Row building in his amusing book *The Longest Cocktail Party*, first published in 1973. He eventually rose to be chief press officer, a post which lasted only a short time. Journalist Anne Nightingale ran a story describing a crumbling Apple empire following some off-the-record remarks Richard made to her, which provided Allen Klein with the ammunition he needed in order to sack him.

Grapefruit Group managed by Terry Doran. John Lennon gave them their name (was it because of Yoko's *Grapefruit* book, the fruit association of the forthcoming Apple organization, or both?) and since Apple Records had not yet been formed, they were signed to Apple Publishing, which was also run by Terry. The group comprised George Alexander (bass), John Perry (lead),

Pete Swettenham (rhythm) and Geoff Swettenham (drums). They had two minor hits on the RCA label: 'Dear Delilah' (RCA 1656) which reached No. 21 in the charts in February 1968 and 'C'mon Marianne' (RCA 1716) which reached No. 25 in August of the same year. Soon after their brief record success they had a disagreement with Apple and severed their relationship.

Mary Hopkin Pretty, blond-haired folk singer, born in Pontardawe, Wales on May 3rd, 1950. Mary appeared on the now defunct British television talent show *Opportunity Knocks*, hosted by Hughie Green, in 1968. Twiggy was impressed by her performance and called Paul McCartney, who was then looking for artists for the Apple label. Paul contacted her and produced her début record 'Those Were The Days', which sold 5 million copies worldwide. It was released by Apple in Britain on August 30th, 1968 on Apple 2 and in America on August 26th on Apple 1801. Paul produced Mary's rendition of the song in Italian 'Quelli Erand Giorni', issued on October 25th, 1968. Paul designed the cover of her *Postcard* album, which he also produced, issued in Britain on February 21st, 1969 on Apple Sapcor 5 and in America on March 3rd, 1969. Paul also produced her version of 'Que Sera, Sera', issued in France on September 19th, 1969 on Apple 16 and in America on June 15th, 1970 on Apple 1823.

Michael J. Pollard American actor who initially rose to fame in the film *Bonnie And Clyde*. He was the first

Paul presents a bouquet to his first Apple discovery, Mary Hopkins

recipient of free clothes at the Apple Boutique when it closed in July 1968. He'd been shopping there for shirts and jackets and when he approached the cashier to settle his bill was told that he could keep the items free of charge.

The Fool A trio of Dutch designers: Marijke Koger, Josje Leeger and Simon Posthuma who had run an Amsterdam boutique called 'The Trend'. They met two PR men in London, Simon Hayes and Barry Finch, and obtained design work at Brian Epstein's Saville Theatre. Barry Finch then joined the team and Simon Hayes was appointed their business manager. They began to design clothes for The Beatles and their wives and girlfriends and also painted the fireplace in George's bungalow, George's guitar and Mini and John's Rolls Royce. They talked The Beatles into advancing them a large amount of money to open a shop and, as Apple Retail, launched the Apple Boutique in Baker Street. Controversy was aroused by a large mural covering the outer walls, designed by The Fool and executed by 40 art students. Local traders demanded its removal. The shop opened on December 7th, 1967 but lost so much money that The Beatles decided to close it down and offer the remaining stock free to all comers. By this time The Fool had made arrangements to move to America and were contracted to Mercury Records. They recorded one unsuccessful album.

Billy Preston Born in Houston, Texas on September 9th, 1946, Billy Preston began to carve a reputation for himself as a support musician in America. He came to the notice of The Beatles when accompanying Ray Charles on tour. He worked quite frequently with the group and is present on their recordings of 'Get Back' and 'Let It Be'. He also signed with their recording company, Apple. Among his Apple releases was a version of 'My Sweet Lord', the George Harrison number which he co-produced with George. It was released in Britain, on Apple 29, on September 4th, 1970 and in the States, on Apple 1826, on December 3rd of the same year.

Trash Glasgow group, formerly The Pathfinders, who were discovered by Tony Meehan (ex-member of The Shadows). They were signed to Apple and

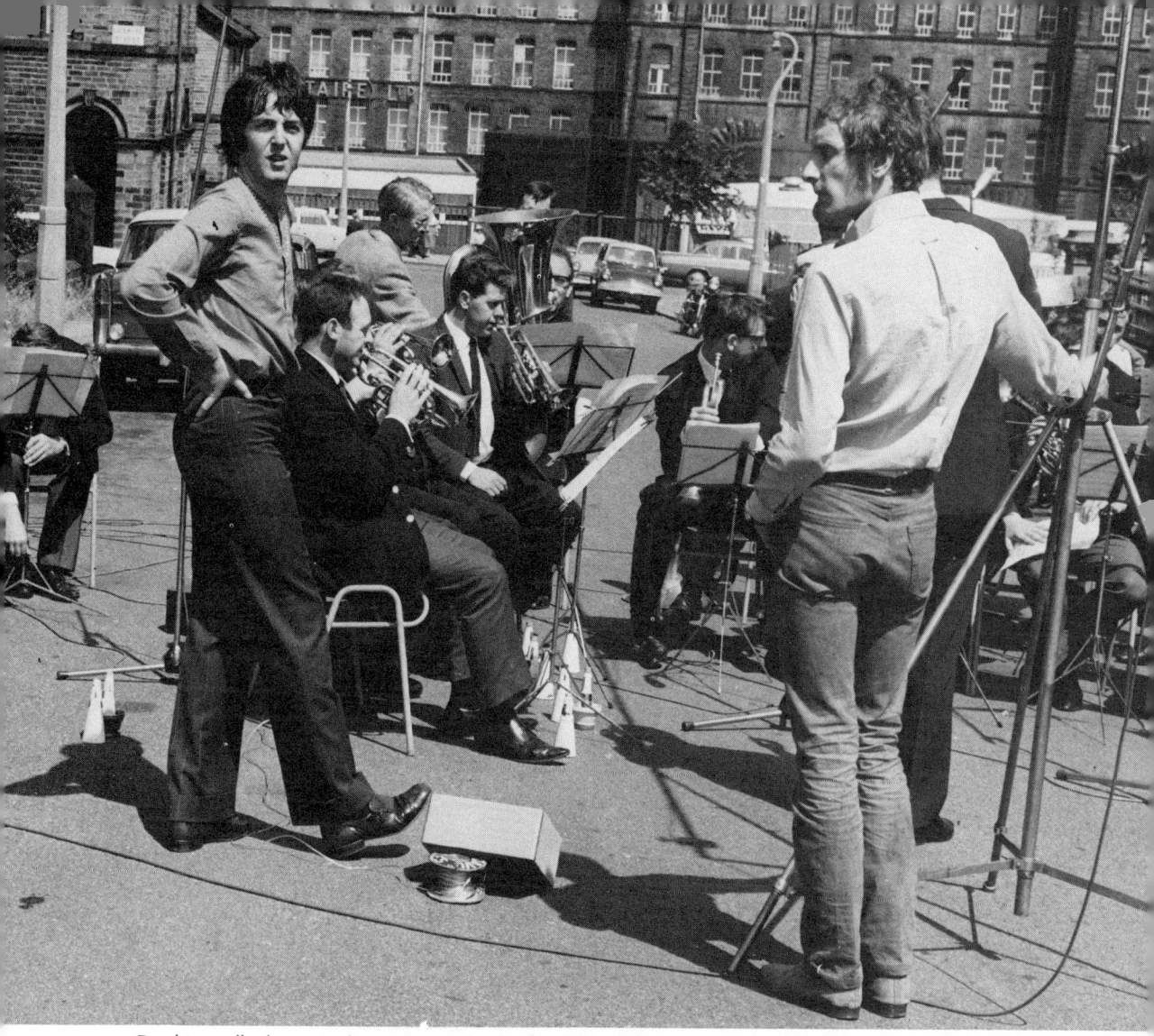

Paul travelled up north to record the famous British Brass Band Award winners, the Black Dyke Mills Band

given the name White Trash by Richard Di Lello. They had difficulty promoting their début single 'Road To Nowhere' because people found the name offensive, so it was shortened to Trash. They recorded The Beatles medley number 'Golden Slumbers/Carry That Weight' (Apple 17) which reached No. 35 in the charts in September 1969. They had no further success and disbanded due to problems within the Apple company. They comprised: Ian Crawford-Clews (vocals), Fraser Watson (lead guitar), Ronald Leahy (organ), Colin Hunter-Morrison (bass) and Tim Donald (drums).

Mortimer A group of musicians from New York who were signed to the Apple label. The Trio (Guy Masson, Tony Van Benschoten and Tom Smith) released 'On Our Way Home' as their début single, a Paul McCartney number.

The Black Dyke Mills Band One of Britain's foremost brass bands, founded

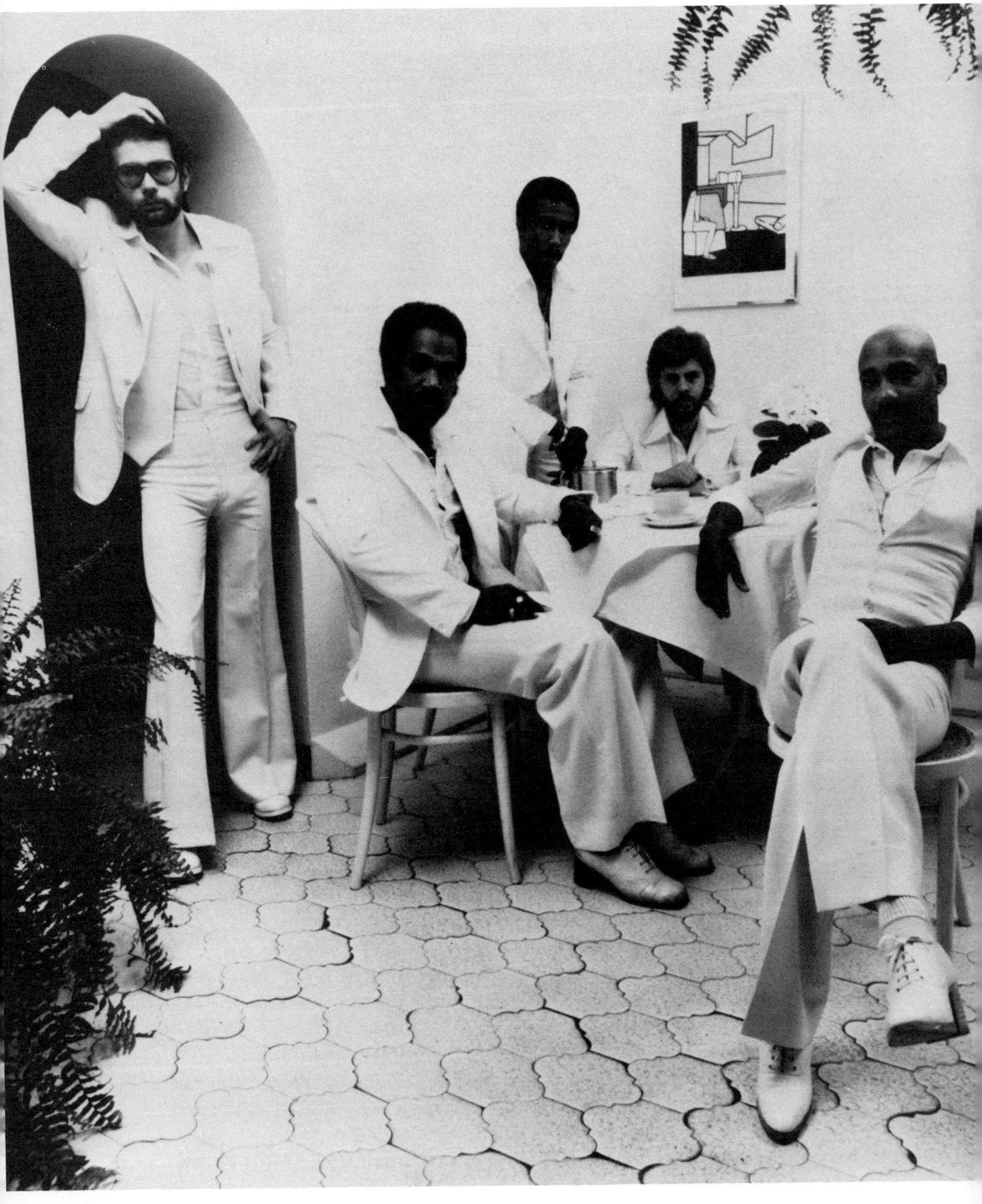

in the forties by the Yorkshire firm of John Foster and Sons. When London Weekend Television were launching a series called *Thingymybob*, they commissioned Paul McCartney to write the title tune. He decided on using the brass band, which comprised 39 men between the ages of 16 and 60 who had won the National Brass Band Championship of Great Britain ten times. He went up to Bradford to produce them and the release was Apple's first non-Beatles single. It was coupled with a new arrangement of 'Yellow Submarine'. The disc was issued in America on August 26th, 1968 on Apple 1800 and in Britain on September 6th, 1968 on Apple 4.

Hot Chocolate I have represented Hot Chocolate as press agent since they first became associate with Mickie Most at the onset of the seventies. A highly popular band, they are the only British group to have had a hit in the UK charts every single year throughout the seventies. When Errol Brown teamed up with Tony Wilson they wanted to record 'Give Peace A Chance', but with some lyric alterations. They needed to ask the permission of the songwriters to do this and sent a tape to Apple. John Lennon arranged to see them and suggested that Apple could release the disc. As they had no group name at the time, Mavis Smith suggested they call themselves The Hot Chocolate Band and John Lennon recommended it, so they adopted the name, although they cut it down to plain Hot Chocolate after they had made their recording début with 'Give Peace A Chance' c/w 'Living Without Tomorrow' (Apple 18), issued in the UK on October 10th, 1969 and in the States on Apple 1812 on October 17th.

Following that release they joined Mickie Most's Rak Records label where they have been ever since and have totted up 30 hit singles and several best-selling albums, including *Brother Louie, Emma, You Sexy Thing, Every I's A Winner* and *No Doubt About It*. Tony Wilson left early in the seventies and the line-up now comprises Errol Brown (vocals); Larry Ferguson (keyboards); Patrick Olive (bass); Harvey Hinsley (guitar) and Tony Connor (drums).

Badfinger A group which started life as The Iveys, during which they appeared at Liverpool's famous Cavern Club. They were originally spotted at Amford Ballroom in Swansea by Bill Collins, who became their manager and for one period they were backing band for the Liverpool singer, David Garrick. They were spotted at London's Marquee Club in early 1968 by Mal Evans who contacted Apple's A&R man, Peter Asher, about them. Asher was not impressed, so Mal asked Bill Collins for a tape and took it directly to Paul McCartney who then asked Mal to play it to George Harrison, John Lennon and Derek Taylor. They were signed to Apple Publishing in April 1968 and to Apple Records in July. Their first release was 'Maybe Tomorrow' c/w 'And Her Daddy's A Millionaire' (Apple 5), issued in November and released in America on Apple 1803. Their original singer Ron Griffiths left and the band now comprised: Tom Evans from Liverpool on guitar, piano, bass; Joe Molland from Liverpool on guitar, piano, bass; Mike Gibson from Swansea on drums and guitar; Pete Ham from Swansea on piano, organ, guitar.

Paul was asked to compose a number for the film *The Magic Christian* which starred Peter Sellers and Ringo Starr and he wrote 'Come And Get It'. Neil Aspinall suggested that the group change their name to Badfinger. They recorded Paul's number which was released in January 1970 reached the No. 3 position on both sides of the Atlantic. Between 1970 and 1973 when they moved to Warner Brothers, they recorded a number of singles, including 'No Matter What', 'Day After Day' and 'Baby Blue'. In the meantime they appeared at *The Concert For Bangladesh* in August 1971 and played on George's album *All Things Must Pass*. They also wrote 'Without You', which Harry Nilsson recorded on his *No Dice* album and became one of his biggest hits when issued as a single.

George Harrison produced four tracks for their *Straight Up* album, Todd Rundgren produced the rest and the cover of the sleeve was by Apple's 'house hippie', Richard Di Lello. The fortunes of the group waned after they left Apple and Pete Ham committed suicide on April 25th, 1975. The group disbanded; then, in the late seventies, Joey Molland and Tom Evans relaunched the band with some new members and have based themselves in America.

Francie Schwartz Born in Pennsylvania, she arrived in London in 1968 and went to the Apple offices in Saville Row to hawk a film script. She met Paul in the reception area and began working for Apple. She frequented the London clubs with Paul when his romance with Jane Asher ended and for a short time moved into his London house. Later, she reported the story of the romance in a *News Of The World* feature, wrote a piece called 'Memories Of An Apple Girl' which was published in *Rolling Stone* and a book *Body Count*, published in America by Straight Arrow Books in 1972.

Maggie McGivern Girlfriend of Paul McCartney for a short time following his break with Francie Schwartz. The couple went on a holiday to Sardinia together.

Harry Nilsson American singer/songwriter, born in New York on June 15th, 1941. He moved to the west coast in 1952. In 1967 former Beatles publicist Derek Taylor, who was also living on the west coast at the time, was much impressed with Nilsson's recordings for RCA and sent them to Brian Epstein. Taylor called him the best contemporary soloist in the world and added: 'He is the something The Beatles are.' Harry's interpretation of Lennon/McCartney material impressed the duo who commented during an interview that he was their favourite singer. He became a close friend of the individual Beatles and had a major hit with 'Without You', a number written by members of Badfinger, the Apple group. George and Ringo performed on his album *Son of Schmilsson* and Derek Taylor produced 'A Touch Of Schmilsson In The Night'. John Lennon produced his *Pussy Cats* album and he appeared with Ringo Starr in two films, *Son Of Dracula* and *Harry And Ringo's Night Out*, both produced in 1974.

Joe Cocker Sheffield singer, born May 20th, 1944. As lead singer with Vance Arnold and The Avengers he recorded the Lennon/McCartney number 'I'll Cry Instead' in 1963. His biggest hit was the *Sergeant Pepper* number 'With A Little Help From My Friends' (Regal Zonophone Rz 3013) which was released on October 19th, 1968 and reached the No. 1 spot in the British charts. He also recorded an album of the same name.

John Dunbar Cambridge graduate who became one of the bright young men of the 'Swinging' London scene in the sixties, marrying pop singer Marianne Faithful and going into partnership with Peter Asher in an art gallery called Indica, situated in Mason's Yard. It was John who, on November 9th, 1966, originally introduced John Lennon to Yoko Ono when the Beatles turned up at the Indica to see her *Exhibition No. 2*.

Robin Cruikshank Designer who launched his own company, Robin Limited, in the sixties. He did some work for Apple, following which Ringo Starr commissioned him to furnish his home and was so pleased with the result that he went into partnership with Robin and the firm's name was changed to Ringo Or Robin Limited. The company proved an ideal outlet for Ringo's latent design talent and he went to work himself on a

Joe Cocker, who hit the No. 1 spot in the charts with 'With A Little Help From My Friends'

variety of intriguing designs, one of the most famous being a Rolls Royce grill table.

Roy Kinnear Portly British character actor who portrayed the bumbling scientific assistant attempting to part Ringo Starr from his ring in *Help!* He also appeared as Private Clapper, a member of the Fourth Musketeers platoon with Private Gripeweed (John Lennon) in *How I Won The War*.

Bob Dylan I first became aware of Bob Dylan when Al Aronowitz of the *Saturday Evening Post* arrived in Liverpool to write a feature about the city and her famous sons. He was full of enthusiasm for Dylan and described the Greenwich Village scene. I immediately went out and bought the album *Bob Dylan*. It was pure magic. Al went on to interest The Beatles in his folk friend and I began to notice the influence he'd had when I heard 'I'm A Loser'. When Dylan arrived in London for a concert tour I went to see him at his reception party. With Al as a mutual friend we got into conversation and I ended up phoning John at home and arranging for Dylan to go and see him there. When Bob was up in Liverpool for his concert at the Odeon, I went to the Adelphi Hotel after the show and he asked me to his room where he introduced me to his manager Al Grossman and we began chatting about Liverpool poets. I told him all about the poetry-to-jazz concert we'd had, the poetry readings of in clubs such as Streates and how Liverpool poets had their own outlook, which was different to that of the beat poets of San Francisco. He then asked if we could take him out to meet some of the poets so we went down to the Blue Angel

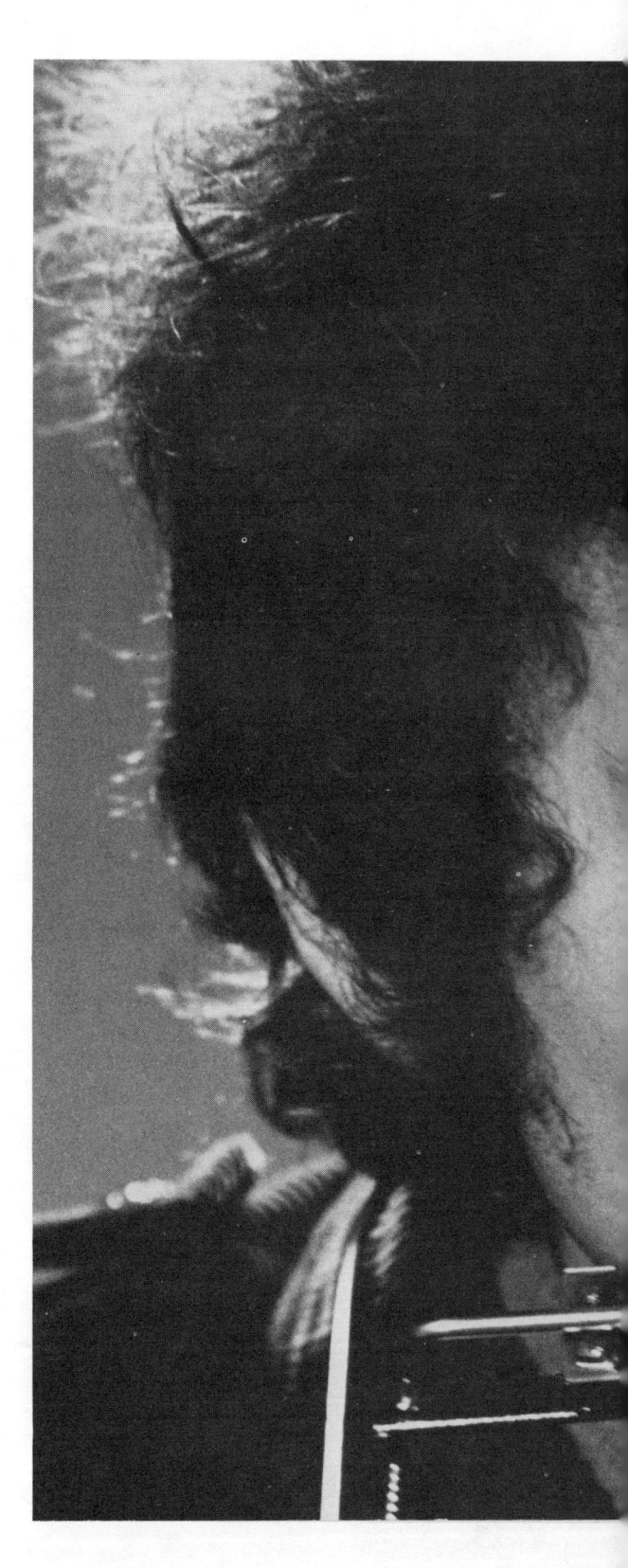

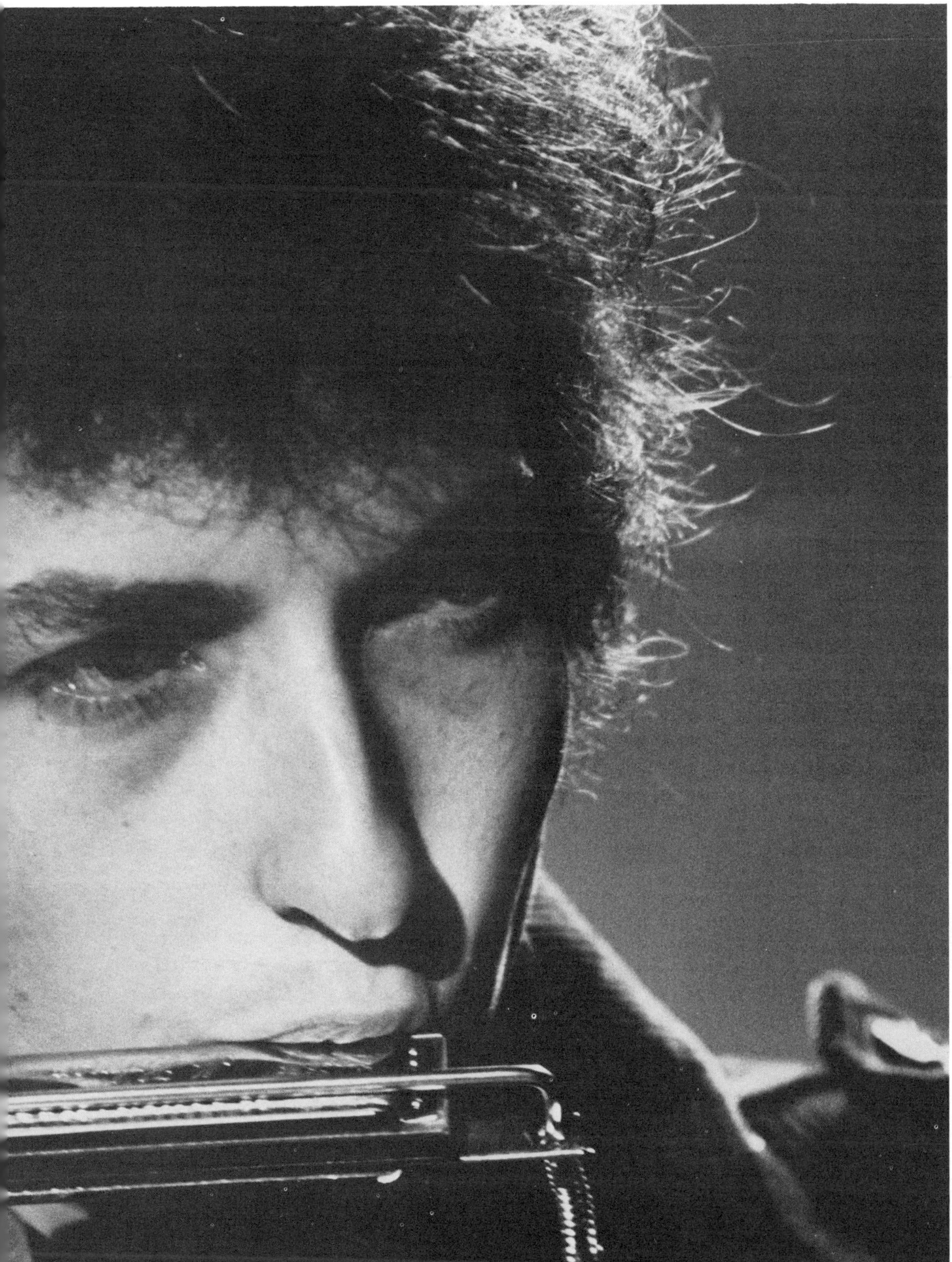

where we met poet Roger McGough and his Scaffold mate Mike McGear. Bob was horrified to discover that the Blue Angel didn't sell Beaujolais wine and suggested we return to the hotel, inviting some friends to join us. Accompanied by Roger, Mike and three delightful black singers, collectively called The Poppies, we returned to the Adelphi where I noticed that one of the tables in his room was neatly packed with about two dozen bottles of Beaujolais. We settled down to conversations which lasted for several hours during which Bob told me about a book he was working on called 'Tarantula'. I next heard that he was so enchanted by The Poppies that he invited them down to London and intended to record them.

Dylan emerged as a superstar soon after The Beatles' own rise to fame. He first heard them on his car radio, performing 'I Want To Hold Your Hand' and was heard to comment: 'They were doing things nobody else was doing. Their chords were outrageous, just outrageous, and their harmonies made it all valid. I knew they were pointing the direction in which music had to go.'

The Beatles and Dylan got on well together and all four attended his London concert in May 1964. It was said that he was the person who first introduced them to marijuana and apart from 'I'm A Loser', 'You've Got To Hide Your Love Away' was said to have been influenced by Dylan. John Lennon also told him that the lyrics of 'A Hard Day's Night' had been influenced by 'A Hard Rain's Gonna Fall'. When The Beatles were on their first major tour they met Dylan again – one of several get-togethers over the years. The influence worked both ways as it was said that 'Tarantula' had been inspired by *In His Own Write*. George and Ringo visited Bob in Nashville during the recording of 'Nashville Skyline' and George and Dylan wrote a song together, 'I'd Have You Anytime', which is the first track on the triple album *All Things Must Pass*. Their most famous association was The Concert For Bangladesh, the benefit organized by George in aid of the refugee children of Bangladesh. Dylan was one of the invited guests and he performed 'A Hard Rain's Gonna Fall', 'Mr Tambourine Man', 'Blowin' In The Wind', 'It Takes A Lot To Laugh, It Takes A Train To Cry' and 'Just Like A Woman'.

The Byrds Californian group comprising Roger McGuinn (guitar/vocals), Chris Hillman (bass/vocals), Gene Clark (vocals), David Crosby (guitar/vocals) and Michael Clarke (drums) who were said to be America's answer to The Beatles after their first hit, 'Mr Tambourine Man', in 1965. In fact, George Harrison once called them 'The American Beatles'. Former Beatles PR man, Derek Taylor, became their publicist when he opened offices in Los Angeles and the group met The Beatles socially on a number of occasions.

P. J. Proby American singer who had a meteoric rise to fame when he came to live in England, began to tour and had a major hit with 'Hold Me'. He recorded the Lennon/McCartney number 'That Means A Lot' which was released in America on July 5th, 1965 on Liberty 55806 with 'Let The Water Run Down' as the flip. The single was released in Britain on September 17th on Liberty 10215 with 'My Prayer' as the flip. Proby also appeared in the television show *Around The Beatles* which was first screened in Britain on May 6th, 1964 and repeated on June 8th of the same year. Edited highlights of the show were screened in the US on ABC TV on July 5th. Proby's downfall was also meteoric, caused by the almost hysterical reaction in the media to the fact that he split his pants on stage. I'd just been contracted to write Proby's life story for him but almost overnight he was finished as a star and his many attempts at a come-back all failed.

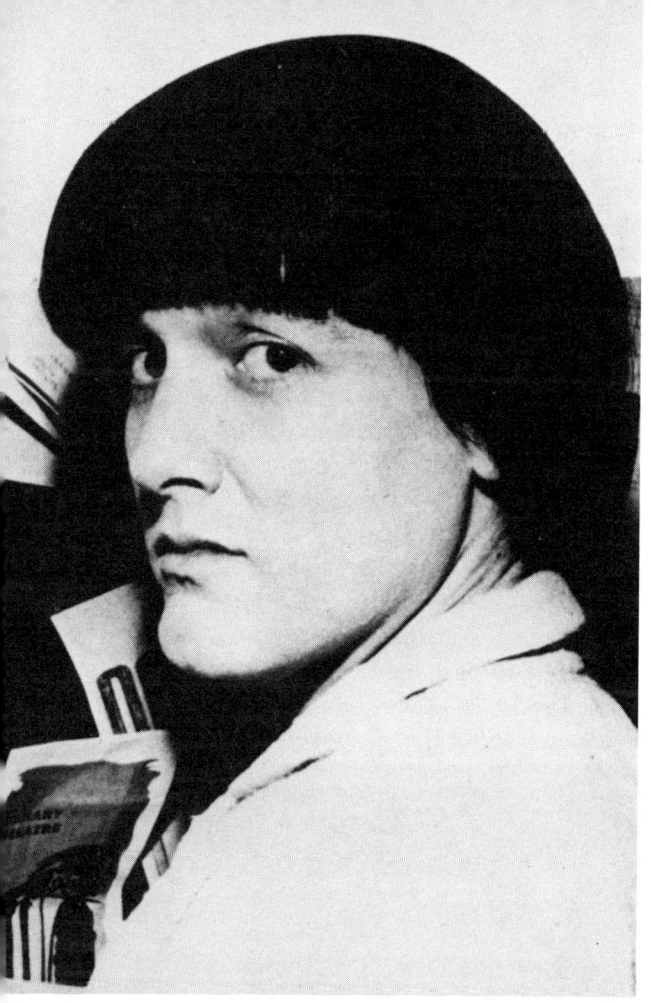

Ethan Russell Photographer who produced the shots for the Get Back book, included in a limited edition boxed presentation with the album Let It Be. Ethan is featured in the first volume of The Beatles Illustrated Lyrics with a double page photograph of John and Yoko illustrating 'Got To Get You Into My Life'. His pics are also to be found in Songs Of John Lennon, a songbook published by Wise Publications.

Angela Williams Angela was a widow who was introduced to Jim McCartney in 1964. On their third meeting Jim proposed and they were married on November 24th, 1964. Angela was more than 20 years younger than her new husband, who formally adopted her five-year-old daughter Ruth. Paul McCartney was particularly fond of Ruth and the family ties were quite strong until Jim's death in 1976. Angie then tried to set up a rock group agency on Merseyside but Paul dissaproved because he felt she might be trading on the McCartney name. Relations between her and Paul cooled and she eventually reverted back to her first husband's name in 1981 following a series of articles, ghosted by Tony Barrow and very critical of Paul, which appeared in the Sun newspaper.

Alvin Stardust His real name is Bernard Jewry and he first achieved a limited degree of fame as Shane Fenton, leading a group called The Fentones in the early sixties. He was a popular singer and I featured him in some Mersey Beat articles. He became friendly with The Beatles and Brian Epstein was interested in managing him, but was turned down. Shane appeared with The Beatles at the Liverpool Empire and after the show Brian approached him and offered him a Lennon and McCartney number which hadn't been recorded. It was called 'Do You Want To Know A Secret?' and Shane turned it down. He married Iris Caldwell, Rory Storm's blond, beautiful sister and the two of them formed a double act. After several years they opened a club outside Liverpool but in the seventies moved to London where Shane changed his name to Alvin Stardust and had several major hit records. The couple were divorced and Alvin married TV actress Lisa Goddard.

Keith Moon Before he died of a drug overdose in 1978 following one of Paul McCartney's annual Buddy Holly promotions, he was known as 'Moon The Loon', the zaniest, most madcap personality on the British rock scene. Drummer with The Who, Keith formed a close friendship with Ringo Starr and they often went clubbing together and even appeared in some movies together, including *That'll Be The Day*. Ringo played on his *Two Sides Of The Moon* album and Keith played on Harry Nilsson's *Pussycats* album which John Lennon co-produced in 1974.

Bonzo Dog Doo Dah Band Multi-talented British group formed by art students in London in 1965. The group appeared in *Magical Mystery Tour*. Their biggest hit was 'I'm The Urban Spaceman', written by Neil Innes and produced by Apollo C. Vermouth. The record was released in Britain on October 11th, 1968 (Liberty LBF 15144) and reached No. 5. It was issued in America (Imperial 66345) on December 18th,

1968. When their album *Urban Spaceman* (Imperial 12432) was issued in the US on June 9th, 1969, Apollo C. Vermouth used his real name, Paul McCartney, for the production credits. Paul also produced their *Tadpoles* album (Liberty LBS 83257) issued in Britain on August 1st, 1969. The group comprised Vivian Stanshall (vocals/trumpet), Roger Ruskin Spear (sax, models), Neil Innes (vocals/piano), Rodney Slater (sax), 'Legs' Larry Smith (drums), Vernon Dudley Bohay-Nowell (guitar/banjo) and Martin Stafford (Sam Spoons) (percussion).

Yoko Ono Yoko Ono (her name means 'Ocean Child') was born to a well-to-do family in Tokyo, Japan on February 18th, 1934. She spent her childhood in her native land and then moved to America with her family when she was 18. They moved into the exclusive Scarsdale area of New York where she was enrolled at the Sarah Lawrence College to study philosophy. She also had lessons on the piano.

In 1957 she married Japanese composer/pianist Toshi Ichiyanagi. Their marriage broke up after seven years and Yoko moved into Greenwich Village where she was keen to find outlets for her creative talents and became an artist, writer, poet and film-maker. She returned to Japan in 1961 but suffered from depression and tried to kill herself. She was sent to a mental hospital and while there was visited by American film-maker Tony Cox. The two of them decided to get married and in 1962 their daughter Kyoko was born and they returned to New York. Yoko moved to London in 1966 and her husband and child followed. The avant-garde artist became involved in a number of projects. She was 33 years of age and decided to make a film called *Bottoms* which would simply portray the bare bottoms of 365 people. Artists, writers and actors volunteered their services and behinds and the film was completed and promptly banned by the British Board of Film Censors. However, the Greater London Council issued it with a special license enabling her to arrange for the film to be screened in the London area. Yoko had also written a book called *Grapefruit* which she promoted by sending 2,000 copies out to reviewers using ladies panties as wrappers.

Yoko first met John Lennon at the Indica Gallery, where she was holding her first major London exhibition. John Dunbar, then married to Marianne Faithful, introduced the couple to each other. The exhibition had not officially opened and John had noticed an exhibit 'Hammer A Nail In'. He asked if he could knock a nail into it and Yoko said it would cost him 5s. As he didn't have any change on him he gave an imaginary five shillings and knocked in an imaginary nail and the two of them began one of the most publicized love affairs of the twentieth century.

They kept in touch and John financed another of her exhibitions at the Lisson Gallery. After John and Cynthia had returned from the Maharishi's ashram in India, Cyn went on holiday to Italy and Yoko visited John at his home in Weybridge where she stayed the night. John informed Cynthia that he wanted a divorce.

Over the years the couple made many records together, beginning with the experimental albums *Two Virgins, Unfinished Music No. 2: Life With The Lions* and *The Wedding Album*. The first LP provided a wave of publicity and hostility. It featured the two of them together, in full frontal nude pose. The fascination they had for each other became intense and John changed his middle-name officially to Ono, wrote and recorded The Beatles single 'The Ballad Of John And Yoko' and created The Plastic Ono Band.

The ensuing years created scores of headlines as they embarked on many ventures. Yoko encouraged John to hold his first art exhibition which opened at the Robert Fraser Gallery in Mayfair on July 1st, 1968. There was a film camera at the entrance which recorded the various people attending the exhibition and there were numerous collection boxes for various charities which John had selected. The main item at the exhibition was a 6 ft circular white canvas, the centre of which contained the handwritten message from John, 'You Are Here'. Three hundred and sixty white helium-filled balloons with the message 'Please return to John Lennon c/o The Robert Fraser Gallery', were released in the West End. The exhibition was dedicated 'To Yoko, from John, with Love' and was the first public declaration of the couple's romance.

John encouraged Yoko in her film experiments and they made several movies together, including *Two Virgins, Smile, Honeymoon, Self Portrait, Rape, Cold Turkey, The Ballad Of John And Yoko, Give Peace A Chance, Erection, Instant Karma* and *Up Your Legs*.

Yoko began to become involved in everything that John did, which didn't help his relationship with the other members of The Beatles and was not popular with the media, who vilified her. Few individuals could have been subjected to such an abusive campaign of hate from the press. She persevered through the dramatic events which followed, including the drugs bust which took place when they were staying at Ringo's Montague Square premises, the police closure of John's exhibition of erotic lithographs of Yoko, the censorship of their nude photos on the *Two Virgins* album, etc. Despite it all they continued to involve themselves in many creative projects – Bagism, Acorns for Peace – in addition to attending film festivals at which their movies were being shown. They also filmed an appearance for a Rolling Stones project 'Rock 'n' Roll Circus', which never received a TV or cinema showing.

Publicity surrounded them wherever they went and following their wedding in Gibraltar on March 20th, 1969 at which Peter Brown and David Nuttall of Apple were witnesses, they flew to Amsterdam to begin a series of bed-ins.

John and Yoko had wanted a child of their own but she suffered two miscarriages. For a time they expended tremendous energy in an attempt to gain custody of her daughter Kyoto and after various court proceedings they decided not to continue any further when they discovered that Kyoto really preferred to be with her father.

The two moved to New York where John remained until his death. They participated, once again, in many artistic ventures and recordings and, for a period of 18 months, John left her and moved to the west coast – in the company of Yoko's secretary, May Pang.

They were reconciled and when their first child, Sean, was born (which also helped John's case for being allowed to stay in America following many efforts to prevent him obtaining a resident's visa because of his drug conviction), John decided to spend his time with his son.

John and Yoko had settled in the Dakota Apartments in New York and they also bought a house in Long Island, a home in Florida and several dairy farms. When John celebrated his 40th birthday on October 9th, 1980, Yoko hired a plane to fly over New York trailing the message: 'Yoko And Sean Love You'. Only a matter of weeks later he was murdered.

Yoko has continued to work on various ventures to perpetuate John's memory and is also writing a book about their life together.

Bill Sargeant American rock promoter. In 1977 he made an offer of $50 million to The Beatles if they would re-form for a show on closed-circuit television.

Linda McCartney Linda Eastman was born on September 24th, 1941. Her mother Louise came from a very wealthy family and her father Lee, who had changed his name from Epstein by deed poll, was also an affluent man — a lawyer specializing in show business accounts. Her family had apartments and houses in the fashionable areas of Scarsdale, East Hampton and Park Avenue. Linda attended Scarsdale High School and when she was 18 her mother was killed in a plane crash. Soon after the tragedy Linda married a geophysicist called John See and they moved to Colorado where her first child, Heather, was born. When the marriage soured, Linda moved back to New York and for a time was receptionist with *Town and Country* magazine. She aspired to socialize in the rock music world and attended a Rolling Stones reception on a boat on the Hudson River on the pretext of being a magazine photographer. In fact, her photographs were published and she entered the field of rock photography, taking pics of mainly British bands who were visiting the States. In 1968 she became house photographer for the Fillmore East in New York. Although an unpaid position, it enabled her to become more fully entrenched in the rock photography scene.

Over a period of time she began to meet Paul McCartney in New York and London and finally moved in with him in his Cavendish Avenue house in St John's Wood. She became pregnant and the couple married at Marylebone Register Office on March 12th, 1969. Paul had been recording the previous night and his best man, brother Mike, was late for the ceremony. Paul and Linda's first child Mary, named after his mother, was born on August 29th, of that year.

The relationship between Paul and Linda grew into one similar to that of the John/Yoko partnership, a unity that involved each other's participation in work and play. A vicious amount of anti-Linda gossip items in the press only drew the couple closer together. Paul taught her how to play electric organ and insisted that she become a member of his new band, Wings. He also wrote a song 'The Lovely Linda' in tribute to his blond-haired wife and encouraged her to develop her creative abilities — which found expression in her photographs, many of which were published in a series of books and calenders, the most noted of which was the 1976 publication *Linda's Pictures*, which included an introduction by Paul. In September 1971 her third child Stella was born but had to be delivered by caesarian operation. Paul's first son, James, was born in September 1977.

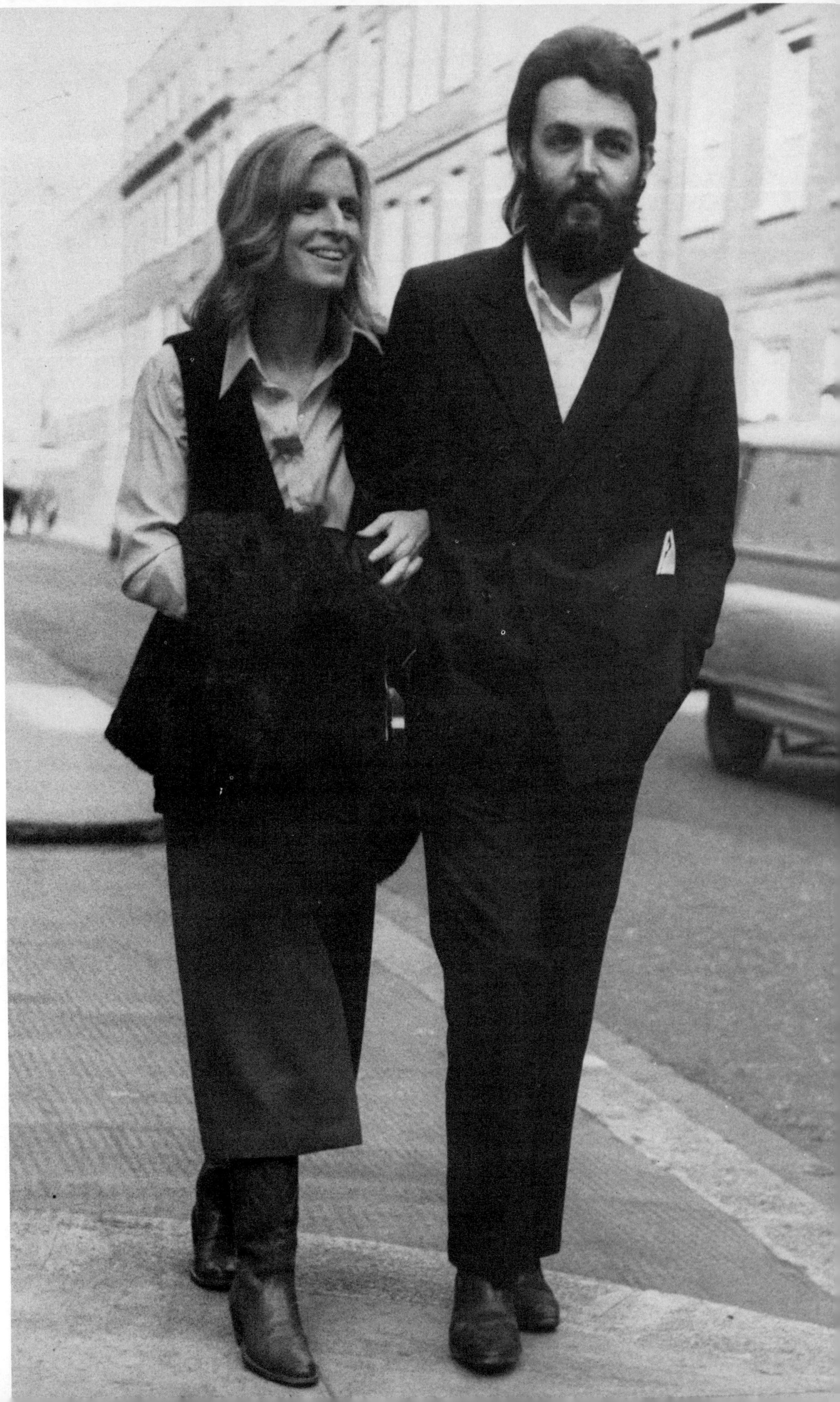

In 1971 Linda wrote 'Seaside Woman' and released the number on a single several years later in 1977 under the pseudonym Suzy and The Red Stripes (Red Stripe being a Jamaican beer). Linda also composed the music, together with Wings, for *The Oriental Nightfish*, an animated short by Ian Emes which won a special award at the Cannes film festival in 1978.

The McCartneys, despite their wealth, have opted for a life devoted to family and friends rather than one involving the celebrity night-life circuit that someone like Ringo Starr favours.

Linda's book of photographs was republished by Pavilion Books in England in 1982.

Joseph Jevans Senior registrar at Marylebone Register Office, London. He officiated at the wedding of Paul McCartney and Linda Eastman and also conducted the wedding ceremony between Ringo Starr and Barbara Bach. Both couples were married in the same room at the Register Office.

Mary Patricia McCartney Née Mohin. Mary was a nursing sister at the Liverpool Hospitals Walton and Alder Hey before she married Jim McCartney in a ceremony at St Swithen's Roman Catholic Chapel. She then gave up nursing and her first son Paul was born, followed 18 months later by Michael. Mary then became a midwife. One month after being told that she had breast cancer she was dead, on October 31st, 1956 at the age of 47, two days after she was admitted to hospital.

Allen Klein Stocky New York financial wheeler and dealer who had a dream of managing The Beatles and almost succeeded in his desire. Klein was born in New York on December 18th, 1931 but spent ten years in an orphanage because his father, a butcher, had abandoned him. He served a short time in the army before embarking on a career as an accountant specializing in the pop music business. He also became a publisher and began managing artists such as Sam Cooke and Bobby Vinton. He took over representation of The Rolling Stones and, while Brian Epstein still handled The Beatles, voiced his ambition of one day becoming their manager himself. He had formed a company, ABKO Industries, using the initials of himself and his wife: Allen and Betty Klein Co.

After the death of Brian, Mick Jagger recommended Klein to The Beatles but Paul McCartney, who had virtually taken over the running of the group after Brian's demise, had been negotiating with Lee Eastman to represent them and John Lennon had raised no objections. When John voiced his comment that he was broke and that Apple was in a financial mess, Klein saw his opportunity and flew to London, where he met John at the Dorchester Hotel. What impressed John most was Klein's knowledge of

A picture from the Clive Epstein collection of Beatles photographs available to members of The Beatles Fan Club

The Beatles' music. In the meantime, Paul had been pressing for the Eastmans to represent them and the lawyers had already made progress in their attempts to buy NEMS Enterprises, which held the group's management contracts and collected royalties on their behalf. A meeting was arranged at which both Klein and Eastman were present and John was so angered by Eastman's attitude and attacks on Klein that he decided to sign with him. John's sense of judgement was purely an emotional one and his decision probably led to the break-up of The Beatles. John wrote to his fellow Beatles to accept Klein as their representative and both George and Ringo agreed. John Eastman, Linda's brother, had almost concluded his arrangements to buy NEMS on behalf of The Beatles but Klein's intervention was a spanner in the works. Clive Epstein, who had wanted the company to go to The Beatles, became so fed up with the problems introduced by Klein's involvement that he sold his family's shares to Triumph Investments, who were able to take over the company. This would probably not have occurred if Klein hadn't been involved. The New York man then instigated a reign of terror at Apple itself, virtually sacking the entire staff, including many of the people who had been involved with The Beatles since the beginning. Old friends, loyal followers, were literally turfed out at a moment's notice by a man The Beatles hardly knew and they never raised a finger to consider their former friends as they were so obsessed with the idea that Klein was about to perform miracles. Paul seemed to be the only one who had doubts.

Klein next decided to participate in their efforts to buy up Northern Songs, the company founded in 1963 and commented: 'The Beatles were almost broke and didn't even have control over their own songs.' He failed in his bid to obtain the company for The Beatles and control of their music went to Sir Lew Grade's company, ATV. Klein was successful however in his dealings with EMI, obtaining a favourable new deal in which the group received 25 per cent of the wholesale price from their American sales. Paul was still disenchanted with the man and was advised that the only way he could prevent Klein from controlling his career and finances would be to sue the other members of The Beatles. Paul reluctantly instigated proceedings and in December 1970 the partnership was officially ended. Klein, however, still continued to reap rewards from The Beatles and in June 1973 sued John for £100,000. Later that year John, Paul and George all sued Klein themselves. Mick Jagger, who had originally recommended Klein to them, had turned sour on his former financial adviser and had broken away from the New York whizkid. He visited Apple one day to warn The Beatles about him but Klein turned up and Mick was reluctant to voice his opinion. In June 1977 The Beatles' company had to make an out-of-court settlement to Klein of over £2 million. Later that same year the lawyer/accountant was imprisoned for two months for tax evasion offences.

His personal story of the association with The Beatles is revealed in a major interview he conducted with *Playboy* magazine in 1971.

Ray Connolly Liverpool journalist who became a feature writer on London's *Evening Standard* in the late sixties. As their main writer covering the rock music scene he interviewed The Beatles on several occasions. He was due to fly to New York to interview John when he received a call from Yoko Ono informing him of the murder. In 1981 he wrote a biography of John, simply entitled *John Lennon 1940–1980*.

Peter Blake With Jan Hayworth he helped to design the cover of the *Sergeant Pepper's Lonely Hearts Club Band* album sleeve. The cost for the sleeve alone was more than the total production costs of most albums being made in the UK at the time. The idea of the sleeve evolved after the title song had been written. Originally the four were to wear Salvation Army suits, but they decided on special brightly coloured uniforms from Burman's, the major costumiers. Sixty-two of their idols were carefully placed in a montage, which also included the Madame Tussaud's waxwork models of The Beatles. The group's name was written in flowers in a setting of artificial grass placed in front of them. It was revealed some time later that one of the patches of grass was marijuana.

Ray Coleman Freelance journalist. Former editor of the British musical weeklies *Disc* and *Melody Maker* throughout the sixties and seventies. He interviewed The Beatles on various occasions and it was to Ray that John Lennon mentioned his feeling that The Beatles would be broke within six months if Apple kept on losing money. Ray left *Melody Maker* in 1981 to set up as a freelance writer and interviewed Yoko Ono for the British national press in 1982.

Lee Eastman Linda's father. A graduate of Harvard University who changed his name from Epstein to Eastman. His wife Louise was killed in an air crash. Together with his son, John, he was sent to represent The Beatles in their financial affairs in 1969 when Allen Klein appeared on the scene with the same idea in mind. Klein won, although the Eastmans continued to represent Paul McCartney in several matters.

Sir Lew Grade Head of ATV who successfully took control of Northern Songs in March 1969 despite a fierce battle by The Beatles to prevent him gaining a foothold in their publishing company. Grade had already lost a similar battle in which he tried to take over Chappell's Music, but this time he was able to do a deal with Dick James who, when he'd been an agent, had been one of his clients. The shares ATV bought off James enabled them to gain a stranglehold on Northern Songs and then obtain a controlling interest. Despite the coup, Paul agreed to work on one of Sir Lew's personal projects, a television special called *James Paul McCartney*. This ATV production was directed by Dwight Hewison and produced by Gary Smith. The programme made its début on American television on April 16th, 1973, and was shown in Britain for the first time on June 7th of the same year. A highlight was the spectacular Hollywood-style musical sequence in which Paul hoofed it with dozens of costumed dancers to the tune of 'Gotta Sing, Gotta Dance'. In contrast there were intimate pieces of film of Linda photographing Paul, Scottish scenes, a Liverpool pub singalong in which Gerry Marsden, former leader of Gerry and The Pacemakers, appeared. Paul's theme from the James Bond movie *Live And Let Die* was used with a clip from the film and Paul sang a Beatles medley. Among the songs featured in the programme were 'Long Tall Sally', 'Live And Let Die', 'Yesterday', 'Michelle', 'Maybe I'm Amazed', 'Blackbird/Bluebird', 'Heart Of The Country', 'Mary Had A Little Lamb', 'Little Woman Love', 'C Moon' and 'Uncle Albert/Admiral Halsey'.

Phil Spector Renowned record producer, born in New York on December 25th, 1940. Spector moved to Los Angeles with his widowed mother in the early fifties and in 1958 formed a trio called The Teddy Bears who had a major hit with 'To Know Him Is To Love Him'. As a producer he became internationally successful, creating a number of rock classics such as The Shirelles' 'Will You Still Love Me Tomorrow' and The Righteous Brothers' 'You've Lost That Loving Feeling'. In January, 1970, he arrived in England at the invitation of Allen Klein who wanted him to work on the many hours of *Let It Be* tapes. Spector met John Lennon who asked him to produce 'Instant Karma' and over

George Harrison with Phil Spector and The Ronettes

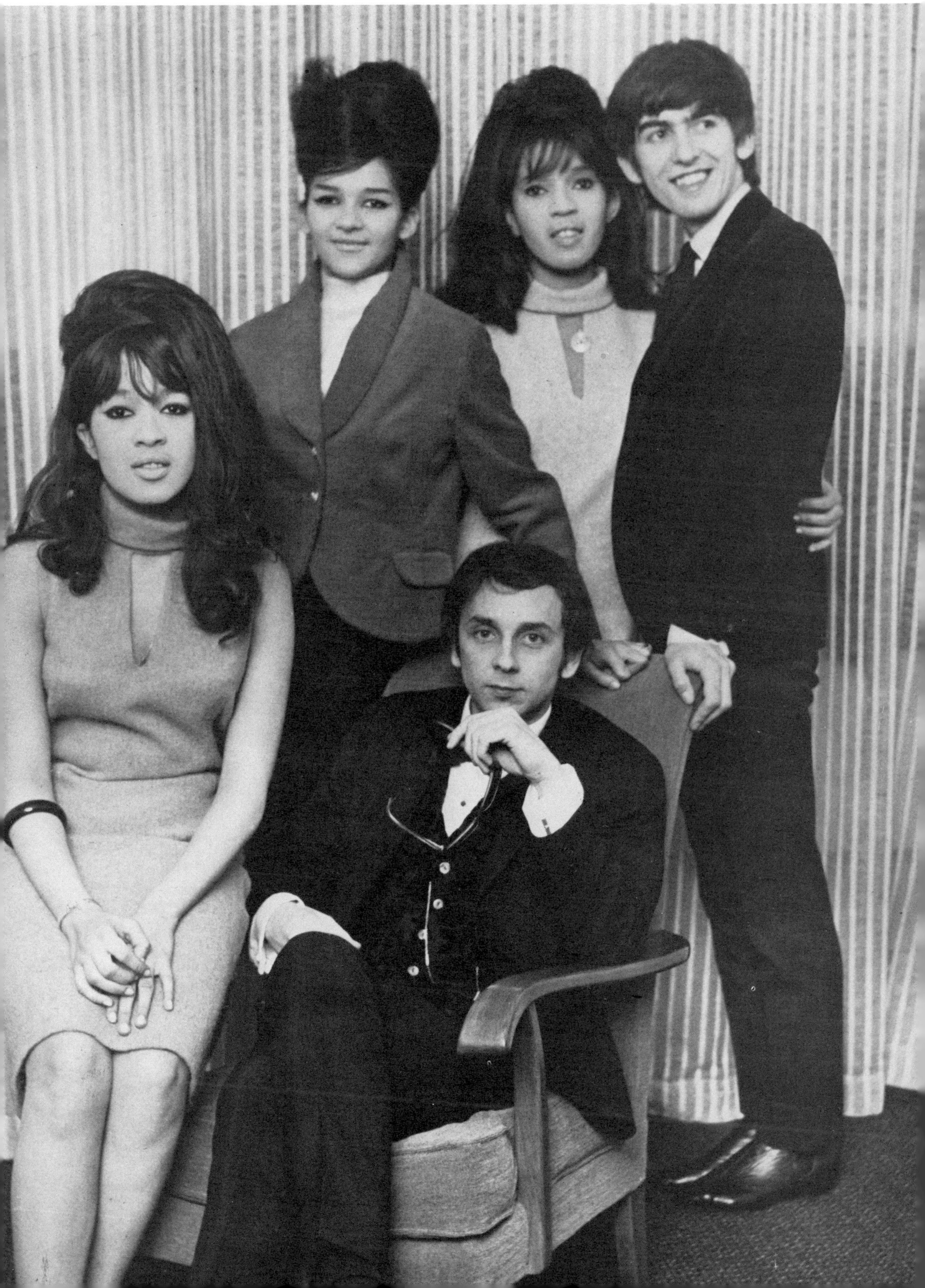

the years he produced several other singles and albums for John, including *The Plastic Ono Band*, *Image* and *Sometime In New York City*. He also co-produced *All Things Must Pass* with George Harrison and *The Concert For Bangladesh* album. However, Paul McCartney was less than pleased with what Spector did with the *Let It Be* tracks, particularly his own 'The Long And Winding Road', upset that Spector had added his own 'wall of sound' trademark to the track. Lennon was also to become disenchanted with Spector. John had the idea of recording his favourite rock numbers for an album tentatively called 'Oldies But Moldies' and when he was in California took the tapes to Spector. For months he was unable to get them back and when he finally did, he found he didn't like what Spector had done to them and considered that only four tracks were salvageable. So he re-recorded the rest of the material and issued them on the album *Rock 'n' Roll*.

Incidentally, in 1964 Spector recorded a novelty single called 'I Love Ringo' with Bonnie Joe Mason who later became successful as Cher.

Denny Laine Birmingham guitarist, born Brian Haynes on October 29th, 1944. He began his musical career with Denny Laine and The Diplomats and achieved initial fame with The Moody Blues and the recording of the No. 1 hit 'Go Now'. In 1965 he left 'The Moodies' and formed the Electric String Band, made up of classically trained violinists and cellists performing on amplified instruments. In 1967 he recorded 'Say You Don't Mind' and for a short time in 1969 was a member of Balls who recorded 'Fight For My Country', but remained together for only ten gigs. During the same period when Balls was in existence he was making appearances with Ginger Baker's Airforce. Tony Secunda produced his solo album 'Ahh . . . Laine' and Denny joined Wings in 1971 and recorded 'Wildlife' with them. Denny remained in Wings and, together with Paul and Linda, formed the core of the group, although he continues to embark on solo ventures. Paul produced his *Hollydays* album in 1977, an LP on which he sang and performed numbers associated with Buddy Holly.

Danny Seiwell American drummer, born in Leighton, Pennsylvania. He was a member of his school band and spent four years in the Army as a bandsman. During the sixties he was a jazz drummer in Chicago, then left for New York, appearing in jazz clubs there prior to becoming a session man. Following auditions Paul selected him to join him on the *Ram* recording sessions between January and March 1971 and then asked him to join Wings. He left the group on August 30th, 1973, before their trip to Lagos, Nigeria.

Henry McCullough An Irish guitarist who originally appeared with showbands and became associated with Chas. Chandler when he joined Eire Apparent, a group who toured with Jimi Hendrix. When the group disbanded he joined Sweeney's Men and then Joe Cocker's Grease Band. The Grease Band and Cocker split and continued on their own for a time. The Grease Band also broke up and, in 1973, McCullough joined Wings. He was only in the band for a short period as he seemed disenchanted with their musical policy and left on August 25th, 1973.

Jimmy McCulloch Glaswegian guitarist, born June 4th, 1953. He turned professional musician at the age of 13 wih 'One In A Million' and experienced his first taste of fame at the age of 16 when he was a member of Thunderclap Newman, who hit the No. 1 spot in the British charts in 1969 with 'Something In The Air'. He left the group to appear for a time with John Mayall and then joined Stone The Crows as a replacement for the late Les Harvey. When Stone The Crows disbanded in 1973 he joined Robert Stigwood's group, Blue. Jimmy had done session work for Paul McCartney on Mike McGear's album *McGear* and had also recorded in Paris with Linda. Paul used him on some Wings tracks recorded in Nashville in 1974 when he was over there recording Peggy Lee. In November 1974 Paul was able to announce that Jimmy had officially joined Wings. He left the group on September 8th, 1977, to join The Small Faces. He was found dead in mysterious circumstances in September 1979.

Marc Bolan British musician, born in 1948, who became a superstar in Britain prior to his tragic death in a car crash in September 1977. Ringo Starr was fascinated by the success of Marc's group, T. Rex, which produced some of the emotional scenes at concerts previously only experienced by The Beatles. They went on holiday to the Bahamas together, in company with their wives, and in 1972 Ringo decided to make a film of T. Rexmania, which he produced and directed for Apple Films at a concert at the Empire Pool, Wembley, in March. The film was only 67 minutes long and was co-scripted by Ringo and Marc, featuring the songs 'Marc's Intro', 'Jeepster', 'Baby Strange', 'Children Of The Revolution', 'Look To The Left', 'Space Ball Pickett', 'Telegram Sam', 'Cosmic Dancer', 'Hot Love', 'Get It On', 'The Slider', 'Union Hall Poem', 'Tutti Frutti' and 'Some People Like To Rock'. Marc was one of the many star names gathered to play on the album *Ringo*.

David Bowie British superstar who collaborated with John Lennon and Carlos Alomar on the song 'Fame'. Bowie was recording his album *Young Americans* at Sigma Sound Studios in Philadelphia and composed the song with John in the studio. John joined in on vocals towards the end of the track. 'Fame' became a million-seller, reaching No. 1 in America, where it remained for two weeks. It was issued in Britain in July 1975 and reached No. 17 in the charts.

Elton John Former office boy for Dick James who became a superstar in his own right. The Lennon/McCartney number 'Lucy In The Sky With Diamonds' provided him with his first single release not written by himself and Bernie Taupin. Issued in Britain on DJM DJS 340 on November 15th, 1974, it reached the No. 3 position and was in the charts for ten weeks. The single, which featured the John Lennon composition 'One Day At A Time' on the flip side was issued in the US on November 18th, 1974, on MCA 40344 and hit the No. 1 position for two weeks, remaining fourteen weeks in the charts. He also played organ and piano on John Lennon's record 'Whatever Gets You Thru The Night' and Lennon reciprocated by joining him on stage for a duet at Madison Square Garden in New York on Novem-

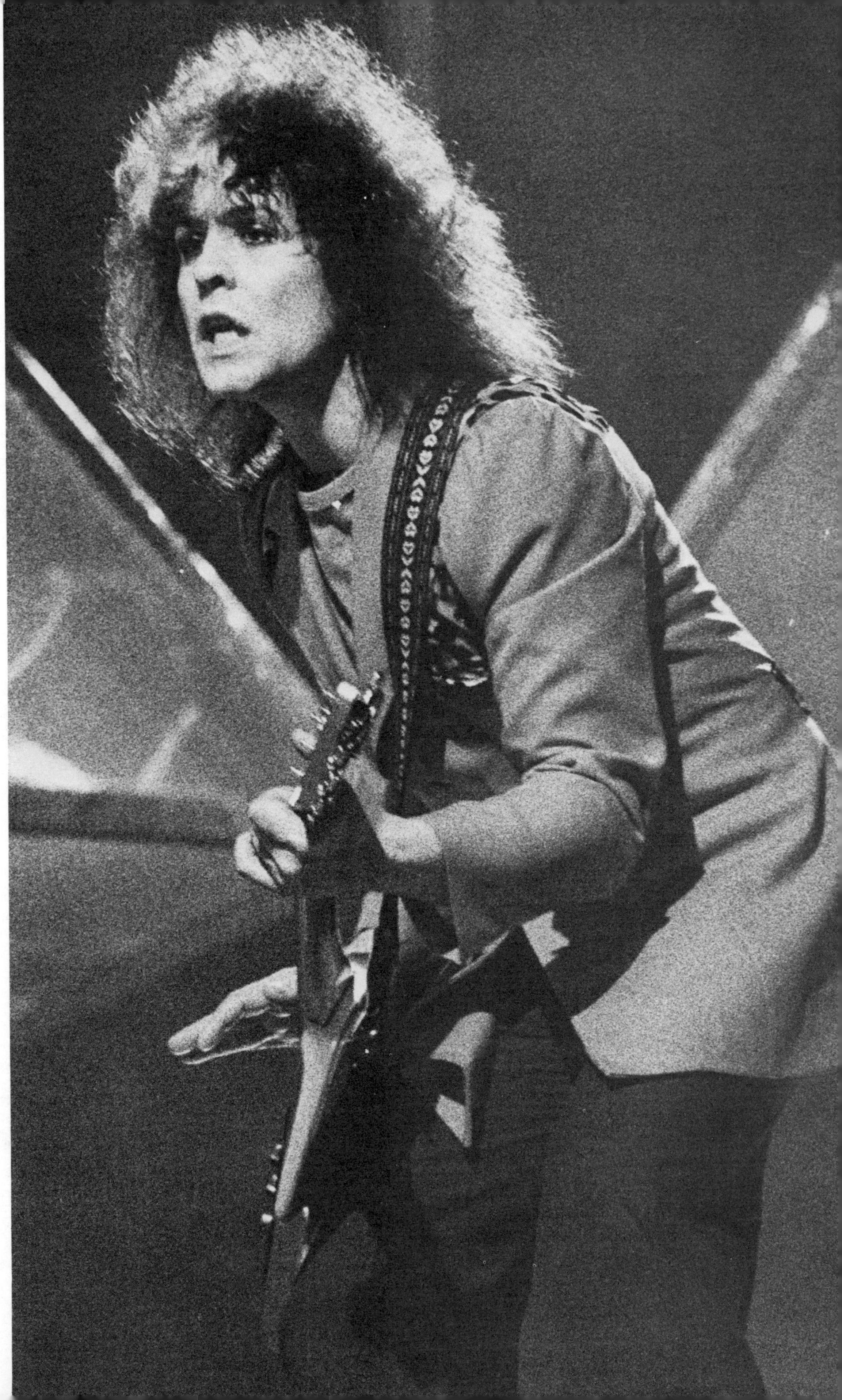

ber 28th, 1974, where they sang three numbers, 'Whatever Gets You Thru The Night', 'Lucy In The Sky With Diamonds' and 'I Saw Her Standing There'. The concert was recorded and the numbers were issued as an EP in Britain in 1981.

Norman Pilcher A detective-sergeant of Scotland Yard's Drug Squad who, with a team, arrived at Ringo Starr's flat in Montague Square, London, on October 18th, 1968, with a search warrant. John Lennon and Yoko Ono were staying at the premises in which cannabis resin was discovered and they were taken to Paddington Green police station and charged. They appeared at Marylebone Magistrate's Court the next day. John maintained that the hash had been planted in the flat. Pilcher was suspended from his job when he himself was arrested some time later.

Anthony Fawcett Born in Hillingdon Heath in 1948, Anthony studied art at Oxford and became an art critic for various magazines. He first met John Lennon and Yoko Ono in 1968 and became involved in organizing a number of artistic projects with them which resulted in his being invited to work full time for them as an assistant. He spent two years with them and his reminiscences of the period are documented in his book *One Day At A Time*.

Eva Majlata Actress who, when she was 21, starred in the film *Rape (Film No. 6)*, which was the first Lennon–Ono film venture to receive a favourable press from the critics. Willie Frischaer wrote in the London *Evening Standard* that it did 'for the age of television what

The late Marc Bolan, close friend of Ringo

Franz Kafka's *The Trial* did for the age of totalitarian justice'. The 73-minute movie produced by Hans Preiner, John Lennon and Yoko Ono had its world premier on Austrian television on March 31st, 1969.

Eva appeared as a Hungarian refugee who is pursued relentlessly by prying cameras which almost drive her mad. The film also received a showing at the Montreux TV Festival. Following the television début, John and Yoko conducted a press conference the following day, April 1st, in the Red Room of the Sacher Hotel in Vienna where they held their discourse with the press within the confines of a large white bag. Commenting on the film, John said: 'We are showing how all of us are exposed and under pressure in our contemporary world. This isn't just about The Beatles. What is happening to this girl on the screen is happening in Biafra, Vietnam, everywhere.'

Joe Davey Joe was a small, slightly stocky figure with a Kaiser Bill moustache and goatee. He ran Joe's Café in Duke Street which became one of the regular early morning haunts for groups seeking a meal after a gig or a drinking session at the Blue Angel club. We usually went there between 2 and 4 a.m. and taxi drivers and ladies of the night were among the clientele. We used to have our chicken curries on the first floor. Brian and The Beatles, in particular, enjoyed the place and Joe was able to build a 'Wall of Fame' in the upstairs room with photographs of his musician customers. He came to like the Mersey Beat scene so much that when the Cavern came up for grabs on April 18th, 1966, he bought it. However, it proved to be a far bigger economic burden than he'd imagined and he sold it again.

Dr Arthur Janov American psychologist who developed a method of psychoanalysis called 'Primal Therapy'. John Lennon and Yoko Ono were so impressed with his book *The Primal Scream* that they undertook a course of his special therapy. Janov flew to England to supervise their initial sessions personally for a period of three weeks in 1971. John and Yoko then spent four months in Los Angeles at the Primal Institute undergoing further analysis.

Sean Lennon John Lennon and Yoko Ono's only child, born on John's birthday, October 9th, 1975, and weighing 8lb 10oz. John commented, 'I feel as high as the Empire State Building' as the couple's previous expectations of a child had ended in miscarriages. John decided to spend five years of his life bringing Sean up and was to enjoy the undoubted pleasures of fatherhood that a growing child can bring.

May Pang Japanese secretary to Yoko Ono in New York who ran off with John Lennon to Los Angeles soon after he'd finished his *Mind Games* album. They lived together in LA for several months and some writers have commented that Yoko herself gave tacit approval to the affair.

Timothy Leary American intellectual and leading figure in the use and exploration of psychedelic drugs in the sixties. His book *Psychedelic Experience* which he co-wrote with Richard Alpert, based on *The Egyptian Book Of The Dead*, inspired John Lennon to write the number 'Tomorrow Never Knows'. Leary visited John and Yoko at the Queen Elizabeth Hotel in Montreal and partici-

On stage with Elton John, a John Lennon session recorded for posterity

pated in the recording of 'Give Peace A Chance' when John had a mobile recording unit installed in his suite. Leary called The Beatles 'divine messiahs'.

Elephant's Memory New York band used to back John Lennon on a few live gigs. It comprised Adam Ippolito, Gary Van Scyoc, Stan Bronstein, Wayne Gabriel and Rick Frank. Lennon also used them on his *Sometime In New York City* album and they were signed to Apple Records in 1972 and released a single, 'Liberation', and an album, *Elephant's Memory*. They also backed Yoko Ono on several occasions.

David Peel Greenwich Village street singer whom John Lennon and Yoko Ono met when they moved to New York to live in 1971. Together they produced an album of him performing his material. Entitled *The Pope Smokes Dope* and issued in America on Apple SW 3391 on April 17th, 1972, it contained one Lennon/Ono number: 'The Ballad Of New York City'. In 1977 he recorded an album and single called 'Bring Back The Beatles' for the Orange label. The album (Orange 004) contained the tracks: 'The Beatles Pledge Of Allegiance'; 'Bring Back The Beatles'; 'Coconut Grove'; 'Imagine'; 'Turn Me On'; 'Lollipop Fish'; 'The Wonderful World of Abbey Road'; 'Apple Beatle Foursome'; 'The Ballad Of James Paul McCartney'; 'With A Little Help From My Friends'; 'My Fat Budgie'; 'Keep John Lennon In America' and 'B-E-A-T-L-E-S'.

L'Angelo Misterioso Pseudonym used by George when he played rhythm guitar on the 'Never Tell Your Mother She's Out Of Tune' track on the Jack Bruce album *Songs For A Tailor*.

George O'Hara Smith Pseudonym used by George Harrison when he played guitar on the 'I'm Your Spiritual Breadman' track on *The Worst Of Ashton, Gardner And Dyke* album. He also used the pseudonym George O'Hara on the Nicky Hopkins *The Tin Man Was A Dreamer* album.

Eric Clapton Born in Surrey on March 30th, 1945, Eric Clapton was to become one of Britain's premier rock guitarists. His first band was called Roosters and for a few weeks in October 1963 he was a member of Casey Jones and The Engineers (the same Casey Jones who once led Cass and The Cassanovas). He then joined the legendary Yardbirds before becoming a member of Cream. His spell in Blind Faith was less successful.

Eric became a friend of The Beatles and played the guitar solo on *While My Guitar Gently Weeps* on the *White Album*. He accepted John Lennon's invitation to play with him in the Plastic Ono Band and appears on the album *Live Peace In Toronto*. He has played on albums by all members of The Beatles in their solo years, including George Harrison's *All Things Must Pass*, *Dark Horse* and *George Harrison*, Ringo's *Rotogravure* and Wings' *Back To The Egg*.

He was invited by John to perform at a Peace gig at the Lyceum, London, the other artists including George Harrison, Keith Moon, Billy Preston and Delaney and Bonnie. He also accepted George's invitation to appear at Madison Square Garden, New York, for *The Concert For Bangladesh*.

His personal life became inextricably wound up with that of his mate George

John with May Pang

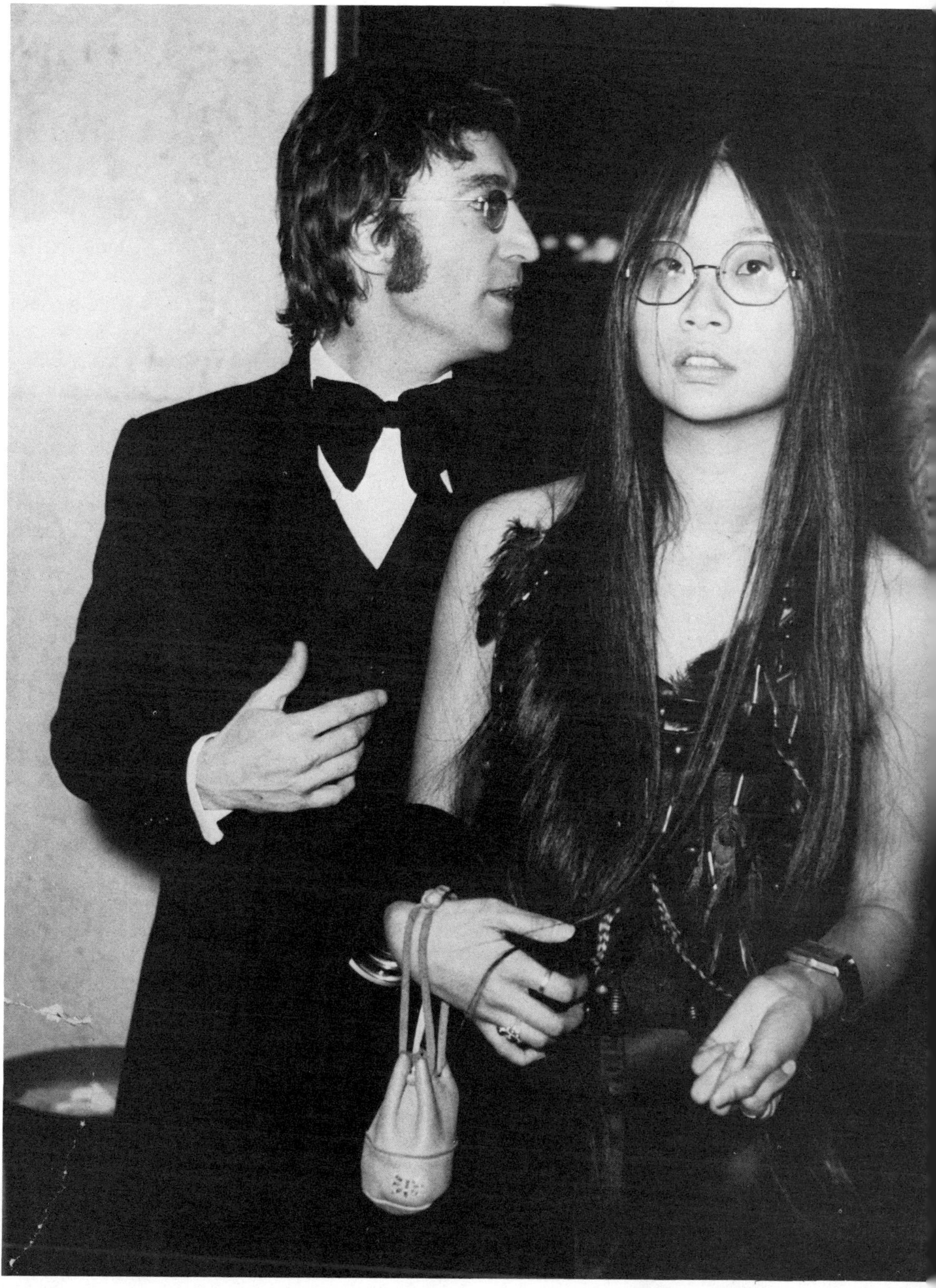

Harrison when he fell in love with Patti. He wrote a love song 'dedicated to the wife of my best friend'. Based on the Persian love story of Layla and Majnun it was called, simply, 'Layla'. Eric recorded it under the pseudonym of Derek and The Dominoes. It barely touched the bottom end of the charts when it was issued at the beginning of 1971 and he became depressed. It was re-issued the following year, however, and entered the Top Ten in Britain in August, having made a high showing in the American charts in May. It was re-released ten years later and entered the British Top Ten in March 1982.

Patti and George were drifting apart and she left him to join her sister Jenny and Jenny's husband Mick Fleetwood in Los Angeles for a time. Eric, who had been in America completing an album, invited her to join him on tour. They married in Tucson, Arizona in March 1979. Two months later they held a party in Britain to which a number of close friends were invited. During the course of the evening Paul McCartney, George Harrison and Ringo Starr took to the stage and began to play, accompanied by Eric and Denny Laine — it was almost like a Beatles reunion!

William Russell Liverpool schoolteacher whose first major stage show was *John, Paul, George, Ringo . . . And Bert*, based on *The Beatles Story* and first presented at the Everyman theatre in Liverpool. It then moved to London's West End where it won a special award from the London *Evening Standard*. An album of the music featured in the play, entitled *John, Paul, George, Ringo . . . And Bert* was issued in Britain on November 8th, 1974, on RSO 2394-141 by the original London cast featuring Barbara Dickson. The tracks were: 'I Should Have Known Better'; 'Your Mother Should Know'; 'With A Little Help From My Friends'; 'Penny Lane'; 'Here Comes The Sun'; 'Long And Winding Road'; 'Help!'; 'Lucy In The Sky With Diamonds'; 'You Never Give Me Your Money'; 'Carry That Weight'; 'We Can Work It Out' and 'A Day In The Life'.

Willie Russell went on to write several plays for television and the stage, all basically featuring working-class Liverpudlians and their biting humour.

Buddy Holly One of rock music's greatest legends who died in an aircrash with Ritchie Valens and The Big Bopper on February 3rd, 1959. Many years later Holly's manager, Norman Petty, was to present Paul McCartney with the cufflinks that Holly was wearing at the time of his death. Buddy Holly was an early influence on The Beatles and in their formative years they performed many of his songs. When they appeared on the talent contest organized by Carol Levis they played two of Holly's numbers, 'Think It Over' and 'It's So Easy'. It has been suggested that the original suggestion of Beetles as a name for the group came about because it was inspired by the name of Holly's backing band, The Crickets. Paul McCartney was the major Buddy Holly fan and his MPL Communications managed to purchase the Buddy Holly music catalogue of approximately 38 Holly copyrights. Paul then began to sponsor a 'Buddy Holly Week' in London each year to tie in with the September 7th anniversary of his birth. John Lennon

Eric Clapton, George's best friend who fell in love with Patti

was to pay his own tribute to Holly on his 1975 album *Rock 'n' Roll* which featured the track 'Peggy Sue'.

Stevie Wonder Stevie Wonder has been blind from his birth in May 1950. He came to the attention of Berry Gordy Jr of Tamla Motown Records in Detroit and his first album was *Recorded Live — The 12 Year Old Genius*. He also topped the American charts with 'Fingertips' when he was 13. In Liverpool the Oriole-America releases of Tamla acts were popular and Stevie came to the attention of people there before he became known in the rest of Britain. Over the years he has produced some superb recordings, developing into a mature songwriter. His albums include *Music Of My Mind, Innervisions* and *Songs In The Key Of Life*. Paul McCartney had always been a Wonder fan and he visited the star's Wembley concerts in London in 1980. He had already decided he wanted to work with Stevie and even invited him to record with him in Montserrat in 1981. The two of them recorded 'Ebony And Ivory' which became a No. 1 hit on both sides of the Atlantic in May 1982.

Charles Manson Leader of a bizarre cult whose members believed him to be some sort of Satanic messiah. Like a Svengali he seemed to hold his 'family' in a mesmeric power. Manson was obsessed by The Beatles' music and believed that the records contained mystical messages which he could interpret. He was certain that The Beatles were the four angels mentioned in the 'Book of Revelations'. If *Sergeant Pepper's Lonely Hearts Club Band* excited him, the *White Album* sent him into paroxysms of delight because he felt he could translate the messages on that particular double LP. 'Blackbird', 'Piggies', 'Happiness Is A Warm Gun' and 'Helter Skelter' were among the numbers which led him to believe that The Beatles had predicted a violent confrontation between the races, leading to a civil war in America. He decided to provide the spark for the coming revolution and sent some of his crazed followers into Beverley Hills where they committed some grisly murders. He is currently serving a life sentence.

Olivia Trinidad Arias Born in Mexico in 1948, Olivia was educated in America and graduated at Hawthorne High School, California. She remained in Los Angeles and went to work at A&R Records as a secretary, where she first met George Harrison in 1974. George was impressed by the serene, dark-haired beauty and engaged her to work for his own Dark Horse Records. The couple became close friends and when George fell ill following a number of problems relating to his marriage breakdown and a slump in his recording career, she recommended that he visit Dr Zion Yua, a noted Chinese acapuncturist, who cured him. George realized that he had found his soul mate and the two became inseparable on his travels around America. George also took her to visit Liverpool. They lived in splendour in Los Angeles for a while but it became apparent that Olivia was not particularly impressed by the lavish life style over there and the two of them moved to the tranquillity of the English countryside, to

James Coburn, Lynsey de Paul, Ringo Starr and Jack Nicholson

George's mansion, Friar Park, in Henley-on-Thames. Their son, Dhani (the word means 'wealthy' in Hindu), was born on August 1st, 1978, and George and Olivia were married by special licence at Henley Register Office on September 7th, 1978.

Nancy Andrews American actress/model who lived with Ringo Starr from

1974 until 1980. Nancy was cited as co-respondent in the divorce case brought by Maureen Starkey in 1975. Nancy moved to Monte Carlo with Ringo but became bored with the place. It's claimed that Ringo promised her that they would get married on several occasions during the six-year period. When Ringo began his relationship with Barbara Bach, Nancy started a law suit, claiming a percentage of his assets as compensation for the acting career which she claimed she gave up in order to look after him. She is credited with co-writing the song 'Las Brisas' with him, a track from the *Rotogravure* album.

Lynsey De Paul Diminutive British singer, noted for her well-publicized romances. She began an affair with Ringo Starr in 1976 which lasted for several months and ended when he left London to become a tax exile. She wrote a song for him entitled 'If I Don't Get You — The Next One Will'.

Stephanie La Motta Adopted daughter of ex-boxer Jake La Motta (featured in the film *The Raging Bull*). She moved to England and became a favourite of the gossip columnists, haunting all the fashionable clubs, such as Tramps and Stringfellows, and revealing details of her affairs with celebrities, such as Liverpool ex-world champion boxer John Conteh, in the newspapers. She had a well-publicized affair with Ringo Starr and in 1981 began taking Julian Lennon under her wing. She bought Julian a white horse for his 19th birthday which she presented to him at Stringfellow's in March 1982 during a party in which models were photographed topless.

Barbara Bach Barbara was born in New York City in 1951. She shortened her surname from Goldbach and became a leading American model. She married and moved to Rome where her European origins (Rumanian grand-

The new Mrs Starr: Barbara Bach met Ringo on the set of Caveman

mother, Irish mother, Austrian father) helped her secure roles in several international films. Whilst in Rome she was divorced from her first husband. She starred with Roger Moore in the James Bond movie *The Spy Who Loved Me*, portrayed the evil Lady Agatha in the Italian sci-fi epic *The Humanoid* and her other films include *Force Ten At Navaronne, The Jaguar lives, The Volcanic Island* and *The Unseen*. She met Ringo when she co-starred with him as Lana, a prehistoric beauty in the film *Caveman*.

The couple were married on Monday, April 27th, 1981 at Marylebone Register Office in London. Wedding guests included George and Olivia Harrison and Paul and Linda McCartney. Sixty guests and relatives then celebrated at the London club, Rags. Barbara wore a cream satin suit, made by the Emanuels, who designed the famous wedding dress for Diana, Princess of Wales.

Roy Carr Special Projects editor of the *New Musical Express* and co-author, with Tony Tyler, of *The Beatles Illustrated Records*. An early contributor to the newspaper, *Mersey Beat*, Roy also pursued a career as a musician before becoming a full-time writer.

Mike Evans Born in Rhyl, North Wales in 1941, Mike moved to Liverpool and became a member of The Clayton Squares. Later he was to join The Liverpool Scene and remained with them until they disbanded in 1970. He was a member of various bands before joining the staff of the Musicians' Union as Rock Organizer. Mike wrote *Nothing To Get Hung About*, a short Beatles book contained in the Liverpool Corporation package *The Beatles Collection*. He also co-authored *In The Footsteps Of The Beatles* with Ron Jones, published by Merseyside County Council in a limited edition of 5,000 copies in 1981.

Tony Jasper Prolific British writer and broadcaster, author of two dozen books, half of them on pop music, the others on religion. Tony wrote *Paul McCartney and Wings*, first published by Octopus Books in 1977.

Nicholas Schaffner American musician/author, born in New York in 1953, who produced several articles about The Beatles for a number of US publications before writing *The Beatles Forever*, his first book, published in 1978, which was followed by *The Boys From Liverpool* in 1980.

Philip Norman I first met Philip Norman in the early seventies when he wrote a lengthy feature on Suzi Quatro for *The Sunday Times*. We were all impressed by the amount of time he spent researching the article, the diligence of his approach and his quiet, friendly manner. Some years later he contacted me when he'd begun to research a book on The Beatles. At the time *The Sunday Times* had been involved in a lengthy strike and several of its feature writers were engaged in book projects. Philip mentioned that he'd been frustrated in his attempts to contact The Beatles directly and I gave him the addresses and phone numbers of various people including Joe Flannery, Millie Sutcliffe, Henri Henriod and Johnny Gustafson. His project took three years and the result was *Shout! The True Story Of The Beatles*, an immediate best-seller when it was published in 1981 and one of the most thoroughly researched and engrossing Beatles books of them all. He then began to tour America and Britain, featuring extensively on radio and television shows to promote the book and while in New York received an invitation to visit Yoko Ono, which resulted in a lengthy and highly detailed *Sunday Times* article. It amazed me how he could remember so much when he never seemed to take notes until I was told that he had the gift of instant recall — almost a photographic memory. Following The Beatles project he became involved in research for a similar blockbuster on The Rolling Stones.

Mark Lapidos Together with his wife, Carol, Mark is now full-time promoter of a stream of Beatles conventions which he presents annually in New York, Los Angeles, San Francisco and Atlanta. Mark launched his first 'Beatlefest' in New York in 1974.

Liz and Jim Hughes Founders of Cavern Mecca, the first-ever Beatles museum, situated at 18 Matthew Street, Liverpool, on the corner of the street where the original Cavern was situated. The couple moved to the premises in 1980 from their former shop where they had sold Beatles memorabilia. The museum, which has 2,000 square feet of space, has a mock Cavern area, a coffee bar and souvenir counter. The two Liverpudlians are dedicated fans and have now instigated annual Liverpool Beatles conventions.

Jaap Eggermont Dutch record producer, former drummer with the group Golden Earrings, who devised the Beatles medley disc *Stars on 45* which took Lennon and McCartney compositions to the top of the American charts for the first time since 1975 when Elton John had a No. 1 hit with 'Lucy In The Sky With Diamonds'. The musicians who simulated The Beatles sound were: Bas Nuys (Lennon), Okki Huysdens (McCartney) and Hans Vermeulen (Harrison).

John Blake Major British journalist, specializing in rock music. Throughout the seventies he provided a daily column 'Ad Lib' for London's *Evening News*, taking over the reins from David Wigg, and on the amalgamation of that paper with the *Evening Standard*, continued with his column in the new revamped publication. He regularly reported on the activities of the former members of The Beatles and in 1981 his book *All You Needed Was Love (The Beatles After The Beatles)* was published. In 1982 he moved to *The Sun* newspaper.

David Wigg David Wigg has been a *Daily Express* show business correspondent for a number of years and formerly produced a music column for the London *Evening News*. He interviewed members of The Beatles on several occasions and a Polydor album containing a compilation of the tapes was issued on Polydor 2683 068 on July 30th, 1976. The double-album set was released following a court case which had taken place because of an injunction on the record. The set came complete with an eight-page booklet of photographs and contains the interviews David conducted between the years 1968 and 1972. The interviews with John Lennon and Yoko Ono are entitled 'Give Peace A Chance', 'Imagine' and 'Come Together'; the Paul McCartney interviews are called 'Because', 'Yesterday' and 'Hey Jude'; the George Harrison interviews, 'Here Comes The Sun' and 'Something' and the Ringo Starr interviews, 'Octopus's Garden' and 'Yellow Submarine'.

John Lennon The senseless murder of John Lennon on December 8th, 1980 shocked the world. It also ended any further hope of The Beatles getting together again for a concert, recording session or TV appearance. The world mourned one of rock's greatest geniuses. For there is no doubt that of all four members of The Beatles it was John who had the most charisma. He was a man bursting with ideas, eager to express himself not only in music but as a film-maker and artist.

When The Beatles finally broke up, John didn't miss them: he was already part of another team. He and Yoko were a duo who aroused controversy, criticism and acclaim. In her, John had found his perfect partner, a mature woman who was able to involve him in many artistic adventures ranging from art exhibitions (including the famous Erotic Lithographs) to film-making. The Lennons made numerous movie shorts, including *Fly, Erection, Rape, Honeymoon, Self-Portrait, Two Virgins, Cold Turkey, The Ballad Of John and Yoko, Give Peace A Chance, Instant Karma* and *Up Your Legs*.

Following the demise of The Beatles he had no difficulty in finding talented musicians to back him, creating The Plastic Ono Band and using the New York group Elephant's Memory.

His albums include: *John Lennon/Plastic Ono Band, Imagine, Some Time In New York City, Live Peace In Toronto,*

John in How I Won The War

Mind Games, Walls And Bridges, Rock 'n' Roll, Shaved Fish and *Double Fantasy*.

His singles include: 'Power To The People', 'Happy Christmas (War Is Over)', 'Whatever Gets You Thru The Night', 'No. 9 Dream', 'Imagine', 'Starting Over', 'Watching The Wheels' and 'Woman' — a relatively small collection of recordings when compared to the releases of Paul McCartney, but this is due to the five or so years of semi-retirement in which John decided he would stay at home and look after his son Sean.

In the early seventies John and Yoko moved to New York. John fell in love with the city and was to remain in America for the rest of his life. Initially he had problems because a deportation order had been served on him on account of his having been convicted for possessing cannabis in England. The deportation order was finally withdrawn, after a long legal battle, in October 1975. In July 1976 he was awarded a Green Card which enabled him to live permanently in America.

For a period of eighteen months, at the time of the *Mind Games* album, John left Yoko and moved to California, taking Yoko's secretary May Pang with him. However, the couple were reunited in New York where they had several apartments in the famous Dakota Buildings. In 1980 John decided that he would record and tour again. Together with Yoko he recorded an album, *Double Fantasy*, at New York's Hit Factory recording studios. A number of interviews with radio disc jockeys and journalists was arranged and John began to make plans for a forthcoming tour. Cruelly, the assassin struck and the world was left the poorer.

Paul McCartney Paul was the one who strove to keep The Beatles together after the death of Brian Epstein and, ironically, he was the one who set the wheels in motion for the group to be disbanded. Reluctant to have Allen Klein control his business affairs, Paul was advised that the only way he could prevent this happening was by taking the other members of the group to court and requesting that the partnership be wound up.

He received a special award from *The Guinness Book Of Records* who acknowledged that he was the most successful songwriter of all time, having participated in 43 songs which sold over a million copies between the years 1962 and 1978.

His albums include: *McCartney, Ram, Wild Life, Red Rose Speedway, Band On The Run, Venus & Mars, Wings At The Speed Of Sound, Wings Over America, London Town, Wings Greatest, Back To The Egg, McCartney II* and *Tug Of War*.

His singles include: 'Another Day', 'The Back Seat Of My car', 'Give Ireland Back To The Irish', 'Mary Had A Little Lamb', 'Hi Hi Hi', 'My Love', 'Live And Let Die', 'Helen Wheels', 'Band On The Run', 'Junior's Farm', 'Listen To What The Man Said', 'Letting Go', 'Venus & Mars — Rock Show', 'Silly Love Songs', 'Let 'em In', 'Mull Of Kintyre', 'With A Little Luck', 'I've Had Enough', 'London Town', 'Goodnight Tonight', 'Old Siam, Sir', 'Getting Closer', 'Wonderful Christmastime', 'Coming Up', 'Waterfalls', 'Temporary Secretary' and 'Ebony And Ivory'.

Following his first solo album which he produced himself and on which he played most of the instruments, he arranged for Linda to participate in his second LP, 'Ram'. He'd decided that

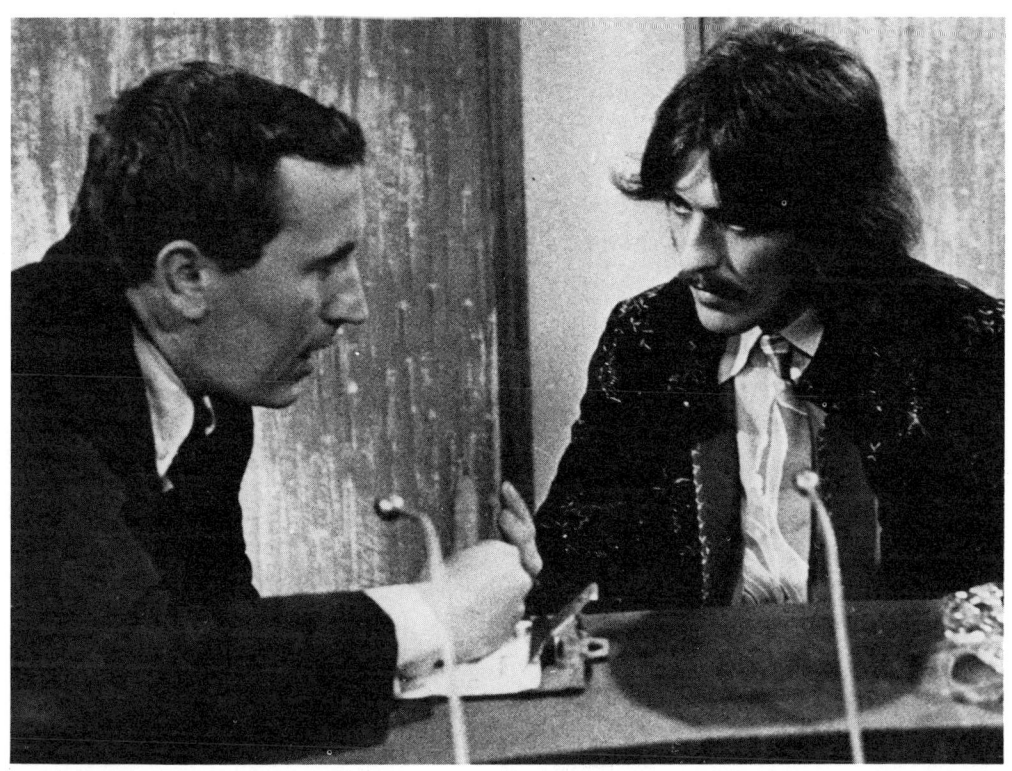

George Harrison guesting on The David Frost Show

Linda should become a part of his world and taught her to play keyboards. Together with Denny Laine, the trio formed the basis of Wings, the group with which McCartney recorded and toured throughout the seventies. Wings finally disbanded in April, 1981. The group had a sensational world tour and a film was made of their concert at Seattle in 1976 and issued as the film *Rockshow* in American cinemas in 1980 and in Britain the following year.

An album was also released of the *Concert For Kampuchea* in which Wings had participated, and on February 23rd, 1981 an album called *The Mccartney Interview* was issued for one day only and immediately withdrawn, making it a collectors' item.

Paul also made a number of drawings to illustrate his songs, these were published in *Paul McCartney: Composer and Artist* (Pavilion Books, 1981).

In addition to his recording career, Paul found himself at the helm of a music catalogue which represented a range of hit material, from Buddy Holly's songs to major stage musicals such as *Annie*.

For some reason writers and critics seemed to resent Paul during the seventies, and he came in for a lot of criticism. His position in The Beatles was also questioned in the TV film *Birth Of The Beatles* and the book *Shout!*, both of which had a John Lennon bias and relegated Paul to a lesser position. He was not one for the headlines, even though he had always appreciated the value of public relations. He decided he wanted a family life and moved out of London, although he still retained his house in Cavendish Avenue. Following the death of John he became unnerved for a time, which probably explains why he disbanded Wings as he was being reluctant to go on the road again. He also had his country house fenced off against intruders, which caused a newspaper to coin the world 'Paulditz' (a reference to the German prisoner-of-war camp, Colditz).

His studio work was not affected, however, and he began to team up with Tamla artists such as Stevie Wonder and Michael Jackson.

George Harrison George, the youngest member of The Beatles, was very much in the Lennon/McCartney shadow during the heyday of the Beatles, although the first story ever written about a Beatles recording, in issue No.2 of *Mersey Beat*, stated that the only original Beatle composition recorded by the group in Germany was George's 'Cry For A Shadow'. When the group began its rise to fame and the Lennon/McCartney songs dominated, I goaded George into writing again. He finally sat down and wrote 'Don't Bother Me', which was featured in *A Hard Day's Night*. Then he seemed to fade into the background once more.

He began to emerge as a major talent in his own right with the interest in Eastern music during the days of the Maharishi and Ravi Shankar. It was Allen Klein who finally saw to it that a George Harrison composition was issued as a Beatles 'A' side with 'Something', a number he'd originally written with Joe Cocker in mind. Although it only reached No. 4 in Britain, it topped the charts in the States. This gave George a degree of confidence and the *Let It Be* film shows him finally preparing to emerge from the shadow of John and Paul. His next major triumph was *The Concert For Bangladesh*.

Following the break up of The Beatles he consolidated his solo career with some fine releases, and although his marriage to Patti Boyd came to an end, he later married Olivia and they had a son, Dhani. George had bought a Victorian mansion called Friar Park in Henley-on-Thames for £140,000 but he paid far more than that for a huge manor house in Letchmore which he bought for the International Society of Krishna Consciousness.

Apart from his own recordings, he produced and appeared on various records using pseudonyms and for a time had his own record label, Dark Horse, which promoted groups such as Splinter, who had a hit with 'Costa Fine Town'.

Throughout the seventies George became interested in motor racing and developed a friendship with drivers such as Jackie Stewart and James Hunt, in addition to paying frequent visits to the Grand Prix circuit. Through another friend, Eric Idle, he helped to finance the Monty Python film *Life Of Brian*, which was a major success, and he took a financial interest in Handmade Films, which produced *The Time Bandits* and distributed *The Long Good Friday*.

Since leaving The Beatles he has had several album releases, including: *All Things Must Pass, The Concert For Bangladesh, Living In The Material World, Dark Horse, Extra Texture—Read All About It, The Best Of George Harrison, Thirty Three And A Third, George Harrison, Somewhere In England* and *By George!*

His singles have included: 'My Sweet Lord', 'Bangladesh', 'Give Me Love', 'Ding Dong', 'Dark Horse, 'You', 'This

Ringo, learning how to smell the roses

Guitar', 'This Song', 'True Love', 'Woman Don't You Cry For Me', 'Blow Away', 'All Those Years Ago' and 'Teardrops'. Of these the most controversial was 'My Sweet Lord'. This was the subject of a lengthy court case due to the resemblance of the tune to 'He's So Fine', an early hit for The Chiffons. George eventually lost the case and in 1981 had to pay £266,000 damages.

He also wrote a book, with the aid of Derek Taylor, called *I, Me, Mine*.

His early interest in film music, evident from his work in *Wonderwall*, was able to find expression via Handmade Films and he wrote the title music for *The Time Bandits*.

Ringo Starr Ringo felt himself to be an outsider when he first joined The Beatles, as they were already Liverpool's leading group. he was not as conventionally handsome as the other three, but his personality soon emerged and he became one of the most popular members of the group in America. Not having the songwriting expertise of John, Paul or George, he found a new outlet of expression in films, following his success with the critics in *A Hard Day's Night*. Apart from The Beatles films, he starred as Emmanuel, the Mexican gardener in *Candy*, as Peter Sellers' son Youngman Grand in *The Magic Christian* and as an engaging bandit in *Blindman*. Other movies followed: with Harry Nilsson as co-star in *Son Of Dracula* and *Harry And Ringo's Night Out*, as the Pope in Ken Russell's *Liztomania*, as Frank Zappa in *200 Motels* and as Mike, a fairground worker, in *That'll Be The Day*, another performance acclaimed by the critics. He also produced *Born To Boogie*, starring his friend Marc Bolan. In 1981 *Caveman*, in which he starred as Atouk, was released.

Ringo's first solo album, *Sentimental Journey*, was followed by *Beaucoups Of Blues, Ringo, Goodbye Vienna, Blast From Your Past, Ringo's Rotogravure, Ringo The 4th, Bad Boy* and *Stop And Smell The Roses*. The December 1973 release *Ringo* was one of his most popular albums, with songs written specially for him by John and Paul and backing music provided by a number of friends including John, Paul and George, Klaus Voorman, Linda McCartney, Harry Nilsson, Billy Preston, Marc Bolan, The Band and Martha Reeves.

His singles included: 'It Don't Come Easy', 'Back Off Boogaloo', 'Photograph', 'You're Sixteen', 'Only You', 'Snookeroo', 'A Dose Of Rock 'n' Roll', 'Drowning In A Sea Of Love', 'Tonight' and 'Wrack My Brain'. His early singles were major sellers and went high in the charts, but lately he has had only limited response to his releases and 'Wrack My Brain' didn't even enter the British charts. In May 1982 Ringo entered a 10-minute video film called *The Cooler* in the Cannes Film Festival. This featured three numbers from his *Stop And Smell The Roses* album and starred Paul, Linda and Barbara.

In his private life Ringo emerged as a playboy, loving the night-life. He hit the headlines frequently and enjoyed a social whirl in the company of many friends, including Keith Moon, Marc Bolan and Harry Nilsson. The London club Tramps was one of his favourite haunts, but he had to leave England for a while and become a tax exile in the South of France. He set up a record company called Ringo-O Records, but it didn't fare so well and was put into cold storage. He also spent some time in California, and while he was there his house was destroyed by a fire in which he lost most of the Beatles memorabilia he'd collected over the years. He lived with an American model Nancy Andrews for some time, following affairs with a variety of minor celebrities, including singer Lynsey De Paul. In 1981 he married actress Barbara Bach, his co-star in *Caveman*, and returned to England to live.

INDEX

Adams, Bob 132
Aldo, Steve 44
Aldridge, Alan 132
Ali, Muhammed 126
Andrews, Nancy 181
Appleby, Ron 51
Applejacks, The 111
Aronowitz, Al 126
Asher, Jane 128
Aspinall, Neil 29
Aulin, Ewa 142
Bach, Barbara 182
Badfinger 153
Bain, Bob 95
Ballard, Arthur 36
Barber, Adrian 40
Barrow, Tony 77
Beatmakers, The 38
Bennett, Cliff, and
    The Rebel Rousers 111
Bernstein, Sid 124
Best, Mona 24
Best, Pete 25
Black, Cilla 79
Black Dyke Mills Band, The 151
Blake, John 184
Bolan, Marc 171
Bonzo Dog Doo Dah Band 160
Bostock, Harry 52
Bowie, David 171
Boyd, Jenny 137
Boyd, Patti 104
Boyle, Bernard 39
Brambell, Wilfred 102
Bramwell, Tony 77
Bratby, John 130
Brown, Bobbie 74
Brown, Ken 23
Brown, Peter 79
Bryce, Leslie 117
Burke, John 106
Byrds, The 158
Byrne, Gay 91
Caldwell, Iris 30
Carr, Roy 183
Casey, Howie 55
Chants, The 73
Charles, Tommy 142

Chipmunks, The 127
Clapton, Eric 176
Cleave, Maureen 107
Cocker, Joe 154
Coleman, Ray 167
Coleman, Sid 84
Connolly, Ray 167
Cox, Maureen 132
Cruikshank, Robin 155
Curtis, Lee 45
Davey, Joe 173
David and Jonathan 110
Davies, Hunter 139
Davis, Pat 55
Davis, Rod 20
Delaney, Paddy 68
Dixon, Jeanne 127
Dooley, Arthur 41
Doran, Terry 74
Dunbar, John 155
Dylan, Bob 156
Eastman, Lee 168
Eckhorn, Peter 61
Eddie Clayton Skiffle Group, The 24
Eggermont, Jaap 184
Elephant's Memory 176
Ellis, Geoffrey 134
Ellis, Royston 41
Epstein, Brian 68
Epstein, Clive 89
Escorts, The 45
Evans, Mal 96
Evans, Mike 183
Farrow, Mia 135
Farrow, Prudence 135
Fascher, Horst 60
Fawcett, Anthony 173
Flannery, Joe 54
Fool, The 150
Fourmost, The 45
Frankland, Rosemary 106
Freeman, Robert 132
Frost, David 127
Fury, Billy 27
Garry, Len 20
Gentle, Johnny 27
Gerry and The Pacemakers 41
Gleason, Ricky, and The Spots 107
Good, Jack 140
Grade, Sir Lew 168
Grapefruit 148
Gretty, Jim 30
Hague, Jonathan 36

Hamp, Johnny 92
Hanton, Colin 20
Harrison, George (Beatle) 188
Harrison, George (journalist) 93
Harrison, Harold 14
Harrison, Louise (Beatle's mother) 14
Harrison, Louise (Beatle's sister) 123
Haslam, Michael 116
Higgins, Henry 116
Hines, Iain 58
Hoffman, Dezo 107
Hollies, The 111
Holly, Buddy 178
Hopkin, Mary 149
Hot Chocolate 153
Howarth, Don 91
Howes, Arthur 91
Hubers, Erika 65
Hughes, Liz and Jim 184
Huntley, Ted 84
Hutchinson, Johnny 27
Idle, Eric 112
Jacobs, David 116
James, Dick 88
Jamieson, Russell 92
Janice The Stripper 46
Janov, Dr Arthur 174
Jasper, Tony 183
Jay, Peter, and The Jaywalkers 95
Jevans, Joseph 165
John, Elton 171
Johnny and The Moondogs 23
Jones, Casey 421
Jones, Davy 46
Jones, Peter 107
Junkin, John 104
Kaempfert, Bert 64
Kane, Art 127
Kass, Ron 144
Kaye, Peter 43
Kelly, Brian 38
Kelly, Freda 73
Kelly, George 132
Kestrels, The 95
Kinnear, Roy 156
Kirchnerr, Astrid 59
Klein, Allen 165
Koobas, The 79
Koschmeider, Bruno 60
Kramer, Billy J. 42
Laine, Denny 170
Lapidos, Mark 184
Leach, Sam 31

191

Leary, Timothy 175
Lello, Richard Di 148
Lennon, Alfred 'Freddie' 14
Lennon, Cynthia 36
Lennon, John 185
Lennon, John Charles Julian 89
Lennon, Julia 12
Lennon, Sean 175
Lester, Dick 99
Lomax, Jackie 53
Lowe, John 'Duff' 19
Mackey, Peter 37
McCartney, James 12
McCartney, Linda 163
McCartney, Mary 12
McCartney, Mary Patricia 165
McCartney, Mike 17
McCartney, Paul 187
McCulloch, Jimmy 171
McCullough, Henry 170
McGivern, Maggie 154
McKinnon, Duncan 27
Maharishi Mahesh Yogi 135
Majlata, Eva 173
Manson, Charles 179
Mardas, Alexis 139
Marmalade 112
Marsden, Beryl 39
Marshal, William 112
Martin, George 84
Matthews, Dick 43
Milligan, Spike 119
Millins, Duggie 117
Misterioso, L'Angelo 176
Mohamed, Jeff 36
Montez, Chris 95
Moody Blues, The 108
Moon, Keith 160
Moore, Tommy 23
Morrison, Ruth 23
Mortimer 151
Motta, Stephanie la 182
Murray, Mitch 97
Murray, Rod 36
Murray The K 122
Nicol, Jimmy 130
Nilsson, Harry 154
Noebel, Rev. David A. 127
Norman, Philip 183
Nurk Twins, The 19
O'Dell, Chris 144
O'Dell, Dennis 144

O'Finley, Charles 125
O'Mahony, Sean 117
Oldham, Andrew Loog 92
Ono, Yoko 161
Orbison, Roy 96
Ormsby-Gore, Sir David 125
Orton, Jo 140
Overlanders, The 110
Owen, Alun 101
Parr, Jack 124
Paddy, Klaus and Gibson 144
Pang, May 175
Paolozzi, Eduardo 64
Parnes, Larry 26
Paul, Lynsey de 182
Pell, David 176
Peter and Gordon 110
Pilcher, Norman 173
Pollard, Michael J. 149
Poole, Brian, and The Tremeloes 83
Popjoy, William Edward 22
Presley, Elvis 125
Preston, Billy 150
Proby, P.J. 158
Quarrymen, The 21
Quickly, Tommy 112
Rainbows, The 22
Rebels, The 22
Remo Four, The 54
Richard, Little 82
Roe, Tommy 95
Rolling Stones, The 108
Rose, Bettina 117
Rossington, Norman 104
Rowe, Dick 83
Rudy, Ed 124
Russell, Ethan 159
Russell, William 178
Rutles, The 113
St Louis Union 112
Sargeant, Bill 163
Scaffold, The 99
Schaffner, Nicholas 183
Schwartz, Francie 154
Seiwell, Danny 170
Sellers, Peter 119
Shankar, Ravi 137
Shannon, Del 120
Shapiro, Helen 95
Shendon, Walter 101
Sheridan, Tony 56
Shotton, Pete 19

Silkie, The 116
Smith, Alan 142
Smith, George O'Hara 176
Smith, Mike 82
Smith, Mimi 16
Smith, Norman 88
Sommerville, Brian 116
Sounds Incorporated 111
Spector, Phil 168
Spencer, Graham 44
Spinetti, Victor 104
Stardust, Alvin 159
Starkey, Elsie 15
Starkey, Jason 134
Starkey, Zak 134
Starr, Ringo 190
Stigwood, Robert 139
Stinton, Roger 92
Storm, Rory, and The Hurricanes 47
Sullivan, Ed 120
Sutch, Screaming Lord 127
Sutcliffe, Mrs Millie 17
Sutcliffe, Stuart 33
Swinging Bluejeans, The 52
Taylor, Alistair 74
Taylor, Derek 93
Taylor, Kingsize 51
Trash 150
Tremlett, George 144
Trends, The 99
Trinidad Arias, Olivia 180
Vaughan, Ivan 20
Vernons Girls, The 99
Vollmer, Jurgen 58
Voorman, Klaus 59
Walsh, Sam 36
Walters, Lu 38
Watmough, Harry 54
Weiss, Nathan 135
Weissleder, Manfred 62
Wells, Mary 96
Whalley, Nigel 19
White, Andy 92
Wigg, David 184
Williams, Allan 30
Williams, Angela 159
Wilson, Harold 139
Winters, Mike and Bernie 117
Wonder, Stevie 179
Woodbine, Lord 33
Wooler, Bob 39
Yolland, Peter 107